MW00658705

THUTMOSE III

Other books by Richard A. Gabriel

Scipio Africanus: Rome's Greatest General (2008)

The Battle Atlas of Ancient Military History (2008)

The Warrior's Way: A Treatise on Military Ethics (2008)

Muhammad: Islam's First Great General (2007)

Soldiers' Lives Through History (2006)

Jesus the Egyptian: The Origins of Christianity and the Psychology of Christ (2005)

Empires at War: A Chronological Encyclopedia, 3 volumes (2005)

Subotai the Valiant: Genghis Khan's Greatest General (2004)

Lion of the Sun: A Chronicle of the Wars, Battles and Great Deeds of Pharaoh Thutmose III, Great Lion of Egypt, as Told to Thaneni the Scribe (2003)

The Military History of Ancient Israel (2003)

The Great Armies of Antiquity (2002)

Sebastian's Cross (2002)

Gods of Our Fathers: The Memory of Egypt in Judaism and Christianity (2001)

Warrior Pharaoh: A Chronicle of the Life and Deeds of Thutmose III, Great Lion of Egypt, Told in His Own Words to Thaneni the Scribe (2001)

Great Captains of Antiquity (2000)

The Culture of War: Invention and Early Development (1990)

The Painful Field: Psychiatric Dimensions of Modern War (1988)

No More Heroes: Madness and Psychiatry in War (1987)

Military Incompetence: Why the U.S. Military Doesn't Win (1985)

To Serve With Honor: A Treatise on Military Ethics and the Way of the Soldier (1982)

With Donald W. Boose, Jr.

Great Battles of Antiquity: A Strategic and Tactical Guide to Great Battles That Shaped the Development of War

With Karen S. Metz

A Short History of War: The Evolution of Warfare and Weapons

History of Military Medicine, Vol. 1, *From Ancient Times to the Middle Ages*

History of Military Medicine, Vol. 2, *From the Renaissance Through Modern Times*

From Sumer to Rome: The Military Capabilities of Ancient Armies

THUTMOSE III

The Military Biography of Egypt's Greatest Warrior King

Richard A. Gabriel

Potomac Books, Inc.
Washington, D.C.

Copyright © 2009 Potomac Books, Inc.

Published in the United States by Potomac Books, Inc. All rights reserved. No part of this book may be reproduced in any manner whatsoever without written permission from the publisher, except in the case of brief quotations embodied in critical articles and reviews.

Library of Congress Cataloging-in-Publication Data
Gabriel, Richard A.
Thutmose III : the military biography of Egypt's greatest warrior king / Richard A. Gabriel. — 1st ed.
p. cm.
Includes bibliographical references and index.
ISBN 978-1-59797-373-1 (hardcover : alk. paper)
1. Thutmose III, King of Egypt. 2. Thutmose III, King of Egypt—Military leadership. 3. Pharaohs—Biography. 4. Egypt—Kings and rulers—Biography. 5. Egypt—History, Military. 6. Egypt—History—Eighteenth dynasty, ca. 1570–1320 B.C. I. Title. II. Title: Thutmose the Third.
DT87.2.G33 2009
932'.014092--dc22
[B]

2009015468

Printed in the United States of America on acid-free paper that meets the American National Standards Institute Z39-48 Standard.

Potomac Books, Inc.
22841 Quicksilver Drive
Dulles, Virginia 20166

First Edition

10 9 8 7 6 5 4 3 2 1

For Suzi
who is the sunrise
and the warmth

In Memoriam
Timmy Mahoney
Bill Dorris and Donna Dorris
Frank Hamilton

"Sunt lacrimae rerum et mentem mortalia tangunt"
(These are the tears of things and our mortality cuts to the heart)
— Aeneas

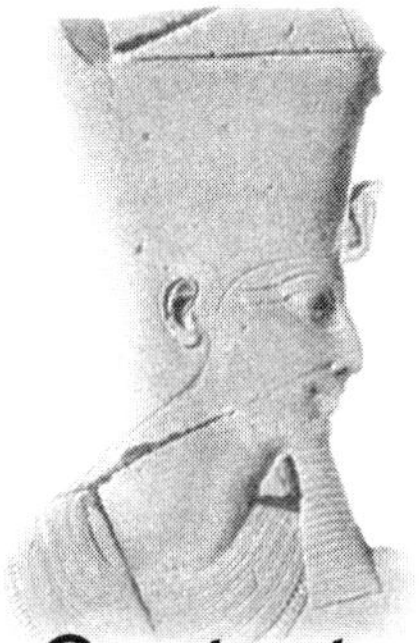

Contents

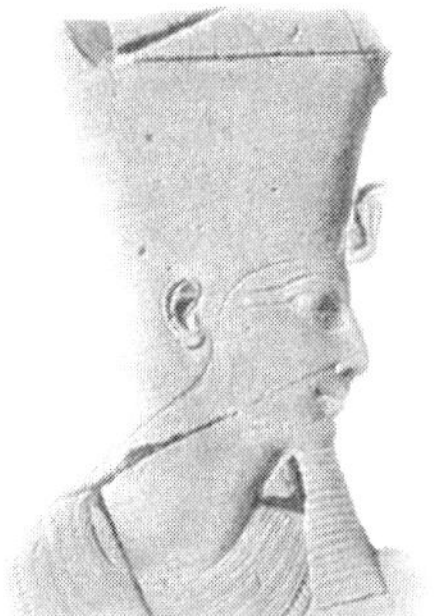

Illustrations

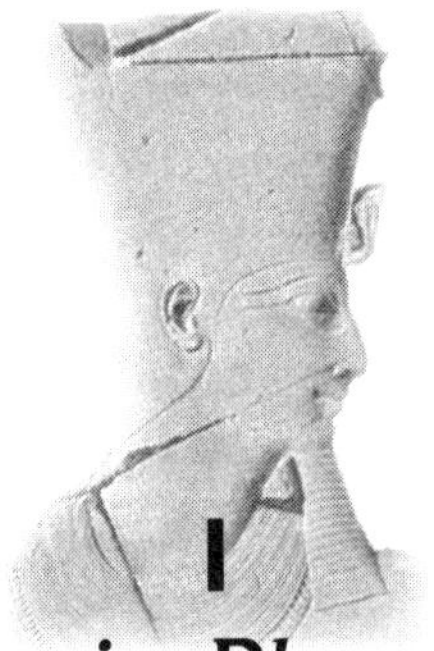

I
Warrior Pharaoh

The Man

The room is not very large, about the size of a small chapel, and dimly lit as if the shadows cast by the soft lights are concealing some ancient secret. The air is chilly, a welcome relief from Cairo's summer heat. Only the background hum of the air conditioner disturbs the reverent silence. This sacred place—a small room set apart in the Museum of Egyptian Antiquities—is the final resting place of the great kings of imperial Egypt, the warrior pharaohs.

Here lies Sekenenre, the great Theban prince who first rose against the Hyksos invaders. His skull is gashed by a penetrating axe, apparently having suffered hideous wounds. There is Ahmose, the founder of the magnificent Eighteenth Dynasty and the hero who drove the despised Hyksos out of Egypt. Thutmose I is here too. This great warrior brought Nubia to heel and "raged like a panther" against his Asiatic enemies, with his armies reaching as far east as the Euphrates River. Next to him rests his son, Thutmose II, who put down the Nubians' revolt with great slaughter and taught the Sand People the meaning of fear.

Off to one side in a casket-like glass case half covered with a cloth of royal purple rests a shrunken corpse, its skin parchment brown and swathed completely in linen wrappings except for those pulled back to reveal his face. The face is oval with full lips, smooth cheekbones, and a prominent brow stretched tightly against the darkened skin. Through the blackened decay one can recognize the set of the jaw and the nose that bears a strong resemblance to that of his father and grandfather. One cannot look upon this face without feeling a sense of awe. Here rests Thutmose III, the greatest warrior pharaoh of the ancient world.

When the king's mummy was discovered in 1881, Egyptologists were horrified to learn that grave robbers in antiquity had almost destroyed the corpse. They had torn all four limbs from the body, and the arms were separated at the elbows. The feet were missing, most of the nose was gone, and the head had been severed at the neck. The sight of this great man desecrated in this manner was so disturbing that the Egyptian government declared a moratorium on future examinations of royal mummies. The ban lasted for five years.[1]

Famed Egyptologist and physician G. Elliot Smith performed the autopsy of Thutmose's corpse. Smith measured the body and declared Thutmose to have been five feet three inches tall. The combination of Thutmose's well-known military prowess and his short stature led Egyptologists to call Thutmose III the Napoleon of Egypt, a description that may have originated with James Henry Breasted, the famous American Egyptologist.[2] It seems, however, that Smith did not account for the corpse's missing feet when taking his measurements. A more recent examination revealed that the king's height was 1.71 meters, or approximately five feet six and one-half inches,[3] which was taller than the average Egyptian of his day and taller than all of the pharaohs of the Eighteenth Dynasty except Amenhotep I.[4] It is fitting that Breasted's description of the great king as an ancient Napoleon Bonaparte should be abandoned, for in his military achievements Thutmose III was, to borrow a line from the British historian B. H. Liddell Hart, "greater than Napoleon." Indeed, Thutmose III was ancient Egypt's Alexander the Great.

He was quite a remarkable fellow, this warrior prince of Thebes and the greatest of all generals in Egyptian history. Unlike many generals before and after him, he did not permit his military training and experience in war to narrow his intellect. He was no military mechanic or a mere technician of war; instead, he was an integral man who retained his interest in things botanical, biological, religious, literary, aesthetic, and architectural to the end of his life. His broad understanding of his world sharpened his already literate, well-read mind, and his early education and training prepared him to reason clearly. He was a brilliant strategic thinker. To him Egypt owes the conception and implementation of a new strategic vision that permitted this once defeated and insular society to become a great nation of imperial dimensions that ruled all the world that an Egyptian would have considered worth knowing for more than five hundred years.

Thutmose III was one of the great captains of the ancient world. His record of military activity is remarkable. He fought more battles over a longer period and won more victories than any other general did in the ancient world. In the 60 years prior to Thutmose's reign, the great warrior kings of Egypt from Ahmose to Thutmose II fought one foreign campaign every 4.6 years. In the 70 years following Thutmose, from Amenhotep II to Amenhotep III, the kings conducted one foreign campaign every 10.5 years. In the 19 years between regnal years 23 and 42 of Thutmose's 32-year reign, he fought seventeen campaigns in Canaan and Syria, or an average of one military campaign every 1.2 years.[5] In addition, he conducted a major foray into Nubia during his last decade of life. In the 6 years between assuming command of the army and ascending the throne in his own right, Thutmose fought a major campaign in Nubia and perhaps another, for which there is only tentative evidence, and led the army that liberated Gaza from the rebels.[6] By the time Thutmose ruled Egypt in his own right, sometime in his twenty-second year, he was already an experienced combat commander. In this first major campaign against the combined Canaanite-Syrian armies at Megiddo in his twenty-third year, Thutmose revealed himself to be a first-rate strategist, tactician, and logistician, qualities he gained through extensive experience in the field prior to ascending the throne.

It is not surprising that this great warrior chose as one of the "five great names," which all pharaohs assumed, a name that is associated with military prowess. Thutmose took as his Horus name Strong Bull Arising in Thebes, a name associated with Montu, the Theban god of war. The famous Blue War Crown also made its appearance during Thutmose's reign. Shaped like a helmet and fashioned of leather, the crown was colored blue and studded with golden sequins. This war crown seems to have been a completely new crown that came into prominence at this time, perhaps reflecting the warrior lineage and military achievements of Thutmose's reign.

At this time also a new symbol of pharaonic authority was introduced. From earliest times the symbol of Egyptian royal power had been the mace. Pharaohs were often portrayed wielding the weapon as the "smasher of foreheads." Under Thutmose, the mace was replaced by the sickle-sword, or *kopesh*. Although the Hyksos had introduced the sickle-sword to Egypt and thus the Egyptian army had probably used it prior to Thutmose's reign, it was probably Thutmose who equipped the army with this weapon on a large scale. It would have been possible only after Egypt had established a strong presence in the Levant from which it could obtain tin to manufacture these bronze weapons in large numbers. In symbol and in fact, therefore, Thutmose transformed Egypt into a military state. With Egypt's great resources at his command, he set events in motion that shaped Egypt and the Levant for the next four hundred years.[7]

More than a hundred portraits of Thutmose III, at least two-thirds of which are life size or larger, have survived.[8] Pharaohs devoted considerable attention to the detail and style of their portraits. While there is a sense that they portrayed themselves in idealistic poses and themes, there is no reason to suspect that there was any great distortion in their physical attributes.[9] Thutmose's portraits reveal a man with the body of a soldier, as befits a person who spent his adolescence and most of his adult life in military service and on campaign. It is not surprising, then, that his physical traits are more in evidence in his portraits than other pharaohs' portraits reveal. The warrior king is portrayed with a broad, thick chest and shoulders; a short torso; and a narrow waist. The legs and calves are muscular and well developed, and even the hands and feet are broad. Art curator Arielle P. Kozloff points out, "These features, together with the physical evidence of Thutmose's mummy indicating that he was fairly tall, at least in ancient terms, add up to quite an imposing figure."[10]

One element of his physique, however, does not appear on his portraits: Thutmose may have suffered from a congenital skin disease. His mummy and those of his father, Thutmose II, and his son, Amenhotep II, show signs of the same disease. The skin on the shoulders, arms, thorax, and buttocks of all three mummies are covered with hundreds of scabrous eruptions similar to those associated with smallpox. Whether these outbreaks represent a congenital condition or some irritant caused by the mummification process is not known.[11] Interestingly, a mummy that was discovered in 2008 and believed to be that of Hatshepsut, the daughter of Thutmose I and the mother of Thutmose II, has the same lesions.

Thutmose's portraits reveal a man with a broad face, steeply sloped forehead, strong jaw, intelligent eyes, and an aquiline nose that is eagle-like in shape and size. The same large beaked nose is evident on his father's and grandfather's mummies and may have been a family trait, as, perhaps, was the steeply sloped forehead. But in ancient Egypt, where the major god Horus was portrayed as a falcon, Thutmose III's subjects would have appreciated the association of Horus's beak with the facial features of their warrior king. Another striking feature in many of Thutmose's portraits is the king's expression of serenity and calm. Even when portrayed at war, the king often seems to be smiling and content, an expression, perhaps, of a man confident in his own abilities and satisfied with his own achievements.

Thutmose is often portrayed as a devout and respectful servant of the gods, and, no doubt, he was. As a young man he trained as a priest of Amun before being sent to the army as a teenager. As Amun's servant, Thutmose later justified his military campaigns as doing the god's will. He gave much of his victories' spoils to the Amun priests of Thebes and other cities. He built the great Festival Hall at Karnak and enhanced the shrine of Montu, the Theban god of war. Thutmose constructed public works, temples, and fortifications throughout the empire, from Buhen in Nubia to the Lebanon Mountains. But always this great warrior humbled himself before the gods of his forefathers.

Despite his great military achievements, Thutmose seems to have retained a strong streak of humility. While the *Annals* carved on the temple walls of Amun at Karnak tell the stories of his battles in detail, they do so in a detached, accurate, and almost reportorial manner. Egyptologists have easily been able to verify these campaigns' details from the *Annals'* descriptions of the terrain, the soldiers' equipment, and the locations of the battles themselves. Absent are the outrageous claims of personal valor and great deeds that have marked so many monuments of antiquity before and since. Even the numbers of enemy slain and the strengths of the armies Thutmose faced, usually the most common source of exaggeration, are believable. Thutmose certainly took care to ensure that those who came after him would know of his achievements, but he did so in a manner that makes him appear very self-effacing indeed.

The man's humility is also reflected in his tomb. Thutmose's tomb is small and sparsely decorated. Compared to other tombs in the Valley of the Kings, Thutmose is buried in the funereal equivalent of the simple military coffin. There are no descriptions of his great military victories inside his burial chamber. It is as if he wished the gods to remember and judge him for other things. Still, no other general in antiquity could claim such a remarkably successful military record as could Thutmose III of Egypt.

Despite his ferocity on the battlefield, the great general seems to have been a compassionate man. In all his campaigns, there are no reports of massacres or atrocities. He often showed mercy to the inhabitants of captured towns. He shared the spoils of war generously with his officers and soldiers and seems to have taken great delight in rewarding his men with decorations for valor in battle. Along with the traditional gold of honor, the king seems to have introduced a number of other military decorations for his troops. Thutmose always remained close to his troops, and they had great trust in him as their commander. One story tells of common soldiers threatening to report their unit scribe, or commissary officer, to the pharaoh if they were not provided with adequate food. Only soldiers who believed their commander to be a fair and just man would dare make such a threat.

That Thutmose cared for his officers and men is clear from the fact that his friends and trusted officials were men with whom he had served in battle and whom he later appointed to administrative positions in the government. As he approached the time when he would be king in his own right, Thutmose began to surround himself with his fellow veterans. Many of these men were of low social origins, but they had proved their mettle in war. Thutmose gave many of them estates from which to draw a living, and others rose to high office in the military and civil administrations.[12] Thutmose also made sure to pass the lesson of caring for one's troops and comrades to his son Amenhotep II. Like his father, Amenhotep was sent to the army as a young man to endure the hardships and learn the skills of military life. Once, after he had become pharaoh, Amenhotep recognized one of the rowers on the royal barge. The rower was Amenemhab, an old veteran of many battles who had fought under Thutmose in Canaan and Syria and had fallen on hard times. Amenhotep had the old man brought before him and said, "I know thy character; I was abiding in the nest [i.e., when I was a child] while thou wert in the following of my father [i.e., serving with him on campaign]." With that acknowledgment, he also gave Amenemhab a royal commission and pension.

Thutmose also possessed an inquiring mind, and his intellectual interests ranged beyond military matters and affairs of state to include history, religion, architecture, pottery, and even jewelry design. His reign witnessed a period of prodigious art production of all forms, and he was one of history's greatest patrons of the arts.[13] He had an abiding interest in botany and while on campaign took along special scribes whose task was to find and record any strange flowers and plants they might encounter. One is reminded of Alexander and Napoleon, for they both took historians, scientists, and secretaries with them on campaign to record the wondrous new things they found in the foreign countries. Indeed, one of Napoleon's secretaries discovered the Rosetta stone during Napoleon's Egyptian campaign. Thutmose saw to it that samples of the strange plants were taken to Egypt and planted there. We know of Thutmose's interest in botany because he had portrayals of these plants inscribed on the walls of the Festival Hall in what has come to be called his Botanical Garden. Animals, too, interested him. He seems to have been particularly enchanted by the story of his father having encountered a white rhinoceros in Nubia. Returning from one of his campaigns, Thutmose spent several days in the vicinity of the marshes of Niya in Syria, studying and hunting elephants.

Thutmose was one of Egypt's great builders. With the possible exception of Ramses II, who enjoyed the longest reign in Egyptian history (sixty-seven years), Thutmose constructed more temples, shrines, votive buildings, pylons, and fortresses than any of his predecessors and all of his successors.[14] The Hyksos invaders had pillaged or destroyed much of the monumental architecture in Middle Egypt, and it was probably not until Thutmose's time that events and resources made an attempt at large-scale rebuilding of the ruined buildings possible. Thutmose also administered an empire that required the construction of new military garrisons and fortifications in Canaan and Nubia.[15] He had an interest in monumental architecture as well and paid great attention to his building program. It was Thutmose who introduced the basilica as an architectural form to Egypt.[16] It is interesting that many of his construction projects took place during the third and fourth decades of his reign, coinciding with the peak of his military activity in Syria and Canaan.[17] To secure his conquests in Asia, Thutmose sometimes transported captured populations to Egypt to serve as laborers. Thus, one of the results of his victories in Canaan-Syria was a large supply of corvée labor that could be set to work on public works projects.

Thutmose's building program speaks volumes about his administrative ability. Egyptian bureaucracy was labyrinthine from ancient times, and at the center of it was the king. The king owned the entire country, and its bureaucracy grew as a means of collecting and redistributing Egypt's produce on behalf of the king.[18] Under Thutmose, the size of the bureaucracy greatly increased. One indication of its expansion is the number of tombs constructed for new government officials: during the New Kingdom the number of these tombs was four times greater than those for any preceding dynasty. Many of the bureaucracy's new officials were the king's military comrades, who appear to have regularly occupied numerous administrative bureaus. This said, its appears that the highest government offices—vizier, overseer of the seal, high priest of Amun, and overseer of the granaries—remained in the hands of the professional bureaucracy, which the powerful traditional elites of the country still staffed.[19]

Thutmose's administrative responsibilities were different and considerably more difficult than those of his predecessors. The wars against the Hyksos and the need to reestablish control over Nubia had led to a gradual centralization of administrative authority in the hands of the pharaoh, but much power remained decentralized until Thutmose III's reign. The need to conscript, train, and equip a large army and a new naval arm and keep both in the field required centralized planning and control over all national resources. While the trend toward centralization was already evident under earlier kings, Thutmose's large-scale and almost constant wars accelerated and increased the trend toward centralization, turning Egypt administratively into a military state. Although Nubia had come under Egyptian administration by the reign of Thutmose I, under Thutmose III Nubia still had to be governed, its goods extracted, its garrisons staffed and repaired, and its occasional revolts suppressed. Further, the great expansion of the Amun priesthood and the remarkable building program, with all that entailed regarding extracting resources and conscripting labor, required constant attention. Thutmose also needed to administer the Egyptian military and economic presence in Canaan while at the same time attending to the threats from Syria and the Mitanni. Unlike any of his predecessors, Thutmose had to govern an imperial realm, and he proved an excellent administrator equal to the task.

The centralization of pharaonic authority permitted a revolution in agriculture, no small achievement in a country where seven million people had to be fed and the army in the field or in garrison supplied.[20] Key to increased agricultural production was a device called the *shadouf*, a long beam supported by two stakes that is weighted at one end and has a bucket at the other. After dipping the bucket into a water source, the weighted beam is used to raise the bucket and empty it into an irrigation channel higher than the water source. Although the Hyksos first introduced the shadouf, it does not seem to have come into widespread use until Thutmose's reign. At the same time, the old wooden plough made of two bent handles that were fastened to the horns of oxen was replaced by a lighter plough with more upright handles that a team of men could draw. These two innovations resulted in more efficient and extensive agricultural production during the New Kingdom.

Early Years

The son of Pharaoh Thutmose II by a concubine named Isis, Thutmose III was probably born in 1504 BCE. Pharaoh's great wife and half-sister, Hatshepsut, produced only a daughter, Neferure.[21] It is probable that Thutmose, while still very young, was married to his half-sister, Neferure. Marriages to sisters and half-sisters were common among the royalty of Egypt since the bloodline of succession was held to follow the female line. Marriage to these royal blue-blooded females was sometimes a means of legitimizing the rule of a nonroyal who had been appointed to succeed a pharaoh who had died without a male heir. The difficulty was, however, that it also permitted powerful male cousins outside the normal line of succession to raise claims to the throne by arranging a royal marriage. Thutmose I had become pharaoh in exactly this manner by marrying the sister of his predecessor, Amenhotep I, who had left no surviving male heir. So, too, did Thutmose II, who was born of a nonroyal mother but married Hatshepsut, the daughter of Thutmose I and his royal wife Ahmose. Thutmose II died while his son, Thutmose III, was still an infant. Although his son was recognized as pharaoh from this early time, real power passed to Queen Hatshepsut, who governed as regent.

In the normal course of things, Thutmose III would have remained in the care of his mother until he was five or six years old and been permitted to scurry about the palace compound stark naked, as was the Egyptian practice with all young children, including the children of the nobility and high government officials. Early on, his head was shaved except for a thickly braided side lock, the Horus lock, that symbolized his youth and adolescence. When a boy turned five or six years old, responsibility for his education passed to the father, who saw to it that the child attended the private academies or was instructed by private tutors. Although his sire was dead and his stepmother-aunt held the throne, Thutmose received the usual education for a child of his age and rank.

We are lacking the details of his early adolescence, but it seems reasonable that the boy-king was sent to one of the temples, a House of Life, or perhaps the scriptorium of the temple at Karnak, where he would have been taught to read and write, first in the common hieratic script and then in the more complex system of hieroglyphics.[22] Egyptians valued literacy highly. They believed that writing, or what they called the divine words, was an invention of the god Toth, who taught it to the Egyptians as a divine gift. Egyptians learned much more than basic literacy in the temples' instruction houses, however; Thutmose would have also been exposed to the books of the temple library, including the historical accounts of his predecessors' accomplishments.[23] When students of the upper classes reached age twelve, they were required to choose a profession and received additional instruction in literary works, poetry, essay writing, medicine, law, science, architecture, astronomy, and mathematics. Egypt was one of the most populous and complex societies of the ancient world and required skilled managers and professionals to make it run smoothly.

It was probably around this age that Thutmose was apprenticed to the priesthood at the temple of Amun at Karnak. The young man would have been placed in the care of the priests to oversee his further education. Thus, it would not have been unreasonable that the priests should have encouraged Thutmose to become one of them. Such encouragement may, perhaps, even have come at the instigation of the queen and her advisers, who might have reckoned that the priesthood was an ideal place to imprison her rival for the throne. So much the better if the boy were to truly follow the religious life. For a few years after his circumcision, Thutmose served as a priest of Amun at Karnak. The experience made him deeply devout for the rest of his life.

An Egyptian boy became a man at age twelve or thirteen, a time of great importance marked by the ceremonies of shaving the Horus lock and of undergoing circumcision. The origins of the Egyptian practice of circumcision are quite obscure and very old, perhaps reaching back to the earliest days of man's original settlement in Egypt. There seems to have been no particularly religious significance to the practice, only a strong social one to mark those men of the nobility as superior to and apart from the other social classes. Among the lower classes, however, circumcision may have been part of the military ritual of induction. The ceremony might have marked the soldier-recruit's commitment to serve the pharaoh, or the warrior god.[24]

One can imagine Egypt's greatest soldier enduring the rite of circumcision as a young man. For the usual nobility, Egyptian physicians operated with the traditional flint knife. But given Thutmose's royal blood, the court physician would have used the star knife, a special scalpel fashioned from nickel steel extracted from meteorites that had fallen to earth. Portrayals of the procedure show the physician kneeling in front of the young man, who is standing. Sometimes others grip the boy and support him should he be rendered unconscious by the pain. One portrait shows what might have been the manner in which Thutmose, a future king, dealt with the pain: we see a young man standing rigidly straight with one hand placed on the physician's head and the other on his own hip in a gesture of calm as he endures the pain without complaint. The ceremony was performed before a gathering of relatives and friends, so a young man's performance on that special day might well mark him as strong and brave or as a weakling for life.

We do not know exactly when Thutmose completed his temple education and went to the army for military training. It may have been a year or so before he reached his age of majority of sixteen years when Queen Hatshepsut appointed him commander of the army.[25] There are no records that tell us about Thutmose's training as an officer in the imperial army at the Stable for Military Education. But whatever his experience, he valued it as most important to forming his character and made certain that his son Amenhotep II was sent to the army at an early age to harden his character. Thutmose was so pleased by his son's performance that he directed a number of stelae to be made detailing the achievements of his son's military training and early career. From these records we are able to obtain some idea of what Thutmose's own military training might have been like.

The training of an Egyptian officer was rigorous and physically demanding. It required familiarization with all combat arms of the fighting force. Amenhotep's stelae tell of his experiences with the infantry, chariot corps, and what seems to have been his favorite arm, the archers. He endured poor food—march rations comprised sour milk, fish with salt, hard bread, and a canteen of water—and forced marches and had to row boats. The Egyptian army held regular field exercises in which young officers participated, and during jousts, mock combats, and weapons competitions, they could demonstrate their skills to their superiors.

Thutmose's introduction to military life likely first involved learning the skills of the infantry, the largest combat arm of the army and its true arm of decision. The roughest and most disciplined of the infantry were the *nakhtu-aa,* or the "strong-arm boys." These tough, disciplined shock troops were armed with the bull hide shield; the *dja,* or short spear; the kopesh, literally the "goat's leg" or sickle-sword; the cast bronze penetrating socket ax; and the *ta-agsu,* or dagger. Life in the infantry has never been pleasant, and it was no less so in the Egyptian army of Thutmose's time. One surviving document offers a soldier's view of life in the Egyptian infantry:

> Come, let me tell you how he goes to Syria, and how he marches over the mountains. His bread and water are borne upon his shoulders like the load of an ass; they make his neck that of an

> ass, and the joints of his back are bowed. When he reaches the enemy he is like a trapped bird, he has no strength in his limbs. If he comes home to Egypt he is like wood that is worm-eaten and becomes bedridden.

If Thutmose's experience was anything like that of his son, the young pharaoh trained and became familiar with a range of infantry weapons, just as ground officers must do today. Perhaps he spent some time training with the *kenyt-nesu*, or the King's Braves. These fellows were the Egyptian equivalent of the U.S. Rangers, elite special operations units of heavy infantry used especially for rushing head-on against difficult positions. Like modern special operations units, the Braves were made up of soldiers who had distinguished themselves in battle. Hardened veterans all, their entry was by merit only.

Service with the light infantry would have gained the young prince an appreciation for the archers—the *megau*, or "shooters"—and how to coordinate their employment with infantry and chariots. Experience with the archers would have also taught the young officer how to use the composite bow to good effect. Egyptian archers and charioteers carried the same bow, an instrument of Hyksos design constructed of a central wood core with thin strips of horn and leather laminated around the belly. The bow was 1.3 meters long, and when drawn to the ear, it could send a reed shaft fletched arrow with a bronze arrowhead through an ingot of copper three fingers thick. Powered by a string of twisted gut, this composite bow was a formidable weapon in a trained soldier's hands. For protection, both archers and spearmen wore textile armor and helmets. The elite infantry and the charioteers wore body armor fashioned of 2-millimeter-thin bronze plates sewn in overlapping patterns on a leather jerkin. One can imagine how uncomfortable and hot the young pharaoh must have found this equipment. But then again, military life was a long way from the comforts of the priests' temple at Karnak or the royal palace.

The chariot corps seems to have been Thutmose's favorite arm of battle, and he used it to good effect when he became commander in chief. But he was still a long way from that day, and before it came he had to learn to master the chariot and use his weapons while racing over the ground at combat speed. Chariot training began with learning to drive a small cart with thick wooden wheels pulled by a single horse, usually some retired warhorse that had survived many battles and had a mind of its own when it came to working with young officers. The cart was very difficult to steer, and attempting to hit anything with the bow even at low speed was a challenge. Once having mastered the heavy cart, the trainee moved to a lighter vehicle and, finally, on to the combat version of this remarkable fighting machine. Thutmose would have been given his own chariot and driver, and then, when proficient, he may have moved on to his first command as a *kedjen-tepy*, or "first charioteer," in charge of a troop of ten machines. Just as his son did after him, Thutmose loved military life and was a natural born leader of men in war. To the end of his life, his most trusted confidants and closest friends remained those he made in military service.

The Rise to Power

Meanwhile, Thutmose's stepmother-aunt, Queen Hatshepsut, governed Egypt as its true "king." Although Thutmose had been very young, perhaps only a nursling, when his father died, he was still recognized as the legitimate king and dated his regnal years from his time as an infant. The effective day-to-day governance of Egypt was then left in the hands of the dead king's great wife, Hatshepsut, who assumed the role of regent for the young Thutmose. There were several historical precedents for an Egyptian queen to assume the role of regent. Hatshepsut's own mother, Ahmose, had been regent for the young Thutmose II for several years. Before that Ahhotep, the mother of Ahmose I, the hero of the Hyksos wars, had played a similar role.[26] But Hatshepsut did something no other female regent had ever done. When Thutmose was seven years old, Hatshepsut declared herself king, assumed the entire titulary of a pharaoh, and even began to dress in male attire, complete with the false beard of Egyptian royalty.[27] The two kings, one male and one female, ruled side by side for some fifteen years, but Hatshepsut wielded the real authority of office. No king of Egypt before or since is known to have undergone Thutmose's experience in which a female regent actually became king and ruled in her own right. It was this unique experience that influenced the first twenty-two years of the young king's life.[28]

The question of Hatshepsut's motives has puzzled scholars for centuries. It has been argued that Hatshepsut's assumption of the Egyptian throne was part of a plot to secure the position until she could pass it on to her young daughter. None of the Thutmosid kings were blood descendants of the royal line of Tao, the great king and founder of the Seventeenth Dynasty. But all the females, including Hatshepsut, were Tao descendants and had been used to legitimize the line of the Thutmosids through royal marriage. If preserving the royal line was her goal, it failed when Hatshepsut's daughter died while Thutmose was still a young boy. There were, however, plenty of royal cousins and ambitious men who might yet mount a claim to the throne based on bloodlines. Hatshepsut may have been trying to protect young Thutmose from rival claimants by assuming the throne outright. Her own claim to royal lineage was unassailable, and as long as she remained alive, no others could raise a credible claim to the throne.[29]

Two facts support this interpretation of Hatshepsut's motives. First, if she really intended to seize power for her own sake, why did she not have the young Thutmose killed? Hatshepsut had her own coterie of court supporters who might have feared their loss of influence and wealth under a regime led by a new king. Surely an accident could have been arranged to befall the young prince. Second, why did she send Thutmose off to the army as a young boy and when he reached his majority at age sixteen then appoint him commander of the army, a position from which he could easily have threatened her? She even trusted him to command her armies on campaigns in Nubia and Gaza. It would have been a foolish sovereign indeed to place the instrument of her own destruction in her rival's hands.[30]

If Hatshepsut was protecting Thutmose, why then did she not step down as king when he reached his majority or, if she still had any doubts about his ability, after he had proved himself as a competent general on the battlefields of Nubia and Gaza? There is, of course, no way to know. Perhaps it was part of the queen's grand design all along that she would continue to look after Egypt's internal affairs while Thutmose led the military campaigns against Egypt's enemies.[31] And this may have been what happened. From the time of his majority at age sixteen until he became king in his own right at age twenty-two, there is no evidence that Thutmose asserted his claim to the throne with any vigor, if at all.

Hatshepsut ruled Egypt with Thutmose for twenty-two years (1504–1482 BCE), all but seven of which as a king in her own right. Her reign is noted for constructing a substantial number of public works buildings and monuments, including her great mortuary temple in the Valley of the Kings, and for sponsoring the famous trade expedition to the land of Punt (Somalia), the record of which is preserved on her temple's walls. She also contributed to the expansion of the great religious complex at Karnak. Under her reign, Egypt was well governed and without civil turbulence, and the general impression from the surviving records is it was a time of general prosperity and peace.

Early in her reign, however, Hatshepsut ordered a military foray into southern Canaan either to put down a small revolt or to deal with the banditry of the Apiru. Later, but still early in her reign, she seems to have personally led a major military expedition into Nubia. One surviving text describes the queen herself as present on the battlefield and supervising the collection of booty.[32] These events suggest that Hatshepsut was an active pharaoh in both the domestic and foreign arenas and that she was clearly aware of and concerned with events and developments beyond Egypt's borders.

While we still ponder Hatshepsut's motives for serving as king, the circumstances surrounding Thutmose's accession to full kingship in 1482 or 1481 BCE remain unclear. It has been suggested that Hatshepsut had been unwilling to resist the encroachments upon Egyptian influence fostered by the Canaanite states. This show of weakness only encouraged additional attempts, including the powerful Mitannian kings' use of proxies to weaken Egypt's hold on the strategic land bridge. Over some time, these encroachments had forced Egypt to withdraw most of its garrisons to the southern fringe of Canaan itself.[33] This move placed Egypt's strategic position and commerce at risk, and it might have raised the fears of the powerful Amun priesthood that the royal revenues and gifts that were the mainstay of its wealth might be diminished.[34] Sometime late in Hatshepsut's reign, she sent Thutmose in command of an army to regain Gaza, long the lynchpin to Egypt's strategic position in Canaan. Shortly thereafter, Hatshepsut was forced to send another army under

Thutmose's command to put down a revolt in Nubia. This campaign took two campaign seasons to accomplish, indicating that the situation was serious.[35] Egyptian foreign policy and its strategic position were under assault, and a strong hand was needed to guide the country.

We do not know the circumstances under which Thutmose assumed his rightful position as sole king of Egypt sometime in 1482 or 1481 BCE or what happened to Hatshepsut, who then would have been older than fifty years of age. It is not unimaginable by year 22 of Hatshepsut's reign that Thutmose, commander of the army and the rightful male king, found it appropriate to press his claim to the throne with the support of the army and court elites and removed his aunt.[36] That many of the important personages of Hatshepsut's court were permitted to continue in office under the new regime suggests as much. It may also be that Hatshepsut had fulfilled her mission to protect the throne for Thutmose, and she handed over the reigns of power to her nephew as she had planned to do all along. It is likely that she continued to live for years while retired from governmental responsibilities.[37] There is no good reason to suspect that she was killed in a palace coup, as some have suggested. Hatshepsut may have simply reached the end of her life and died. Within six months of coming to the throne of Egypt, Thutmose III saw Canaan explode in revolt. Egypt was threatened with another foreign invasion.

Strategist

Thutmose III's great achievements on the battlefield inevitably lead one to think of him mostly in military terms, that is, as a great general who excelled in the art of war. It is certainly true that few generals of the ancient world can claim a record of battlefield achievement equal to that of the great pharaoh. Still, there is more to greatness, even military greatness, than winning battles. Often an appreciation for the political dimension of war and the personal dimension of leadership give victories on the battlefield any meaning beyond the body count and the movement of boundaries. Thutmose knew and appreciated these dimensions of military performance and demonstrated them often.

Perhaps the most important and far-reaching of Thutmose's achievements was how he changed the psychology of Egyptian national character. In the same manner that Alexander did for the Greeks, he set forth a new paradigm that altered the way Egyptians thought about themselves and their world. For more than two millennia Egypt had been an isolated society, almost hermetically sealed by its vast desert borderlands from the great cultural changes that were occurring in the rest of the Levant. Thus, Egyptians rarely thought about the world beyond these borders. Strange and little-known lands were of no concern to the land of the gods, the land that gave the world the concept of resurrection.[38] Throughout their recorded history, Egyptians had lived as if there were no other lands at all. In all this time one is hard pressed to find any significant examples of cultural or technological change within Egypt that occurred as a consequence of contacts with lands and people beyond its borders.

The Hyksos invasion (circa 1650 BCE) and their subsequent 108 years of occupation provided a shocking awakening to this peaceful view of things. But even then, the Egyptian leaders' goal was simply to rid *Kemit*, or the "Black Land," of the invaders and return to their former ways. It was Thutmose III who first realized that there was no going back. The strange lands of the Asiatics could no longer be safely ignored. To return to the past would achieve nothing and only place Egypt at risk once more. Thus, Thutmose led a closed society into a new era of awareness and interaction with other cultures. Those of us who remember the uncertainty that accompanied the end of the era of American isolation after World War II and the difficulties the United States confronted in adjusting to its new international role can only marvel at Thutmose's achievement. It was one thing for the barely two-hundred-year-old United States to make such a significant change in its psychological perception of the world. How much more traumatic it must have been for the Egyptians to abandon their two-thousand-year-old history and worldview! Thutmose succeeded in providing Egypt with a new vision of itself and its place in the world, and that vision remained unchanged in its essentials for the next five hundred years.

The new Egypt required a new national security strategy to guide its policy in the changing and hostile environment in which it was forced to live. Thutmose developed a strategic vision of Egyptian security that guided Egyptian diplomatic, commercial, and military policy for half a millennium. In this view, Egypt had no safe borders. Instead, the nation's security lay in Egypt's ability to control the political and military developments in Canaan, Lebanon, and Syria. The goal of Egyptian policy was to prevent any major power or coalition of Asiatic city-states from assembling an alliance powerful enough to threaten Egypt. This policy required Egypt's full involvement in the politics, economics, and military affairs of the states on the land bridge. Egyptian policy was dynamic and proactive, requiring preventive and reactive military interventions in support of political objectives. After the battle of Megiddo, Thutmose intervened with military force in the area no fewer than sixteen times. His son, Amenhotep II, was kept busy with one campaign after another in a similar fashion, as were most of the succeeding pharaohs for the next five hundred years.

New empires and great powers rose and fell during this time, and most challenged Egyptian hegemony on the Canaanite land bridge at one time or another. Two centuries after Thutmose had defeated the Mitanni, Ramses II fought the Hittite forces to a draw at Kadesh. A century and a half later, Ramses III defeated the Sea People in a great land and sea battle at the mouth of the Nile, saving Egypt from the devastation that had overwhelmed and destroyed every major city from Syria to Canaan. And so it went, on and on, with Egyptian policy guided by the same national security goals and strategic vision that Thutmose had forged for Egypt so many centuries before. It was "a sustained military and administrative effort unequaled in Egyptian history."[39]

Thutmose's success on the battlefield provides a case study of those personality traits that make a general great. First and foremost is a penchant for clear thinking unclouded by ideology or religious precepts. The battlefield is the most empirical and, thus, most unforgiving place of a soldier's existence. Thutmose was a deeply religious man who believed in and attended to the gods. Yet, when it came to war, he appears to have assessed situations with a cold, calculating eye. As far as we know, he fought no wars for ideological purposes. He rarely destroyed the temples of other people's gods and then only to make a political point. Second, Thutmose was a commander who was open to new ideas, and his inquisitive mind permitted him to find them everywhere. Whether it was adopting new weapons, using the four-wheeled wagon for the first time in Egypt's history, dragging rafts over mountains, or recognizing the value of naval power to ground warfare, Thutmose was an innovative commander who carefully considered things large and small. The willingness to accept innovation is the mark of a stable, self-confident personality, one who trusts his own experiences and intellect to make sense of his world. It is, unfortunately, a rare trait among military men.

The strength of Thutmose's personality is revealed, too, in his willingness to challenge the unknown. He moved armies eight hundred miles from Egypt into foreign territory about which Egyptians knew little. Time and again he forged ahead into unknown land, trusting in his ability to learn and adapt to its very strangeness. In the twenty-first century, with so much of the world known and mapped, it is difficult for us to appreciate the apprehension such journeys could generate in the ancient mind. These ventures would cause great trepidation, one suspects, especially for the Egyptians with their millennia-long history of isolation. To challenge the unknown requires a strong and confident personality, and Thutmose's strength of will was prodigious. It was revealed, for instance, when he overruled his senior officers' objections to his plan of advance at Megiddo and imposed his own tactical vision upon the battle plan. One can only imagine how many more times the young and adventurous pharaoh overruled his more conservative military advisers. The risks and scale of the Euphrates campaign against the Mitanni must have shocked his generals. It is a maxim of military leadership that an army is an instrument of a commander's will. If so, then it is a good idea to have as its leader a commander who possesses a will of iron, as Thutmose did.

Brilliance, clearheadedness, a sense of risk, and a strong character are the qualities of a good general, but other qualities must augment them if soldiers are to willingly follow a commander into battle and risk their own deaths. No soldier dies for grand strategy or for the glory of his king or country. Men cannot be managed to their deaths; they must be led. Thutmose possessed the traits of a good combat commander, including the all-important willingness to share the risks his soldiers faced, as Thutmose did at Megiddo when he personally led his army down a dangerous narrow track. The lesson was clear: if he made a mistake and the enemy ambushed the column, he would have been the first into the fight and the first to die. During the battle itself, Thutmose led the chariot attack in the center of the line, a place of great danger but also of high visibility. As every combat officer knows, officers must be seen by their men when it comes time to fight and die. In every one of his campaigns for which we have records, Thutmose is portrayed as always participating fully in the battles.

A great combat commander must also be responsible for his men. Thutmose seems to have taken great care to be close to his troops and ensured that they were well fed and well trained. He rewarded bravery in battle often, and many stories indicate he bestowed gold and other awards upon brave men. He seems to have taken a special pleasure in presenting common soldiers with the Fly of Valor, a solid gold housefly on a chain that was the highest Egyptian decoration for bravery in battle and one that Thutmose himself introduced. He was one of those great captains of antiquity who shaped his world in ways that most men of his time could not have imagined.

The Egyptian Alexander

Thutmose III set in motion a series of events that shaped and influenced the Levant and Egypt for the next five hundred years, and his reign can be considered a watershed in the military and imperial history of the entire eastern Mediterranean.[40] In this regard he may rightly be compared with Alexander the Great, whose achievements served as a turning point for Greece a thousand years later; however, in numerous instances Thutmose was even greater than Alexander. For example, Alexander's father, Philip of Macedon, built the military establishment and force structure that Alexander later used as an instrument of his conquest. It was Philip's genius, not Alexander's, that saw the need to abandon traditional Greek infantry tactics and replace them with cavalry. In Philip's new tactical doctrine, infantry was relegated to a platform of maneuver with cavalry becoming the battle arm of decision.[41] Thutmose, meanwhile, had inherited only a rudimentary military establishment that was gravely inadequate to the task of fostering his imperial ambitions. It was Thutmose who forged the new model army of the New Kingdom, introducing major reforms in logistics, conscription, weapons, chariotry, and a new naval arm capable of supporting ground operations far from Egypt itself.[42] Had he not done so, Egypt's conquest and administration of the eastern Levant would have been impossible.

The army that Thutmose brought into being lasted almost four centuries without major changes, remaining a reliable instrument of force projection in the hands of his immediate successors throughout the rest of the Eighteenth Dynasty and during most of the Nineteenth. After Alexander's death, however, his army proved largely ineffective in the hands of his successors, whose meager reforms included the use of lesser-quality infantry and the introduction of the elephant. Alexander's successors seem not to have continued his one tactical innovation, the use of catapults as covering artillery.[43]

On the one hand, the strategic vision that made Alexander's victories possible was not Alexander's creation. It was Philip's. It was Philip who conceived the idea of an attack on Persia and forged the new military instrument to attempt it. Both men, however, were not motivated by any calculations of national security or national economic interest, something that would have required a genuine sense of Greek nationhood that transcended city-state, clan, and regional rivalries and did not yet exist. Instead, Alexander was motivated by the traditional Greek ideal of military glory, with the conquest of Persia being merely the arena in which personal glory and fame might well be sought. The very nature of the Greek city-states, with their small populations, paucity of wealth and resources, and part-time militia armies, made it almost impossible for long-term strategic goals to be achieved by Greek arms.

Thutmose, on the other hand, created a new strategic vision for Egypt based solidly in calculations of national self-interest. Unlike Greece, Egypt already possessed a sense of national identity. Achieving Thutmose III's long-term strategic goals made it possible for his heirs to keep Egypt safe for generations. Thutmose was certainly aware of the millennia-old Egyptian ideal of the warrior king who protected Egypt from its enemies and triumphed gloriously on the battlefield. But the search for glory in Egyptian terms had to be sought in the protection of the nation and its security interests and not in the performance of a king seeking glory (*arete*) for himself alone.

In twelve years Alexander demonstrated his brilliance as a tactician while fighting four major battles (Granicus, Issus, Arbela, and the Hydaspes River), four short sieges (Miletus, Halicarnassus, Tyre, and Gaza), and a number of running bloody battles and sieges with tribal armies in what is now Afghanistan and India. All the other potential adversaries—the city-states of the Phoenician coast, Egypt, and key satrapies of the Persian Empire—surrendered to Alexander without a fight. Thutmose, by contrast, took part in twenty campaigns in two distant theaters of operations—Canaan-Syria and Nubia—and ruled for thirty-two years. Alexander neither governed the empire that he brought into being nor concerned himself with public works, improvements in the army, creating a new naval force, foreign policy, diplomacy, and rebellions. Thutmose had to attend to all these things as well as oversee the governance of an empire that stretched from Asia to Nubia.

Alexander's victories were achieved against mostly second-rate armies and third-rate generals. Persia itself was rotten to the core well before Alexander attacked it. Indeed, the political assessment that Persia was corrupt prompted Philip to conclude that only a slight push was needed to make the empire collapse. The Persian army that faced Alexander, though very large, was ill led, ill equipped, incapable of maneuver or controlled retreat, and had officers who were selected more for their political reliability than for their military competence. When Alexander struck, the Persian army collapsed just as Philip had predicted. Only in India did Alexander confront competent professional armies, and with the exception of his battle with King Porus at the Hydaspes River, Alexander refused to engage them.

The Canaanite armies that Thutmose faced in Canaan-Syria were professional armies, led by competent commanders who were members of a professional military aristocracy, and were equipped with the most modern military equipment of the day: the sickle-sword, body armor, composite bow, penetrating ax, and chariots. Most of Thutmose's adversaries in that theater of operations also had the advantages of interior lines along which to logistically support their field forces and of strongly fortified cities upon which to fall back and from which to carry on the war even when defeated on the battlefield. Only in Nubia did the Egyptians face adversaries who were weaker than they were. Egypt's ability to prevent Nubia from obtaining adequate supplies of tin to manufacture bronze reduced its armies to using bows, arrows, and spears.[44] If the greatness of a field commander is judged by the ability of the enemy he faces—both the opposing commander and the armies he commands—then compared to Alexander, Thutmose must rank as the greater field commander for his success in defeating stronger adversaries.

Alexander's victories permitted Greek rule to be imposed on what was the Persian Empire and resulted in Greek cultural and military influences replacing the Persian in most of the Levant. This change ushered in the Hellenistic Age, a period in which Eastern influences in all areas flooded into the West at a level not seen before, and permitted the diffusion of new ideas and technologies throughout the Mediterranean basin. But Alexander's empire existed in name only, for upon his death it was divided among his successors into three competing imperial states that frequently warred against one another. Once this internecine warfare commenced, Alexander's imperium came to an end in a practical sense.

Within a generation, the Ptolemies of Egypt, Alexander's successors, had become thoroughly Egyptianized to the point of calling themselves pharaohs. Even the traditional Greek gods were expressed in Egyptian terms.[45] By the battle of Raphia (217 BCE), Egyptian troops outnumbered Greeks in the Ptolemies' armies. The rulers of mainland Greece witnessed the beginning of their empire's end at the hands of Rome after the battle of Cynoscephalae (197 BCE) and suffered the coup de grâce at the battle of Pydna thirty years later. The Syrian branch of Alexander's empire fell to the Romans at the battle of Magnesia in 190 BCE. By the time of Carthage's destruction in 147 BCE, for all practical purposes the empire of Alexander's successors had ceased to exist. By contrast, the empire Thutmose III created in Canaan, Syria, and Nubia remained the dominant cultural and military force in the Levant for more than five hundred years.[46] Seen in context, then, Thutmose III was at least Alexander's equal as a military commander and a force of history, and in many respects this Egyptian warrior king was even greater than the Macedonian.

Succession

At the beginning of his third decade of rule, or regnal year 42, Thutmose was still actively campaigning in Syria, this time against the cities of Kadesh and Tunip. His program of domestic public works was in full swing, and the great shipyard at Perunefer north of Memphis was producing the new seagoing ships to transport Egyptian troops and supplies to Asiatic battlefields. At the height of his power Thutmose began to think about the problem of succession. None of the Thutmosids were of Tao blood, and each had legitimized his rule by marrying a woman of the royal line.

Now Thutmose faced the same problem. As a young boy Thutmose was probably married to Hatshepsut's daughter, Neferure, but she died soon after the union. He then married Queen Satiah, probably of royal blood. She bore him a son, Amenenhet, who would have been a legitimate heir had the boy not died around age eight. Thutmose then took another wife, Meryetre-Hatshepsut, who was a commoner. She bore him four girls—Nefertari, Isis, Baket, and Meryetamun—and a son, Amenhotep II, who eventually became heir to the throne.

But just as all Thutmosids before him, because Amenhotep II's mother was not of royal blood, the legitimacy of his succession was in question and raised the ambitions of royal cousins and others who had married royal women. To forestall any challenge to that succession, in year 42 Thutmose embarked on a systematic campaign to erase the official memory of Hatshepsut in all Egyptian texts and monuments. He attempted to rewrite the account of his reign by carrying out history's first great political purge of the official record and deleting Hatshepsut.

Thutmose ordered artisans to remove all representations of Hatshepsut in reliefs, texts, cartouches, and wherever else they appeared and to recut the resulting blank spaces with other images, usually those of offering tables. Where possible, these spaces were replaced with the names of the first two Thutmosids and in some instances even with Thutmose's name itself. All of the freestanding portraits, sphinxes, and statues of Hatshepsut were smashed and the pieces buried. Thutmose even ordered Hatshepsut's tomb opened and had the body of her father, Thutmose I, which she had moved to a sarcophagus in her tomb, reinterred in his original tomb in the Valley of the Kings.[47] Thutmose I was the first king to have been buried there and to have his tomb located apart from his mortuary temple.

At this time Thutmose's portraiture took on a new form. Many of his portraits prior to Hatshepsut's proscription show him with a round, soft, almost feminine face fashioned in the image of the ruling queen. Now Thutmose's portraits took on a more masculine character and began to reflect his physical features more realistically. The new portraits stressed the physical features that the king shared with his father and grandfather as if to say they, and he, were the legitimate heirs to Egypt and not the women of the Tao bloodline.[48] The idea seems to have been to present himself and his male forebears as the true royal line and thus remove any rationale for a challenge to his son's claim to the throne.

When he was forty-two years old, Thutmose mounted his last campaign in Syria-Lebanon. In the last years of the king's life Amenhotep II was sent at the head of an army to put down a rebellion in Syria. This time the population was slaughtered, and the rebellious princes hanged head down over the prow of Amenhotep's barge as he sailed up the Nile to present his father with a great victory. Unlike his father, Amenhotep did not shrink from slaughter.

Thutmose III spent his last years building temples and indulging his intellectual interests. Two years before his death, to further strengthen his boy's claim to the throne, Thutmose made Amenhotep co-regent, probably when the boy reached his majority at age sixteen and after having seen to his military education and giving him experience in war.[49] Perhaps Thutmose remembered his own youthful inexperience and wanted Egypt's next pharaoh to be more prepared to deal with the dangerous world of war and international politics. And then one day the greatest of the warrior pharaohs was gone, dead from natural causes.

> Lo, the king completed his lifetime of many years, splendid in valor, in might, and in triumph; from year 1 to year 54, third month of the second season, the last day of the month under the majesty of King Menkheperre [Thutmose III], triumphant. He mounted to heaven, he joined the sun; the divine limbs mingling with him who begat him.

He had lived fifty-three years, ten months, and twenty-six days, and in his time had changed Egypt forever. For his having lived, the world was never the same again.

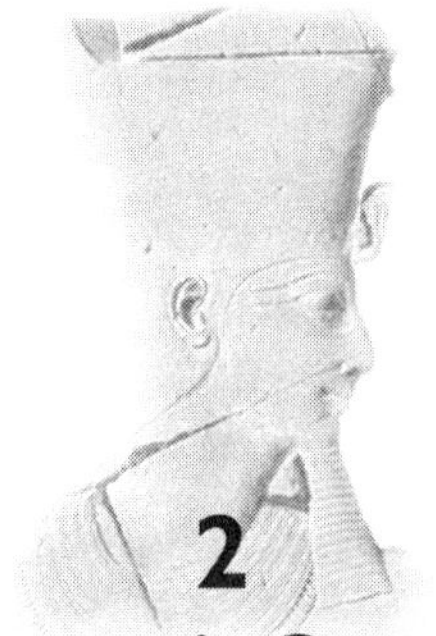

2
Strategic Setting

Egypt

In order to understand Egyptian national defense strategy on the eve of Thutmose III's ascension to power, it is necessary to understand the evolution of Egyptian foreign policy that preceded it. Egypt is one of the oldest continuous national entities on the planet. Egyptian society of 4000 BCE was formed around province-like entities that the Greeks later called *nomi* and that were ruled by individual *nomarchs,* or chiefs. Over time, these nomarchs assembled in loose feudal arrangements into two clusters of kingdoms, Upper and Lower Egypt. Sometime around 3200 BCE the king of Upper Egypt, known variously to history as Narmer or Menes, united the two kingdoms by force into a single Egyptian state.[1] His successor, Hor-Aha, established the first national irrigation control system and founded the national capital at Memphis. Thus began the reign of the pharaohs of the Early Dynastic Period, which lasted for almost five hundred years.

The social order that evolved was similar to the feudal orders of the early European Middle Ages. Egypt's national authority, in the person of the pharaoh, was constantly at odds with rival local barons (nomarchs) who provided military forces to the national sovereign in exchange for local privileges and land. Over time, these rival barons represented a considerable threat to the national state's integrity, and Egypt's early history was punctuated by periods when coalitions of local barons virtually controlled the national authority.

The kings from 3100 to 2686 BCE expanded the Egyptian state. Successful campaigns were launched against Nubia to the south and the Libyans to the west. Expeditions were also undertaken in the Sinai, and trade was established with the principalities in Canaan, Lebanon, and the Jordan Valley. During this period a state bureaucracy was developed, writing was introduced as a tool of centralized administration, and political institutions transformed Egypt from an assembly of chiefdoms into a theocratic state ruled by a pharaoh, who was regarded as divine and was supported by religious and administrative castes.

Over the centuries, however, the pharaohs of the Old Kingdom Period (2575–2150 BCE) were able to create a national identity, conscript armies, fight wars on Egypt's borders, and develop a national defense policy that kept Egypt free from foreign invasion and occupation. That geography isolated Egypt from genuine security threats made this task somewhat easier. To the west was the vast Libyan desert populated by wandering nomadic tribes whose occasional forays represented more of a nuisance than a threat to Egyptian security. To the east were the Sand People of the Sinai and the Canaanite land bridge whose level of societal organization and military sophistication were generally low, rendering them incapable of mounting military operations of sufficient size and strength to challenge Egyptian security. To the south, the Nubians, or "vile Kush" as they were known in Egyptian documents for millennia, represented only a limited military threat. But even here, the cataracts of the Nile helped provide good defensive terrain from which to resist military incursions. Frequent conflicts were fought between Egypt and Nubia for thousands of years, but the Nubian armies' limited sophistication could not really threaten Egypt's existence. To the north the Mediterranean Sea, known to the Egyptians as the Great Green, presented a strategic barrier to invasion, for shipbuilding had not yet evolved to build ships that could transport large numbers of troops across the open sea with any degree of safety. For more than a thousand years Egypt was under no significant military threat from outside its borders.

The Egyptian social order was larger, more sophisticated, and more organized in form and content than almost any other in the region except the Sumerian civilization of southern Mesopotamia. By 3000 BCE Egypt's population was almost 1 million people,[2] and its agriculture could support

2.1. THE ANCIENT NEAR EAST

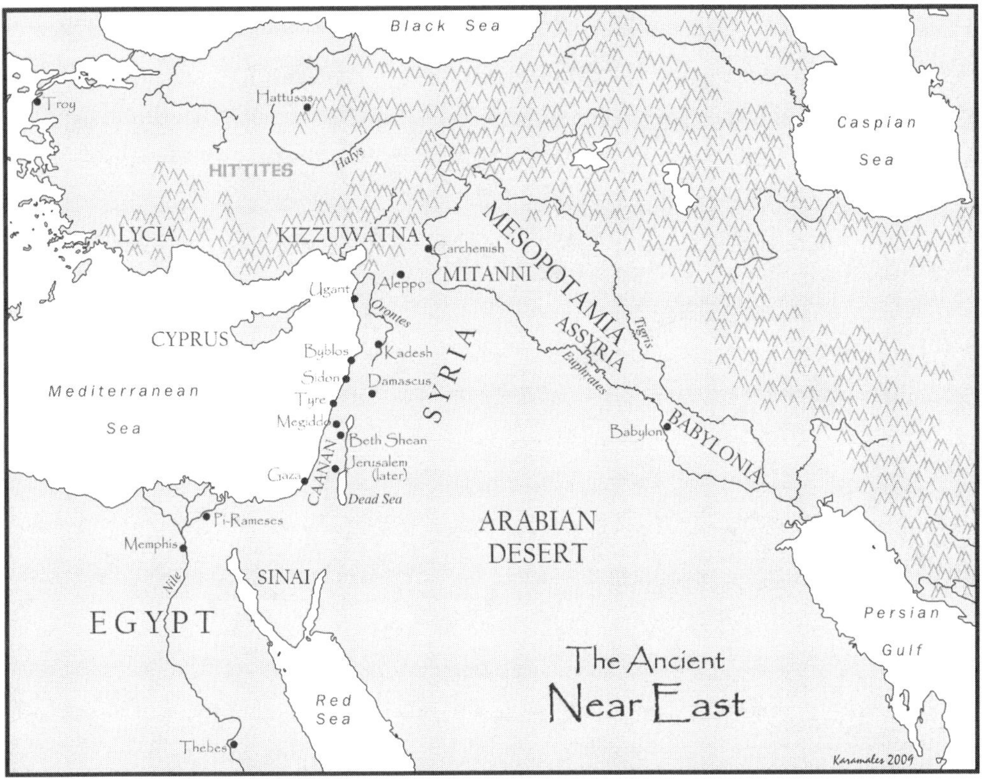

450 people per square mile.[3] Egypt's destruction would have required a degree of shock far beyond its traditional enemies' ability to deliver. Safe behind its natural borders, mesmerized by its unique theology,[4] and well administered by a highly structured governmental system, Egypt was almost hermetically sealed off from the larger military and technological developments occurring in the rest of the Near East, most particularly in Mesopotamia, where military technology and warfare had reached levels far more advanced than those in Egypt.

During the Old Kingdom, Egypt pursued a national defense policy of preclusive security. Egypt focused its efforts on the frontiers to the south and east, the sources of the two most troublesome threats. A series of fortresses called the Wall of Princes was constructed along the Isthmus of Suez and permanently garrisoned. These fortifications were the first and last line of defense against the hit-and-run raids of the Canaanites. To the south, along the First Cataract of the Nile, a series of forts were also constructed to meet the threat of Nubian incursions. Thus, Egyptian national security policy was both strategically and tactically defensive.

None of this discussion about Egypt's defensive posturing is meant to imply that the Egyptians were unaware of the larger world in which they lived or that Egypt did not, from time to time, conduct military expeditions beyond its defensive perimeter. Egyptian governmental functionaries, mostly trade consulates, were stationed in Canaan, Syria, and Lebanon, where they conducted trade, gathered intelligence, and carried out diplomatic activities. It was also Egyptian practice to conduct punitive military raids beyond their line of forts in both directions to punish any transgressions of its borders. These operations were never major campaigns or of long duration, however, and they did not result in the establishment of permanent garrisons in territory beyond Egypt's borders. By the end of the Old Kingdom, the traditional defensive strategy had worked successfully for almost half a millennium to keep Egypt safe from foreign invaders.

The problem of national authority versus local barons had occasionally resulted in periods of domestic unrest and instability, and civil wars precipitated the demise of the Old Kingdom. Events were contained, however, and at the dawn of the second millennium BCE, Egypt entered the Middle Kingdom Period (1975–1640 BCE). As national authorities gained more power over local barons, it was possible to raise larger armies and conduct a more active and aggressive national defense policy. The Middle Kingdom saw the development of a new national defense strategy premised on the creation of buffer zones beyond the walls and forts to the south and east. This strategy also saw more frequent and larger military operations into hostile areas. No longer did Egypt merely react to military threats; now it attempted to preempt them.

Along the eastern border Egyptian armies pressed the security zone farther out from the Wall of Princes and established a major military garrison in southern Canaan. From this forward base, the Egyptians conducted search-and-destroy operations into Canaan proper, on one occasion reaching as far north as Samaria in north-central Canaan to reduce the garrisons of the Asiatics. They made no attempts, however, to permanently occupy strong points in the area of military operations.

In Nubia, Egypt expanded its area of military control almost to the Second Cataract of the Nile, constructing no fewer than twenty-one permanent fortresses in the area of operations. This effort was classic defense in depth, but again the Egyptians did not make any attempt to colonize the new area. Instead, it was turned into a military defense zone designed to make it expensive for the enemy to penetrate the Egyptian homeland. Still reflecting the old policy of strategic defense, the military used offensive tactics to preempt and protect the buffer zone from enemy encroachments. The idea was not to take the war to the enemy, however, but to prevent a large-scale war by preempting his military preparations and punishing him whenever the need arose.

This national defense strategy worked well for almost three centuries. Egypt then entered another period of domestic turmoil in which civil war broke out between local and national authorities. While the Nubian threat remained unchanged, events in Canaan took a more ominous turn. For reasons still unclear, the people of the area, known collectively to the Egyptians as the *Heqau Khasut* or, as rendered later in Greek, the Hyksos,[5] had obtained the superior military technology of the Mesopotamians. While the Hyksos armies had chariots, horses, helmets, body armor, the composite bow, and the penetrating ax—all of which the Mesopotamians introduced to warfare almost five hundred years earlier—the Egyptian armies possessed none of these combat technologies. The result was a greatly increased military threat to the Egyptian eastern border as the Hyksos awaited the opportunity to take advantage of Egyptian domestic instability. Sometime around 1650 BCE, the Hyksos armies struck.[6] With sudden and devastating military force, they invaded Egypt, pressed the national army as far south as Thebes, and occupied the fertile delta region.[7] Establishing their capital at Avaris (modern Tanis), they remained on Egyptian soil for 108 years.[8]

Egyptian power was driven south to Thebes. Sometime during this period, the Nubians overran the southern defenses and established themselves above the First Cataract. Foreigners then occupied Egypt in the north and south while Egyptian national authorities occupied only slightly more than a third of the country. This period saw great national humiliation for the proud Egyptians and was one they never forgot. The Hyksos invasion and occupation had an enormous impact on the Egyptian national psyche.[9] Egypt had gone from a period of security to invasion, occupation, and national peril in a few short years. Ejecting the Hyksos and the Nubians from the country and reestablishing Egyptian national identity became the primary national security goals of the Theban princes. Even after achieving these goals, though, the fear of invasion remained permanently embedded in the Egyptians' national psyche. The result was a new national security policy built around the aggressive use of military force to protect the state.

The struggle against the Hyksos required several generations to succeed, and it began in earnest sometime in the 1550s BCE as the first great warrior pharaoh, Kamose, conducted a series of wars against the Hyksos enemy. The Egyptians' anger against the occupiers was captured in Kamose's words to his council, which opposed hostilities. Kamose understood the role of power in a statesman when he rebuked his councilors:

> Let me understand what this strength of mine is for! One prince is in Avaris, another is in Ethiopia, and here I sit associated with an Asiatic and a Negro! . . . No man can settle down, despoiled by the imposts of the Asiatics. I will grapple with him, that I may cut open his belly! My wish is to save Egypt and to smite the Asiatics.[10]

Having assembled the Egyptian armies under his command at his capital in the city of Thebes, Kamose began his war of liberation.

Kamose gained some initial success, defeating the Hyksos in a series of battles, capturing some of the northern towns, and expanding his control of the Theban ascendancy. He was killed in battle and did not live to see his dream of expelling the hated Asiatics from Egypt. He was succeeded by his brother, Ahmose I (1539–1514 BCE), who ruled for twenty-five years and waged unrelenting war against the occupiers.[11] Ahmose succeeded in driving the Hyksos from Egypt and pressed them back to their strongholds on the Canaanite border. He achieved his goal by

2.2. GEOPOLITICAL SITUATION IN EGYPT DURING THE HYKSOS PERIOD

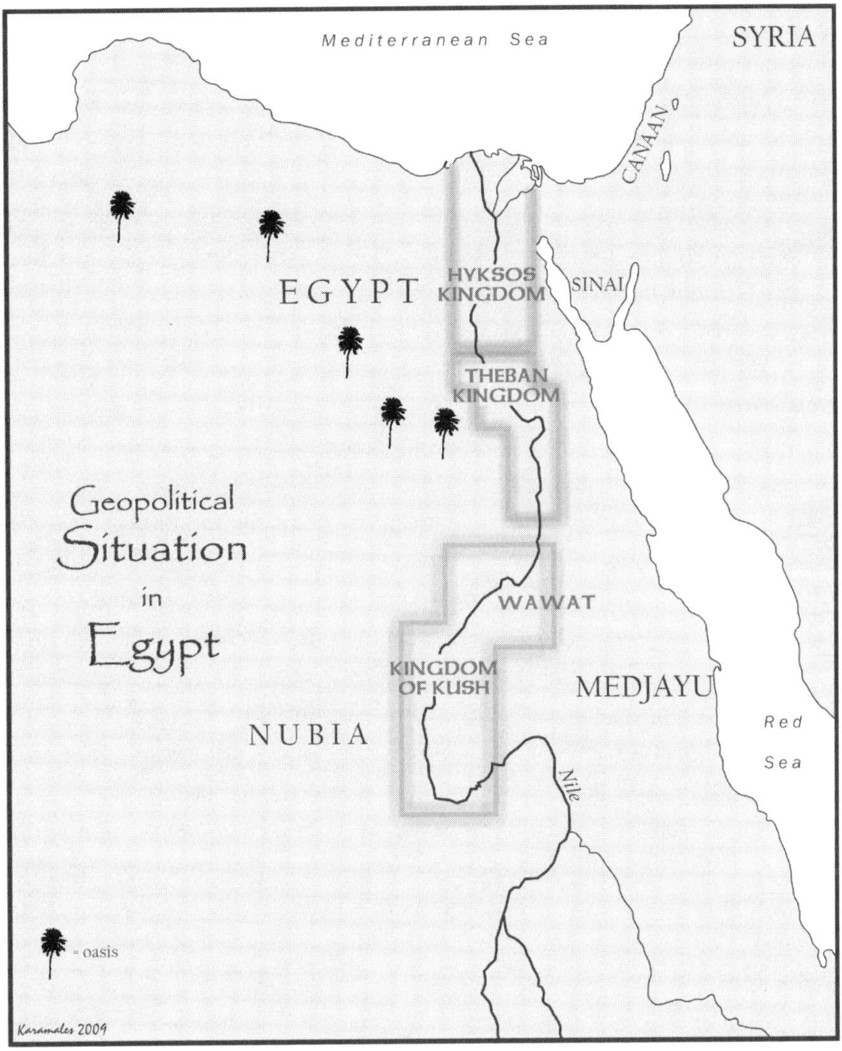

redesigning the army and reducing once and for all the power of the local barons. The new Egyptian army became a national instrument with which to pursue national objectives.

During the war with the Hyksos, Ahmose also conducted holding and spoiling operations against the Nubians in the south. With the primary front secured, he turned his armies southward, driving the Nubians back behind the First Cataract. At the end of his life, Ahmose had restored the territorial integrity of Egypt from the Sinai to the Nubian border, established Thebes as the new capital, redesigned the army into an instrument of national military power, and passed his achievements on to his son, Amenhotep I (1514–1493 BCE). Ahmose also founded the Eighteenth Dynasty of Egyptian kings. Over the next two centuries this dynasty produced fifteen kings, eight of which were great warrior pharaohs. Throughout all of Egyptian history, before or since, there has never been such a long line of talented rulers to oversee Egypt's security.

Under the Eighteenth Dynasty, Egyptian power extended beyond the Sinai into Canaan and Syria. The rulers abandoned the old geographically based defensive strategy and replaced it with a new national defense policy wherein Egypt attempted to influence events in Canaan through diplomacy, treaties, and alliances with various small client states. Egypt developed a sophisticated strategy in which diplomacy, intelligence, and trade were used to influence the Canaanite states' behavior and prevent the emergence of any rival coalition with sufficient strength to threaten Egypt itself. Behind the diplomacy and commercial inducements was Egypt's new modern army, a powerful and mobile instrument of force that could be used to coerce rival states, go to their aid to protect them, and, if need be, to attack any rival coalition of forces that diplomacy failed to prevent. Although military garrisons and strong points were sometimes constructed within the client states as a guarantee of the Egyptians' commitment, for the most part there was less reliance on fortifications and more on the army's ability to move and strike quickly with overwhelming force. Using political, economic, and military assets in the service of clear national policy goals aimed at preventing the rise of a rival military power was a masterpiece of policy integration. Later, Thutmose III gave full expression to this new national defense policy, with the result that he set in place an Egyptian Empire supported by military power that lasted for more than five hundred years.

Egypt's new security strategy was partially dictated by a change in the nature of the threat the empire faced. The Sand People of the Canaanite land bridge, whom the Egyptians continued to view as the descendants of the hated Hyksos, had matured to the point where they constructed sophisticated and powerful military establishments and fortifications.

These circumstances, when taken together, meant that the armies of the small states of the area, especially in coalition, were dangerous and powerful instruments that had to be dealt with if Egypt was to be secure.

At the same time, new and more powerful kingdoms were emerging. The most proximate threats came from the Mitanni, who occupied the land beyond the Great Bend of the Euphrates in northeast Syria and whose client states extended south and west to the Litani River into southern Syria and modern Lebanon. To the northwest the powerful and dangerous Hittites were also beginning to appear as major players on the international scene. Both states eventually became competitors with Egypt for hegemony in Syria. The key to the dominance of Canaan, and thus to protecting the Nile, was the ability of Egypt to control events in Syria. The larger city-states of the area, particularly Kadesh, Qatna, and Tunip on the Orontes River, could affect Egyptian influence considerably. It is testimony to the sophistication of the Egyptians' strategic thinking that they realized that the defense of the Nile began far away in the mountains of Syria.

As noted earlier, the waning of Egyptian influence among the client states of Canaan marked Queen Hatshepsut's reign. The unclear line of royal authority also created domestic difficulties in Egypt. During this uncertain time, the king of Kadesh led a coalition of states and attempted to take advantage of Egypt's domestic political difficulties while the states of northern Canaan also began to maneuver for political advantage. The king of Kadesh saw an opportunity to increase his influence in the key Syrian zone and to weaken Egyptian influence in northern Canaan. These maneuverings did not go unnoticed by the Egyptian diplomatic and intelligence services. Once Thutmose's grip on power was secure, he moved immediately to restore Egyptian power in the critical strategic platform of central Canaan. The result was war.

The Land of Canaan

From 1800 to 1550 BCE climatic conditions improved on the Canaan land bridge and cultural development flourished, permitting the people of Canaan to rebuild their old cities into powerful, new, fortified urban centers. During this time both the first written documents in Canaanite appear and Canaan as a recognizable entity with its own culture can be said to have come into being.[12] Egyptian documents from the time of Senusret II (1897–1878 BCE) tell of a previous era when a number of independent Canaanite kingdoms ruled by warrior princes from fortified towns grew into city-states that challenged Egypt's power in the area. Of these early Canaanite fortified towns two of the more famous were Sodom and Gomorrah. We can deduce from the famous Egyptian story of Sinuwe and his travels in Canaan and Syria that during this time Canaanite society was based on tribes, and each was ruled by a warrior chieftain (*melik*) who held his position by virtue of being the tribe's fiercest warrior. These chiefs maintained household guards (*henkhu*) as part of their personal retinues, which constituted their main combat elements in tribal wars.

The name Canaan is very old and in antiquity denoted that territory between Gaza in the south and the upper reaches of Lebanon north to Ugarit. To the east the land of Canaan ran to the base of the central mountain massif of later Judah and Samaria and then north through the Jezreel Valley to include the Beqqa Valley up to Kadesh. Later Canaan was subject to the passage of a group of warrior tribes, originating somewhere in northern Syria, that moved over the land bridge until they entered Egypt itself. They settled in the Nile Delta near Avaris and defeated the Egyptians by force of arms. These people were the Hyksos. While their origin remains uncertain, undoubtedly these militarily sophisticated people introduced their military technology to Canaan, where the rival princes of the Canaanite city-states adopted it.[13] The origin of the Hyksos' sophisticated equipment is uncertain as well, but it might have come from the technology of the Mitanni-Hurrians of the Upper Euphrates.

The military influence of the Hyksos, and later the Mitanni, brought a number of new weapons to Canaan that revolutionized warfare on the land bridge. From the Hyksos the Canaanites acquired the horse-drawn chariot as a new weapon of war. The composite bow, socket ax, and the sickle-sword also made their appearance in Canaan at this time.[14] The coat of mail used as body armor also came into use at approximately the same time, but at first it was probably worn only by the armed charioteer. Later, we find Canaanite infantry wearing body armor as well.

The Canaanites' new military sophistication during this period was reflected in another development when the Canaanite cities changed the nature of their military fortifications. Canaanite princes began constructing their cities atop a new kind of massive rampart, a slanted bank of packed earth called a glacis. The glacis joined an exterior ditch, or fosse, that obstructed the most likely avenues of approach. During this time Canaan had extensive contacts with the Mitanni-Hurrians, and likely they became the predominant influence on the Canaanites' method of war. The Mitannian influence on the new architecture, for example, is also seen in two powerful cities in northern Syria, Carchemish and Ebla, which used the same fortifications.[15]

The influence of the Mitanni-Hurrian culture during this period was strongly reflected in the transformation of Canaanite society itself into one derived from the Mitannian model. In Canaan a feudal warrior noble caste based on heredity and land possession came into existence. As in the land of the Mitanni, these warriors were called *maryanna*, and like their Mitannian cousins, they were an elite group of chariot warriors. This elite ruled over a half-free, Semitic-speaking class of peasants and farmers *(khupshu)* without a middle or merchant class in between.[16] There is some evidence that the feudal barons were of non-Semitic stock, another similarity with the Mitannian social order. The transformation of Canaanite military technology and social organization produced a society able and willing to fight wars, especially in resistance to the aspirations of the great powers to the south (the Egyptians) and to the north (the Hittites and the Mitanni).

The presence of foreign influence did not prohibit the Canaanite princes from fortifying their important cities and towns. The entire country was heavily fortified even though an independent king or chief ruled each city-state. Although there was no Canaanite high king to direct it, the countrywide Canaanite fortification design was so well integrated as to suggest at least some degree of cooperation among the princes. The purpose of these fortifications was to protect the lucrative trade routes that crisscrossed the country, linking it to Syria and Egypt, and to protect Canaan from the predations of migrating nomadic tribes. Taken together, the system of fortifications was designed to permit the Canaanite princes to mount a mobile defense in depth, using mounted chariot warriors. Only as a last resort did Canaanites permit themselves to be besieged in their cities.

Illustration 2.3 portrays the Canaanite strategic defense system. Each of the major fortified cities served as a base for chariot units to disrupt

2.3. CANAAN: STRATEGIC PASSES, ROADS, AND FORTIFICATIONS

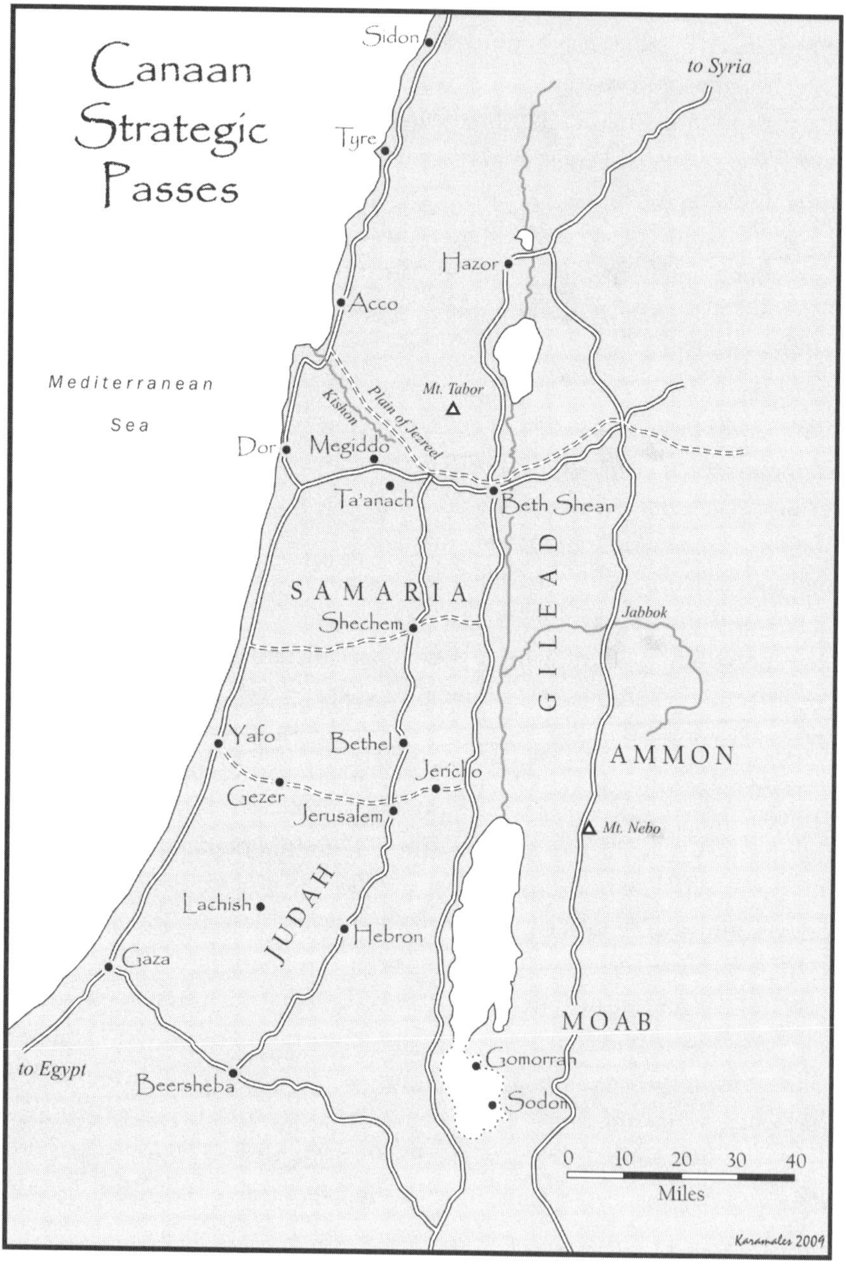

and neutralize an enemy threat. Hazor, the largest of Canaanite cities whose kings ruled over all of northern Canaan, sat astride a key road junction that controlled the route leading to Damascus and the Lebanon ports. Megiddo controlled the access to the Jezreel Valley from the coastal road—known as the Way of Horus to the Egyptians and the Via Maris to the Romans—leading east to the Transjordan. Beth Shean was located at the far eastern exit of the Jezreel Valley and controlled the entrance to the Jordan plain, blocking the logical route of the migrating desert tribes. Shechem, in the middle of the country, controlled the crossroads of the lateral routes across the land bridge. Closer to the coast sat Gezer, which presided over the southern junction of two ancient trade routes—the Way of Horus connecting Egypt and the main road leading inland up to Jerusalem and the gateway to the central mountains. And Jerusalem itself, situated on the northern central ridge, controlled the north-south route running along the spine of the mountains. It also sat astride the continuation of the road leading from the Mediterranean Sea east into Jordan.[17] Operating either independently or in concert, depending on the size and nature of the threat, the Canaanite princes were able to mount a fierce defense of their territories from these strategically located urban fortifications. From a military point of view, the city-states of Canaan represented a formidable defensive array against Egyptian encroachment.

The Mitanni

The people known as the Mitanni appeared on history's stage for only a short time, perhaps less than two centuries, before disappearing forever. In that period the Mitanni built a powerful nation around which swirled the great power conflicts of the armies of the Near East from the fourteenth to the twelfth centuries BCE. The Egyptians, Assyrians, and Hittites were all at one time or another allies or enemies of the Mitanni. The latter's geographic position astride the main trade, transportation, and communication routes of Anatolia, Mesopotamia, and Egypt forced it to play the role of balancer among the great powers in order to preserve its own security. The Mitanni occupied the area of the northern Euphrates plain, or the steppe between the Euphrates and Tigris rivers. The Assyrians called this area Hanigalbat, a term that became synonymous with the Mitanni. It encompassed the area of what is today southeastern Turkey, northern Syria, and northern

Iraq, or approximately the area corresponding to Kurdistan. Its capital, Washukkanni (Ushshukana), probably lay at the head of the Khabur River Valley. From here the power of the Mitanni spread eastward over the east Tigris region and Assyria, where it reduced the country to vassalage. All the Assyrian kings between 1500 and 1360 BCE were vassals of the Mitanni,[18] and there is evidence of Mitannian military units stationed in Assyria at this time.

To the north, Mitannian power held sway in the ancient land of the Urartu, or modern Armenia.[19] In the northwest the borders of Mitannian influence touched on Anatolia, the land of the powerful Hittites, and for more than a century tension and frequent wars marked the relations between the two nations. Northern Syria to the west marked the point where Mitannian power rubbed against the northern frontiers of the Egyptian empire and where, at one point, Mitannian influence ran to the Litani River and the city of Megiddo.[20] For more than two centuries northern Syria was the hub of great power politics and the place where the influence of three powerful states—that of the Hittites, the Egyptians, and the Mitanni—collided and rubbed each other raw.

With few natural boundaries protecting their homeland, their routes to sources of strategic metals and materials terminating in hostile territory, and hostile powers surrounding them, it is not surprising that the Mitanni became skillful warriors as their Hittite and Egyptian adversaries did. For two centuries the Mitanni kept Assyria under its heel, stationing troops throughout the country to secure its loyalty. Early in the seventeenth century BCE, the Mitanni invaded the land of the Hittites and inflicted a major defeat. From that time forward, the Mitanni consistently intervened in Hittite domestic politics, provoking civil wars among Hittite vassals and aiding foreign tribal people in their conflicts with Hittite rulers. The Mitanni forged alliances with powerful vassals along the Hittite homeland's borders to form a ring of buffer states that would keep Hittite power contained beyond the Taurus Mountains and the Cilician Gates. In Syria, Mitannian diplomacy aimed at establishing alliances with powerful city-states such as Kadesh, Tunip, and Aleppo, whose rulers saw these alliances as a counterweight to Egyptian influence there. It was just such a Mitanni-inspired coalition that sought to test the mettle of the new Egyptian king at Megiddo.

Thutmose III's policy of expanding Egyptian power to the Orontes River succeeded in pushing the Mitanni back across the Litani River. Over the next century, however, a rough parity between Egyptian and Mitannian influence in Syria developed so that during the reigns of Amenhotep II and Thutmose IV (1479–1400) the two nations signed a mutual assistance treaty directed at containing Hittite ambitions in northern Syria.[21] With the ascent of the religious fanatic Akhenaten to the Egyptian throne (1353–1336), Egypt turned its attention elsewhere and proved to be a weak reed in upholding its military obligations under the treaty. With Egypt on the sidelines, the Hittites saw their chance to drive the Mitanni from Syria.

The origins of the Mitanni are uncertain but seem closely related to the history of the Hurrians, about whom we know only slightly more. The Hurrians are first mentioned in the Amarna letters (diplomatic correspondence) and again in the Bible (Genesis 36:20–30), where they are called Horites. The Hurrian language is neither Semitic nor Indo-European but seems vaguely related to the Asiatic group whose nearest relative is the language of the Urartu. It is likely then that the highlands of Armenia are the original homeland of the Hurrians.[22] The Hurrians appear to have been a people given to migration or clan travel, and there is evidence that colonies of Hurrians had been extant in various parts of Mesopotamia for millennia. For example, evidence shows a Hurrian element in ancient Sumer before 2000 BCE, and during the Akkadian period that followed a Hurrian community appears to have been in the area of the Upper Tigris from which it migrated into the Fertile Crescent proper.[23] By 1800 BCE, the Hurrians were a majority in the Syrian town of Alalakh, situated between Aleppo and Antioch, and a century or so later they were a majority in northern Iraq itself. During this time they occupied the city of Gasur, changed its name to Nuzi, and adopted the language and customs of the former Semitic community there.[24] After 1600 BCE, the Hurrian element became dominant in northern Syria.

Hittite texts dating from the middle of the seventeenth century BCE record a major attack on the Hittite homeland by a people called the Hurri, but the texts suggest that they were not yet a unified people established in a single homeland but instead a confederation of people organized along clan lines. Probably around this time a warrior caste of Aryan (Indo-Iranian) dynasts imposed themselves upon the Hurrian people and became a new aristocracy in command of war and the government.[25] By 1550 BCE, Hittite texts report a major Hurrian-based kingdom, then known as the Mitanni, had been established east of the Euphrates River while other smaller Hurrian states were also extant in northern Syria at the same time. During this period the Mitanni established their dominance over Assyria and became a major competitor to Hittite and Egyptian influence in Syria. While the Assyrians called this powerful kingdom of the Mitanni Hanigalbat, the Egyptians called it *nhrn* (Akkadian for "river"), which was rendered as Naharin.

Just when and how the Hurrians were eclipsed or subsumed under the people who called themselves Mitanni are uncertain. One widely accepted idea is that the Indo-Aryan Mitanni were equipped with the horse chariot, and that weapon permitted them to rapidly conquer the area. Another view is that the Mitanni were an Indo-European people of the Russian steppe.[26] That the Mitanni were of Indo-Aryan origin seems probable, however, in that their gods and several of their famous kings, including Tushrata and Mattiwaza, have names that are linguistically of Indo-Aryan origin. Wherever the Mitanni came from, there is no dispute that by 1500 BCE or so (and perhaps earlier) the Mitanni had imposed themselves as the new leaders of the Hurrian state. The name of the Mitanni king, Paratarna, appears around 1480 BCE, by which time Mitannian influence is already evident as far south as Qatna and Ugarit.

What did the Mitanni bring to the Hurrian society that permitted them to rise to such heights of power and prestige? Two answers suggest themselves. First, the Mitanni seem to have imposed themselves upon the Hurrians relatively peacefully and to have adopted the culture of the land they entered. Their main contribution seems to have been to introduce a new form of political and social organization that was more effective at mobilizing and employing resources for war.[27] The organizational pattern was a familiar one among Indo-Aryans; that is, a strong king was drawn from a great family and tied by blood to his vassals, who acted as a council of advisers. This system also permitted a council of elders and perhaps an assembly of free men (warriors) from the tribe to act as advisers, and their consent may have been required for the king to undertake certain tasks.[28] The Mitannian system was not unlike that found earlier among the Hittites, whose origins are, like those of the Mitanni, obscure and involve the superimposition of a new warrior caste upon the then extant Hatti society.

Second, the Mitanni were probably the first to truly exploit the horse as an instrument of war, most particularly using it with the spoked-wheel chariot as a combat vehicle. They did not, of course, introduce the horse to Mesopotamia, where it had been known from at least the Sumerian period. During the Akkadian period the animal was known as *sisu* in Akkadian.[29] It is likely that the Hurrians first used the horse as a draft animal for agricultural purposes, even before the migrations. What is clear, however, is that the spoked-wheel war chariot made its first appearance among the Mitanni sometime soon after the their arrival in the Hurrian land, or about circa 1600 BCE. Almost simultaneously, the war chariot appears in Kassite Babylonia, among the Hittites and the Hyksos, and a short time later among the Egyptians. The validity of the Mitannian claim as being the first to use this weapon can be deduced from the era's Hittite texts, which recount the story of Kikkuli of the Land of the Mitanni whom the Hittite king hired to instruct his army in the breeding and use of horses.[30] H. M. F. Saags suggests the evidence is sufficient to award the claim of this chariot's first use, if not outright invention, to the Mitanni.[31] Whatever the case, the war chariot's appearance as a major weapon of war in the Near East coincided closely with the arrival and emergence of the Mitanni in the former Hurri states. While neither the horse nor the chariot can be attributed to the Mitanni with certainty, it is highly probable that the Mitanni were the inventors of and first to use the chariot system, an innovation that changed the face of battle among the armies of the Near East for the next thousand years.

Nubia

The land the Egyptians called Ta Nehesy from time immemorial extended south from the First Cataract of the Nile near modern Aswan to the Fifth Cataract, some four hundred miles as the crow flies but closer to six hundred miles by boat. We know almost nothing certain about the ethnic constitution of the country, its social structure, or its political order.[32] All that we can reasonably discern is that Nubian society seems to have been made up of various small kingdoms ruled by local chiefdoms. From time to time a high chief emerged who was able to assemble several of these kingdoms into a larger political-military order and bring their combined troops to bear against Egyptian incursions. But these larger entities usually did not persist for very long. The country was not highly urbanized, and even those areas closest to the Egyptian border had few towns of any size.

Egypt was originally attracted to Nubia for chiefly economic reasons, and from the Twelfth Dynasty Period Egypt fortified and controlled northern Lower Nubia (Wawat) and competed with the Kingdom of Kerma for influence in Upper Nubia (Kush). The Egyptians built fortresses and troop garrisons to exert their influence over the region. Nubia's economic resources included large amounts of alluvial land that supported extensive farming and animal production, resources that permitted it to support a relatively large population. Nubia's eastern desert was the source of substantial gold deposits, and the country was also the source of such highly desired trade goods as ivory, ebony, and panther skins.[33] The rich grasslands south of the Third Cataract produced great quantities of grain and other cereals. Later, under Egyptian occupation, Nubia became an important source of wood, and there is evidence that the Nubians produced ships for the Egyptians, although it is likely that these were small river craft for moving trade goods rather than Egyptian naval vessels.[34]

While Egypt and Nubia had engaged in running skirmishes for centuries, Nubia presented no strategic threat to Egyptian security until the period of the Hyksos invasion. When the Hyksos began occupying the Nile Delta in the north, a powerful new kingdom emerged below the Third Cataract in the Dongola reach centered on the town of Kerma.[35] Taking advantage of Egyptian weakness, the military forces of Kerma moved north into Upper Egypt itself, destroying its temples, towns, and forts.[36] The Nubians established close ties with the Hyksos in the north, squeezing Theban Egypt between them. When the Theban prince Kamose mounted his attempt to eject the Hyksos from Egypt, the Hyksos appealed to the Nubians to attack Thebes from the south. The Hyksos' letter to the Nubians was intercepted, and Kamose moved troops to close the eastern desert caravan route around Thebes. The incident revealed the strategic threat from Nubia, and before marching north against the Hyksos, Kamose moved south to drive the Nubians back beyond the First Cataract. Kamose likely moved his army overland through the desert rather than up the Nile by boat and struck the Nubians' position from the rear.[37]

2.4. EGYPT AND NUBIA

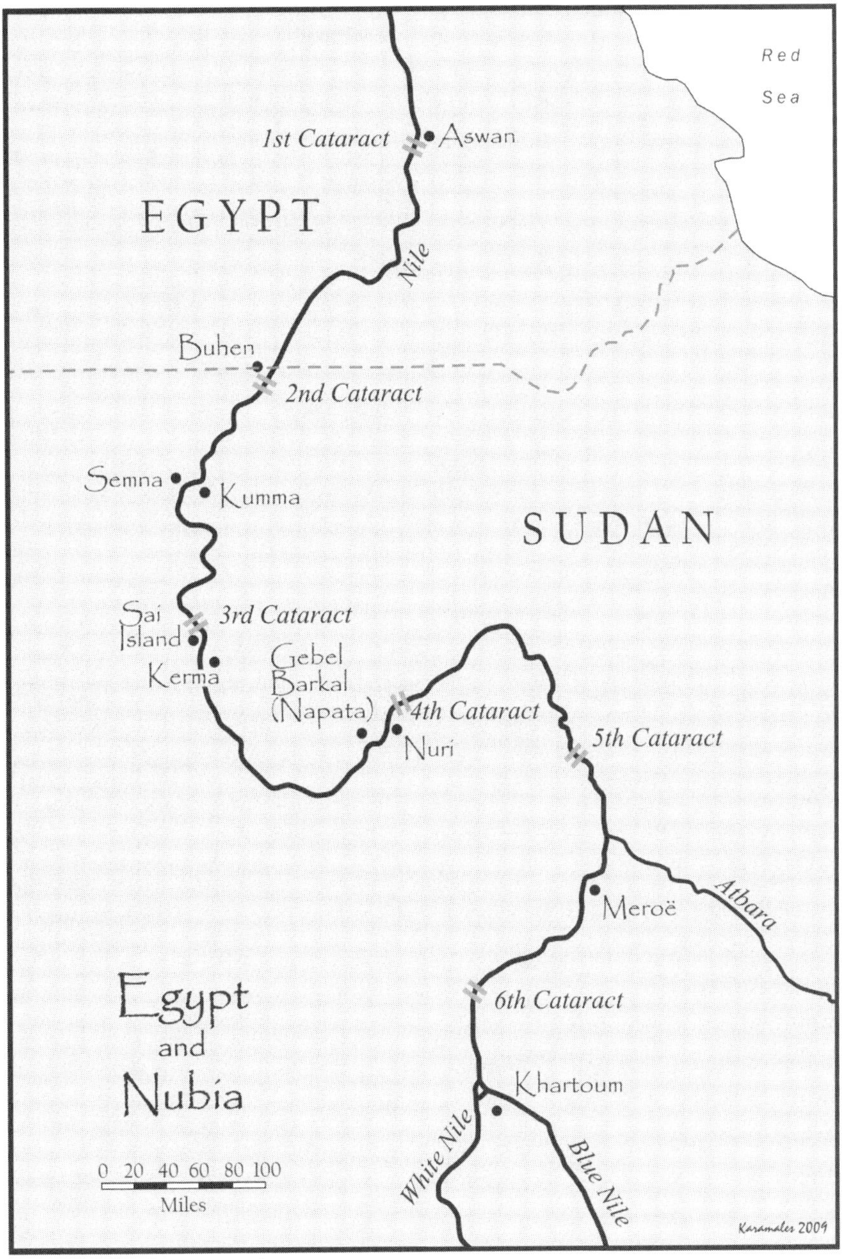

The Egyptians marched south as far as Buhen, recaptured the fortress there, and established a defensive line to contain any further Nubian encroachments to the north. From this time on, Egypt always regarded Nubia as a potential strategic threat as well as a region to be exploited economically; consequently, wars and invasions occurred sporadically in the area over the next eighty years.

When Ahmose succeeded his brother to the Theban throne, the situation in Nubia had already been stabilized. Ahmose turned his attention to the task of driving the hated Hyksos from Egypt while Egyptian forces in Nubia went over to the strategic defensive to prevent further incursions into southern Egypt. In the later half of his second decade of rule, after driving out the Hyksos, Ahmose moved against Nubia. He established new political and economic institutions in Lower Nubia to incorporate the area into southern Egypt proper. He then marched beyond Buhen and reached the Second Cataract, defeating the Nubians as he went. With this area pacified, Ahmose moved farther south and put down a series of disturbances and revolts between the Second and Third cataracts.[38]

Amenhotep I, Ahmose's son, continued to put pressure on Nubia and invaded the land to extend Egypt's boundaries. The problem he encountered was the Kingdom of Kush. Amenhotep moved his army overland instead of by boat, swung hard east, and then attacked Kush from the rear.[39] Thutmose I followed up with another major military incursion, this time reaching as far south as the Fifth Cataract and chasing rebels and hunting down desert raiders. The campaign was a combination of search-and-destroy and clearing operations but extended too far from its base, and no attempt was made to hold the land south of the Third Cataract. Thutmose did manage to establish firm control over Upper Nubia and divided the territory into five administrative regions, each controlled by a local chief whose loyalty was sworn to Egypt. The system broke down when some of the chiefs failed to prevent rebellions, and early in his reign Thutmose II was forced to send an army into the area to put down the disturbance. That the pharaoh himself did not lead the expedition, however, suggests that the problem was not serious. Nonetheless, Thutmose II imposed a new administrative structure on Nubia, so by the end of his reign all of Upper and Lower Nubia had been amalgamated into the Egyptian state and was now peacefully administered.[40]

Events in Nubia during the joint reign of Hatshepsut and Thutmose III are unclear, but it is likely that Hatshepsut was forced to send troops into Nubia no fewer than four times to put down disturbances of one sort or another.[41] There is evidence that the queen herself accompanied one of these forays, suggesting that the Egyptians regarded these events as important.[42] On one of these forays it is possible that Thutmose III commanded the operation. Whatever the nature or extent of the Nubian problem, by the time Thutmose III assumed his sole occupancy of the Egyptian throne, the situation was sufficiently stabilized so that he could turn his full attention to the problems facing Egypt in Canaan.

Later in his reign, Thutmose ordered the construction of many fortified settlements, temples, and forts in Nubia and imposed a regular economic and administrative structure on it so that the country was thoroughly integrated into the Egyptian political and economic system. In Thutmose's regnal year 42, he led a demonstration of force expedition down the Nile that reached the Fourth Cataract, where he erected the famous Gebel Barkal stela. In regnal year 50, he led a large force farther south and reached the Fifth Cataract. The Egyptians never fully controlled the area south of Gebel Barkal, however; minor incidents occurred there frequently. But from Gebel Barkal to the north, Nubia was strongly tied to Egyptian power and culture, so much so that within a few hundred years, the people of the area came to think of themselves as Egyptians. Anthony J. Spalinger sums up Thutmose III's achievements in Nubia correctly when he says, "If Thutmose III is famous owing to his Asiatic warfare, he ought to be equally renowned for effecting the final pacification of Nubia."[43]

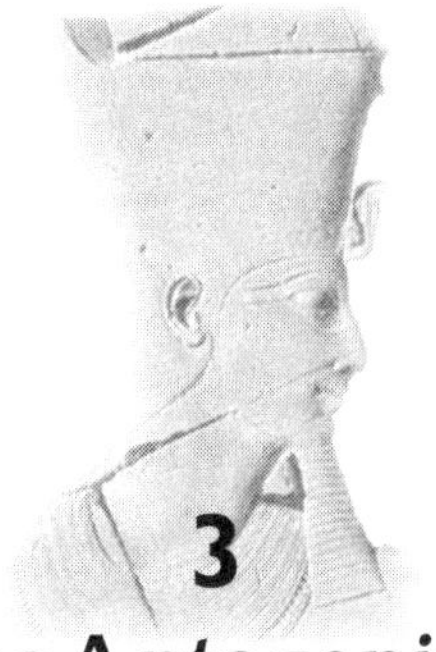

3
The Antagonists

Pharaoh's Army

A definable military organization first emerged in Egypt during the period of the Old Kingdom (2575–2150 BCE).[1] Although united in a single kingdom, Egypt's political order was fragmented, and local nomarchs remained sufficiently powerful to obstruct pharaonic power. The nomarchs raised and maintained their own military forces and often controlled strategic resources and important trade routes. The situation was similar to feudal Europe, where the power of the king depended on his ability to control his local barons.[2]

The national army arose from the pharaohs' needs to defend the state against Libyan and Nubian raiders and to deal with the nomarchs' periodic revolts. Pharaoh's army consisted of a small standing force of several thousand regular troops organized in the manner of household guards. Egypt introduced conscription, levying one man in ten to service each year, but even then the nomarchs provided these troops.[3] The best of the conscripts went to the army, where the small force of regular officers organized and trained them. Others were sent to labor battalions. Nubian auxiliaries in the pay of the king augmented the standing armies.[4]

The army mostly comprised militia units organized under the local nomarchs' command. These barons were required to provide specific troop levies to the pharaoh during times of emergency. In normal times, however, the troops were raised, trained, and kept at the local level. The political relationship between the king and the local rulers largely determined if and how many troops would be made available for dealing with national problems. A large number of conscript troops levied under the system of national conscription did not go to regular combat units. Instead, these soldiers received some military training and were used to garrison the frontier forts and furnish corvée labor for public works projects. It is unknown how long the term of service for conscript soldiers was, but apparently soldiers remained with local militia units for some time after completing their initial period of national service.

The organizational structure of the army of the Old Kingdom is unclear, but it is evident that distinctions were made between regular officers and men of other ranks. A number of military titles appear for the first time, including those of specialists in desert travel, frontier and desert warfare, garrison troops, frontier troops, quartermaster officers, and scribes who seem to have functioned as senior noncommissioned officers.[5] There are also titles that refer to "overseers of arsenals," "overseers of desert blockhouses and royal fortresses," and "caravan leaders."[6] The army's size remains a mystery. Weni, a commander in the army of the Sixth Dynasty (2345 BCE), recorded that his army was many tens of thousands strong.[7] A string of twenty mud brick fortresses was built around approximately 2200 BCE to guard the southern approaches to Egypt, each requiring up to three thousand men to garrison. This number suggests an army of at least sixty thousand in the frontier force alone.[8] With Egypt's population approaching two million at this time, these force levels could have easily been achieved.

The Egyptian armies of the Middle Kingdom (1975–1640 BCE) became more structurally articulated as Egypt struggled through periods of anarchy and the weakening of its centralized authority, which eventually emboldened the Hyksos to invade and occupy the territory. This period saw a constant tug and pull between the pharaohs and the nomarchs who still controlled their feudal armies. The pharaohs retained their standing armies, which were augmented by conscription, and still employed Nubian auxiliaries. Then a clearer command structure emerged with the pharaoh acting as a field commander on major campaigns and with general officers in charge of safeguarding the frontiers and managing logistics. There were also clearer distinctions among junior officer ranks and titles.[9] Titles appear for commanders of shock troops, recruits, instructors, and commanders of retainers, or personal bodyguards of the king. The title of assault troop commander appears for the first time. The progression in rank for junior officers began with a command of a unit of seven men, then to a company of sixty men, and finally to a unit of a hundred men.[10]

The proliferation of formal titles during this period implies that the army's administrative mechanisms had become more complex. For the first time there is evidence of a military intelligence service, which is reflected in the title Master of the Secrets of the King in the Army.[11] The army also seems to have organized troops on the basis of their experience and age. Names and titles appear for companies and regiments, although the strengths of these units are not known. Terms for bowmen, garrison troops, police patrols, district officers, and military judges make their appearance. While the army of the Middle Kingdom appears more formally organized than that of its predecessor, it is difficult to determine to what extent this difference may be a function of the survivability of their records more than anything else.

By 1700 BCE the centralized government of Egypt began to lose ground to the rebellious nomarchs, and the national army proved insufficient to control them. Taking advantage of the disarray, the Hyksos invaded Egypt sometime around 1650 BCE and established themselves for more than a century as the rulers of Lower Egypt. One of the more intriguing military mysteries of the Hyksos is how they were able to overwhelm the Egyptians so quickly. Much of the answer lies in their ability to bring effective military technology to bear on the battlefield, technology that was unknown in Egypt at the time. The Egyptian army was an infantry force organized into units of bowmen, spearmen, and axmen. By contrast, the Hyksos army was an army of mobility and firepower. The centerpiece of the Hyksos field army was the composite bow archer mounted on the horse-drawn chariot, and their infantrymen were equipped with helmets, body armor, sickle-swords, and socketed penetrating axes.[12] These weapons conveyed a decisive military advantage, especially when wielded by the Hyksos military professionals.

These new weapons must have terrified the Egyptian soldier. While the Egyptians were forced to anchor their positions with exposed infantry formations, the Hyksos archers could kill them from a distance with their composite bows, whose range exceeded that of the Egyptians' simple bows by two hundred yards. Egyptian formations were immobile while the Hyksos mounted chariot charges from all directions. The psychological impact on the Egyptian soldiers of facing the horse must also have been significant, for the horse was generally unknown in Egypt. The Egyptian blade ax was no match for the killing power of the penetrating ax, and without body armor the sickle-sword took a heavy toll in close combat.

The Hyksos established their capital at Avaris (modern Tanis) and then captured the Egyptian capital of Memphis. For the next century they controlled most of Lower Egypt while Upper Egypt remained largely in the hands of the Theban princes.[13]

The wars of liberation Kamose and Ahmose waged brought profound changes in Egyptian society and its governing institutions. For the first time a truly professional military caste came into being. Amenhotep I, Ahmose's son, instituted the practice of awarding landed estates to his battle-hardened officers and thus began a professional officer corps to lead the national military establishment. These military families retained the land grants from generation to generation only so long as they continued to send at least one son into career military service.[14] The army rid itself of the local militias, reorganized its structure, and became a genuine national force based in conscription. The local militias continued to exist, but the nomarchs lost the ability to withhold troop levies from the king. Over the next thirty years the Egyptian army completely changed its weapons and tactics. First, all the weapons of the Hyksos—the chariot, composite bow, penetrating ax, sickle-sword, helmets, and armor—were incorporated into the Egyptian army. Great improvements in the chariot's physical design and the tactical doctrines that governed its use on the battlefield were also implemented.[15] The combination of the composite bow archer mounted on the improved chariots produced one of the most important military revolutions in ground warfare yet seen in the Near East. The result was a modern fighting machine, which Thutmose III used to create the Egyptian empire.

Modernizing the Egyptian military establishment took some fifty years and could begin only after the Hyksos had been driven from the country. Even then, it proceeded slowly. The Hyksos' occupation of the Nile Delta made it impossible for the Theban princes to adopt the superior weapons and technologies of the occupiers.[16] By controlling the trade routes to Canaan and Syria, the Hyksos denied Egypt access to the sources of strategic raw materials from which the new weapons and machines were manufactured. Producing bronze weapons required expensive and rare tin that had to be imported from merchants in Canaan and Syria, and as long as the Hyksos controlled the Egyptian ports and overland routes to Canaan, they could deprive the Theban princes of this precious strategic material. Different woods required to manufacture chariots also had to be imported. Ash for chariot frames, axles, and felloes; maple for the floors; elm for the wheel spindles and yokes; and bark from the silver birch to waterproof the glued joints and leather that held the machine together all had to be imported from Syria and Anatolia. Composite bows were also made from imported goods like ash and birch bark, which was used to waterproof the laminations of the weapon.[17] Further, while there is some evidence that the horse was used in Egypt before the invasion,[18] their presence in large numbers and their use as implements of war resulted after the Hyksos' invasion.[19] With the Hyksos limiting overland trade, however, they prevented the Egyptians from obtaining horses in any significant numbers. To modernize its armed forces, Egypt would first have to break the Hyksos' stranglehold on Egyptian trade routes and obtain access to important strategic materials.

The armies of Kamose and Ahmose that drove the Hyksos from Egypt were not state-of-the-art military machines; instead, they were the traditional infantry forces armed with the same weapons the armies of the Middle Kingdom used. The next army, that of Amenhotep I, also showed little change in its weaponry and no evidence of chariots, except to mention them as vehicles for transporting the pharaoh. The same held true for Thutmose I's army, although he likely was the first pharaoh to begin seriously reequipping the army with modern weapons and vehicles. The process of acquiring and adopting new military technologies required much more than simply gaining access to raw materials. It also required a knowledge of their manufacturing methods; the availability of suitably skilled craftsmen, which, in the case of the Egyptians, meant finding and importing foreign craftsmen; a political or social need for the new technology; and a suitable strategic context that supported operational plans and strategies within which the new technologies would be used.[20] These requirements were not immediately fulfilled in Egypt when the Hyksos left, and they took considerable time to develop.[21]

The departure of the Hyksos did not likely immediately improve Egyptian access to strategic raw materials, for instance. The Canaanite city-states, some of which had maryannu elites imposed on them by the retreating Hyksos, could hardly have seen it in their interests to supply the Egyptian colossus with the materials and the technical knowledge from which their own destruction might be fashioned. More likely it took years before the needed materials made their way in sufficient quantities to Egyptian military workshops. One of the reasons for Thutmose I's raid into Canaan and southern Syria may have been to demonstrate Egyptian power and to stimulate the flow of strategic materials from the Canaanite city-states. Moreover, Egypt had to find the monetary resources to pay for these expensive materials. Perhaps gaining access to its gold mines pressed the Egyptians to attack and occupy Nubia almost immediately after they drove the Hyksos from Egypt. Without a new strategic vision and operational doctrine that defined how the new weapons were to be employed, the Egyptian military's modernization would have also been slowed.

Until Thutmose II's reign, Egyptian strategy had been occupied first with ejecting the Hyksos and second with reestablishing Egyptian control of Nubia, both of which were accomplished with traditionally equipped Egyptian armies. While it must have been obvious that bronze weapons, armor, and the composite bow increased the Egyptian infantry's combat power, it was by no means clear that the chariot would do so as well. Egypt proper was not particularly well suited to chariot warfare. Except for a few places in the Nile Delta, there were no wide-open plains upon which to maneuver as there were in Canaan and Syria.[22] Once beyond the narrow fertile belt, which was crisscrossed with streams, irrigation canals, villages, and ditches, the Egyptians encountered mostly rocky plains and desert. The same topography is found in Nubia. Military movement in Egypt then was best accomplished via boat up and down the Nile and not overland by oxcart or chariot. For millennia the Egyptians referred to their navy as the army because it provided the army's strategic and tactical transport until the military services were separated under Thutmose I.[23]

It is always interesting to ask if technology follows a paradigm shift or if the reverse is the case. By the reign of Thutmose II and his immediate successor, Hatshepsut, the process of Egyptian military modernization was still incomplete and unsupported by a new strategic doctrine to underpin its implementation. As long as Egypt remained a strategically defensive power, the relatively small existing military establishment, equipped with bronze weapons but without large chariot squadrons, would suffice. When Thutmose III came to power, he provided a new strategic vision and shifted the Egyptian strategic paradigm from defense to offense.

In this new strategic perspective, Egypt's defense required the military and political subordination of the city-states of Canaan and Syria. Given the nature of these enemy forces, which were equipped with bronze weapons and armor; of their fortified cities; and of the open terrain, which would require rapid movement and maneuverability to dominate it, Thutmose also required a newly structured military force. To achieve its strategic goals the new army would have to be larger, better equipped, and better organized logistically to carry out expeditionary campaigns almost without rest. Garrisons had to be constructed and manned, the professional cadre expanded to organize and train large numbers of conscripts, and new administrative roles had to be created and staffed. Transporting Egyptian forces by sea also required expanding and modernizing the navy, meaning Egypt needed new shipyards and a large shipbuilding program. Egypt also had to secure the sources of important strategic materials and establish thousands of new workshops manned with skilled craftsmen to produce the necessary modern weapons and war machines in substantial numbers. While the army's restructuring program probably began under Hatshepsut and incorporated previous improvements in supplying new weapons, most of the credit is owed to "the military genius of Thutmose III."[24]

Thutmose III's strategic vision brought about another important development, the Egyptian imperial navy. Egypt could not hope to bring Canaan and Syria under its control if it had to move its army overland each time that control was threatened by a revolt. The overland march had numerous disadvantages. It was 350 miles long, took a high toll on the army's men and machines, was difficult and expensive to support logistically, conceded the tactical initiative to the enemy, and took too much time, sacrificing any possibility of surprise. In addition, the transit time through Canaan reduced the effective campaign season to such a degree that the Egyptian army would be incapable of conducting sustained operations against the Mitanni across the Euphrates.[25] Maintaining permanent troop garrisons of sufficient strength in Syria was expensive and probably not possible in terms of manpower. To achieve Egypt's strategic goals in Canaan and Syria, then, Thutmose had to find a way to move his army quickly into the zone of operations and to do so at a low cost.

Thutmose's solution was to transport his army by ship along the Canaanite-Lebanon-Syrian coast, land it in secure harbors logistically prepared in advance, and then strike inland against his adversary. Instead of invasions, Thutmose planned to conduct rapid expeditionary operations. The Egyptians had been sailors and shipbuilders from time immemorial but only on the Nile and never on the open sea. The navy had been an integral part of the army until Thutmose I and had considerable experience in transporting troops and equipment over long distances up and down the Nile. The wars against the Hyksos and the conquest of Nubia had been successfully achieved with naval operations transporting troops to the battle areas, sometimes over distances of more than a thousand miles. To fulfill Thutmose's mission, however, the navy had to construct more and larger ships, to learn how to transport and unload horses, and, most important, to learn how to sail upon the Mediterranean Sea.

Early in his reign, Thutmose ordered the expansion of the military's presence at the new town of Perunefer (literally, "good sailing" or "bon voyage"), which was located on the western edge of the old Hyksos capital of Avaris and on the Pelusiac branch of the Nile leading to the open sea.[26] A large army, logistics, and naval base was constructed there and became the main operational base from which troops and equipment were transported to carry out military operations in Asia.[27] A large dockyard for building ships was established, and the Egyptians began to construct new and larger ships, including seagoing horse and troop transports.[28] Six years after Thutmose's attack on Megiddo, he transported his army by sea, landed on the Lebanon coast, and attacked Kadesh, conducting the "first great amphibious operation in history."[29] Over the next three years Thutmose gained control of numerous Lebanon port cities, converting them into safe harbors and logistics bases for future expeditionary operations. From this time forward, Egypt had no rival for control of the coastal Mediterranean region.[30]

The new Egyptian national army was raised by conscription, with the levy being one man in ten instead of the traditional one man in a hundred.[31] It was trained by professional officers and noncommissioned officers, and the pharaoh himself stood as commander in chief and personally led his troops in battle. The vizier operated as the minister of war, and an army council served as a general staff. The field army was organized into divisions, each of which was a complete combined-arms corps that included infantry, archers, and chariots. These divisions contained approximately six thousand men, including logistics and support personnel, and each was named after one of the principle gods of Egypt. Later Ramses II organized Egypt and the empire into thirty-four military districts to facilitate conscription, training, and the supply of the army.[32] The army's administrative structure was also improved, with professional schools established to train and test officers and scribes in the military arts.

The two major combat arms of the Egyptian army were chariotry and infantry. The chariot corps was organized into squadrons of 25 machines, each commanded by a charioteer of the residence, who was equal to a modern company commander. Larger units of 50 and 150 vehicles could be rapidly assembled and employed in concert with other forces.[33] It was common practice to assemble units whose size depended on the nature of the mission and terrain, an example of the modern practice of tailoring a unit to a specific function. Supporting the chariot corps logistically were staffs to procure and train horses and craftsmen to maintain and repair the machines. Egyptian divisions also had mobile chariot repair units to ensure the vehicles' operability when the army was in the field. That the pharaoh was often portrayed as leading a chariot charge suggests that the chariot forces were the status elite of the army, if not its primary combat striking arm.

It is paradoxical that in an age of bronze the most innovative and destructive weapons of the day, the chariot and the composite bow, were made entirely of wood. The Egyptian chariot of the New Kingdom was constructed of a light wooden frame, covered by stretched fabric or hide, and weighed about seventy-five pounds.[34] Two men could easily carry the vehicle over streams and rough terrain. On the march, however, it was common to remove the wheels and transport them on donkeys, and human porters carried the much lighter chariot bodies. The chariot's floor, which supported the rider and archer, was made of stretched leather thongs covered with hide or matting and fashioned in the shape of a *D*. A surviving example of this floor matting was made from a special kind of cloth involving a dense layer of long loops. The springiness of the looping helped cushion the riders in the shaking vehicle.[35] The cab was 1 meter wide, 1.25 meters high, and 0.75 meters deep. Two horses, usually geldings, pulled the vehicle, which was attached to a central yoke pole attached to the horses by outer races and reins. The vehicle was capable of reaching the speed of a galloping horse, or about twenty-five miles per hour, but at that speed the chariot was an unstable firing platform for the archer. The combat speed of the chariot was more likely in the range of eight to twelve miles an hour, which was slow enough to provide the stability the archer needed. Experiments have shown that at this speed the archer could hit his targets more than 80 percent of the time.[36] Belly bars and leg straps helped steady the riders at high speed. Arrow and spear quivers and an ax were attached to each side of the cab for easy access in battle.[37]

By the reign of Thutmose III the Egyptians had modified the chariot into the finest fighting vehicle in the ancient world.[38] The chariot workshop was probably the most complex manufacturing facility in the ancient world because of the diversity of materials involved and the wide range of technological skills required.[39] Some of the manufacturing techniques needed for chariot construction were already known in Egypt before the Hyksos invasion. As far back as the Twelfth Dynasty, Egyptians had learned how to steam and bend wood to make bows.[40] They were excellent carpenters and expert at lathe turning and using mortise and tenon joints. Egyptians were also practiced leather-workers and weavers of weft-loop textiles before the Hyksos arrived. The Egyptians' familiarity with these basic techniques may have reduced their learning curve when constructing chariots and led to innovations in the machine's design.

Three major innovations in chariot design may be credited to the Egyptians: the position of the axle, the six-spoked wheel, and the *U*-joint connecting the yoke pole to the chariot cab. They were the first to move the axle to the far rear of the carrying platform, thereby increasing the vehicle's speed, stability, and maneuverability.[41] They also introduced an improved wheel. Hyksos chariot wheels had four spokes. As the wheel rolled over the ground, the spaces between the rim and the spokes flexed at the top and bottom-most positions, causing an inherent washboard effect of up-and-down movement that was quite pronounced even on smooth ground.[42] This flexing increased the wear on the axle and hub that, in turn, caused the wheel to slant outward. At speed, the four-spoked wheel had a tendency to break under this side load.[43] The chariot with four-spoked wheels was neither very fast nor very maneuverable and did not provide a stable platform for the archer when in motion.

We cannot be certain that the six-spoked wheel was an Egyptian invention, but it seems likely.[44] The six-spoked wheel reduced the washboard effect considerably for having more spokes stabilized the wheel rim. Also, by using spokes that were elliptically shaped (not round) and tapered from the hub to the wheel rim, they were ideally oriented to resist the bending movements of side loads, further reducing axle wear.[45] A chariot with six-spoked wheels was thus much more stable at speed and ran less risk of having side loads collapse its wheel in a turn.[46]

Egyptian chariots' *U*-shaped socket joint can be counted as one of the great inventions of ancient engineers. The tail of the yoke pole bent under the chariot body, where it was not firmly attached to anything but loosely nested in a *U*-shaped socket joint. The socket permitted the screwdriver blade–shaped end of the pole to slide back and forth and tip from side to side. It always kept the pole centered on the axle and smoothed out the roughness of the chariot's horizontal motion by allowing the pole to key the position of the axle to the position of the yoke.[47] Thus, the axle was held closely to the horizontal at all times by the pole's flat blade even when bouncing over rough ground. At the same time the *U*-socket helped dampen the vehicle's rotational displacements about its pole, greatly reducing the machine's tendency to roll over in a turn.

Taken together, these technical advances produced a vehicle that was fast, stable, and highly maneuverable, and it required less frequent repairs than the chariot bequeathed to Egypt by the Hyksos. If, as the evidence suggests, these advances occurred during Thutmose III's reign, then the Egyptian chariots had a significant operational advantage over the Canaanite-Syrian chariots, which lacked these advances during Thutmose's campaigns in Canaan and Syria. Originally the chariot was

3.1. EGYPTIAN CHARIOT

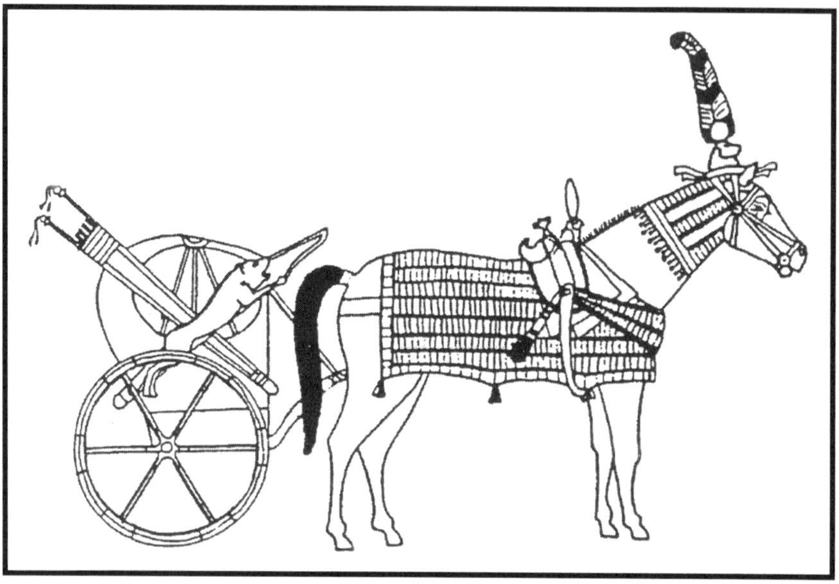

little more than a slow-moving, fragile platform for archers. With the Egyptian advances in chariot design, the vehicle acquired new tactical functions. It could be used to engage the enemy with arrows at long range while closing to deliver shock in massed formations. Once the enemy was engaged at short range, axes and javelins were brought to bear. After the enemy force was shattered, the chariot could be used in lethal pursuit, and its archer could kill with the bow.[48] The Egyptian chariot combined the innovative dimensions of shock, lethality, and mobility, making this weapon the only one in ancient armies that could participate in all phases of the battle—the movement to contact, engagement, and pursuit—with equal killing power.[49]

Egyptian infantry was organized into 50-man platoons commanded by a "leader of 50." A *Sa*, or company, contained 250 men in five platoons plus a commander, quartermaster, and scribe. Each company was identified by the type of weapon it carried: swords and spears, axes, and bows.[50] Units were further identified as being made up of recruits, trained men, or elite shock troops. The next higher unit in the chain of command was the regiment, commanded by a standard-bearer, although we are not certain of its strength. Above the regiment was the *Pedjet*, or "brigade," composed of 1,000 men who were commanded by a captain of a troop. This rank was also assigned to a fortress commander and may have been a general officer or senior colonel rank. A typical Egyptian field division was organized into five Pedjets, three heavy infantry brigades, and two archer brigades.

Egyptian infantry regiments were organized into axmen, archers, and sword and spear infantry (see illustration 3.2). The latter carried shields and six-foot-long spears. Their task was to protect against and

3.2. THREE TYPES OF EGYPTIAN INFANTRY

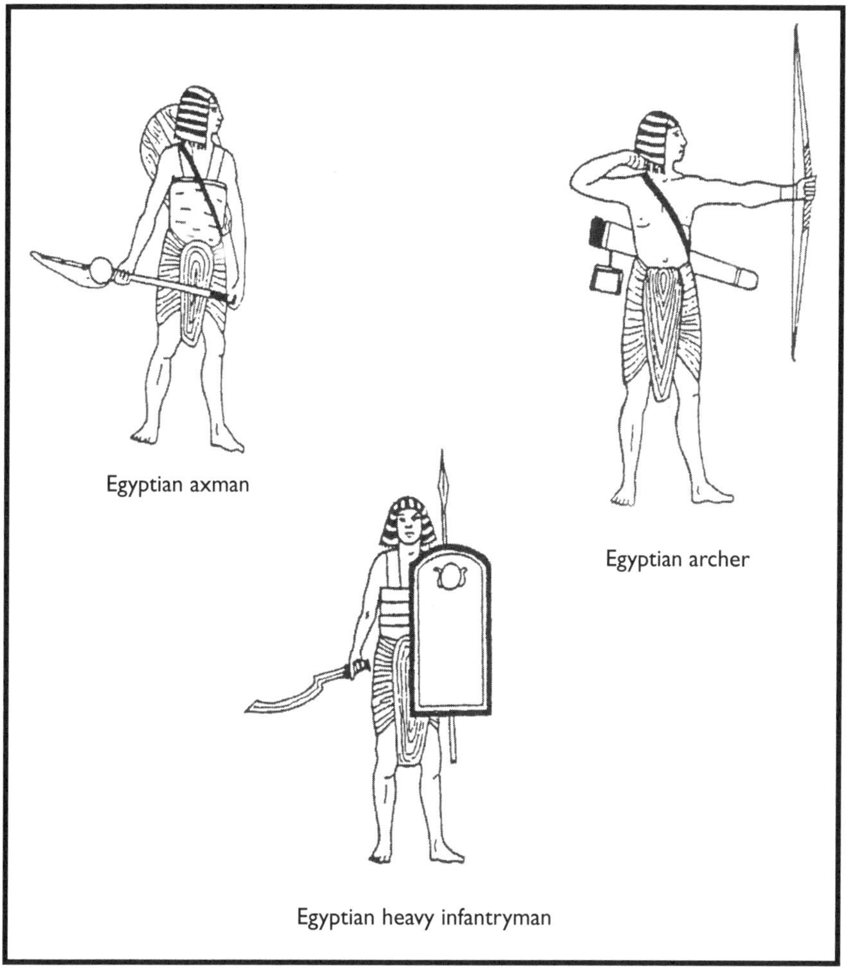

disrupt hostile charges aimed at the chariot units. The infantry, the true arm of decision in Egyptian tactical thinking, fought in formations five men deep with a ten-man front in fifty-man platoons. These units could quickly form marching columns ten men wide, providing a degree of tactical flexibility in infantry employment. The division contained special elite infantry units as well. The *kenyt-nesu*, or King's Braves, appear to have been the Egyptian equivalent of elite special operations units of heavy infantry used especially for overcoming difficult positions. Like modern special operations forces, the Braves were made up of hardened infantry veterans who had distinguished themselves in battle. Membership was by merit only.

Egyptian light infantry comprised mostly archer units called megau, literally "shooters" and "slingers."[51] Egyptian archers and charioteers carried the same composite bow. Constructed of a central wood core with thin strips of horn and leather laminated at the belly and protected by birch bark covering, the composite bow was 1.3 meters long and came in two types, recurved and triangular.[52] When drawn to the ear, it could send a reed shaft fletched arrow with a bronze cast arrowhead through an ingot of copper three fingers thick. The bow was powered by a string of twisted gut and was a formidable weapon in the hands of trained infantry or chariot-borne archers. Both archers and spearmen wore textile armor. Elite infantry and charioteers wore body armor fashioned of 2-millimeter-thin bronze plates sewn in overlapping patterns on a leather jerkin.[53] The bronze helmet that Canaanite and Mitannian soldiers favored does not appear to have gained wide use in the Egyptian army probably because of its weight and its tendency to get unbearably hot. Even Thutmose's famed Blue War Crown was not made of bronze.

The addition of 500 chariots organic to the field division brought the Egyptian division to approximately 5,500 fighting men with a supporting force of between 700 to 900 technicians, carpenters, quartermasters, scribes, logisticians, intelligence officers, and so on for a total of more than 6,000 soldiers. To place the logistical burden of the chariot corps in perspective, one need only consider that 500 chariots require 1,000 horses with 250 in reserve. A horse consumes twelve to fourteen pounds of hard fodder (grain) and fourteen to sixteen pounds of green (grass) or dry (hay) fodder a day. In addition, horses need between twenty and thirty-five quarts of water per day and more in hot climates.[54] The logistical requirement for a single chariot brigade therefore was 13,000 to 15,000 pounds of grain and fodder and 2,500 to 4,000 gallons of water a day to keep the animals in fighting trim.

A royal prince or important retainer commanded a division, but it is likely that the division's day-to-day command and operations were in the hands of a senior general called the lieutenant commander of the army. This system is analogous to that used by the German army between 1860 and 1918. The organizational structure of an Egyptian division is portrayed in illustration 3.3.

The Egyptian army's well-developed tactics were supported by excellent logistical functions. The use of store cities, depots, resupply by ship, donkey pack trains, and human porters worked in concert to keep the army well supplied in the field. Its tactical expertise was increased by a

3.3. ORGANIZATION OF AN EGYPTIAN DIVISION IN THE EIGHTEENTH DYNASTY

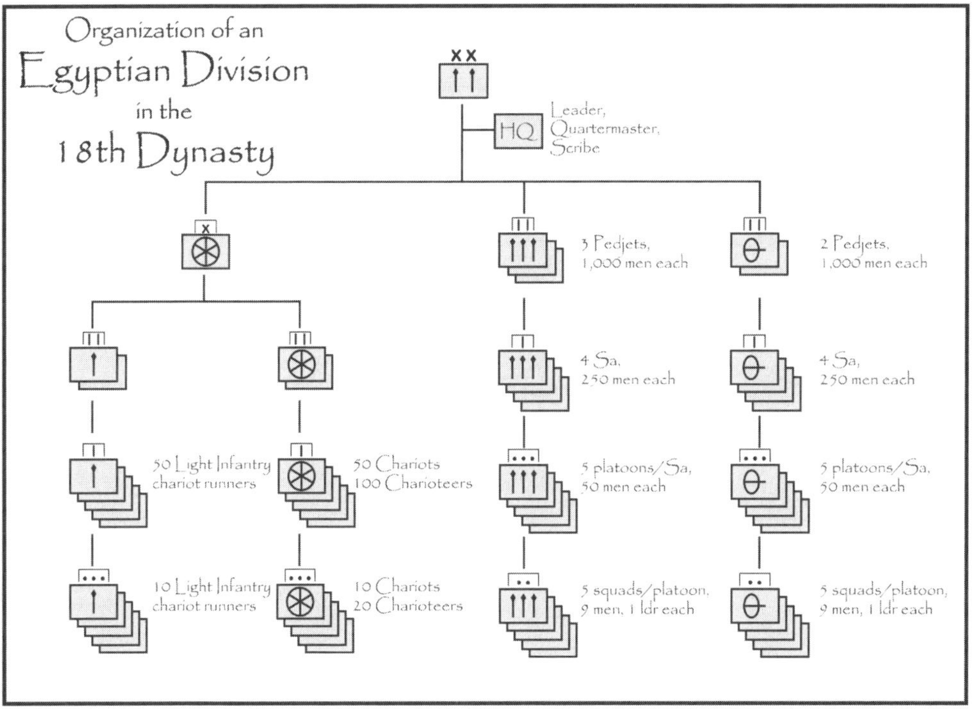

professionally trained officer corps experienced at maneuvering various types of large units on the battlefield. With careful and integrated use of field intelligence gathered through patrols and special collection units of spies, scouts, translators, interrogators, and so on, the Egyptians were adept at moving large armies over considerable distances and maneuvering them on the battlefield. At Megiddo, for instance, Thutmose moved his army three hundred miles and arrived outside his objective without being detected. In his war against the Mitanni, he transported scores of raft-like landing craft on carts more than three hundred miles and used them to cross the Euphrates and surprise his enemy. Egyptians also used counterintelligence and deception to gain maximum surprise. Prior to the final formulation of battle plans, Egyptians used the commander's conference in which officers were urged to criticize the proposed strategy and offer frank advice. It resulted in sound battle plans.

On the battlefield Egyptian forces usually deployed chariot units to act as screens for infantry and to cover their maneuver during a movement to contact. Engaging the enemy with the long-range composite bow, the chariot archers began killing at a distance as they closed with the enemy. Archer units deployed ahead of the infantry, firing as it moved to contact. Once the enemy was close, the archer units retired through the infantry's ranks or to its flanks and continued to deliver indirect plunging fire into the main body of the enemy's formations. The infantry then closed at a dead run to maximize shock, and a general melee resulted. Chariot units engaged the enemy at any exposed point, sometimes dismounting and fighting as infantry once in contact or using their axes and javelins from aboard their chariot platforms. If the enemy gave ground, chariots could be committed to exploit the weakness. The chariot's mobility allowed the use of mobile reserves that could be committed at a propitious moment to turn a flank or exploit a breakthrough. It offered a military capability that had never existed before in military history. If the enemy broke and a rout began, chariot archers could engage in rapid pursuit with devastating effectiveness. If tactical surprise had been achieved, chariot units could engage an enemy not yet fully deployed for battle. If something went wrong, chariots could then be used to rescue a desperate situation.[55]

The Egyptian army lacked cavalry formations, an innovation the Assyrian army would introduce six hundred years later. Egyptian units did make use of mounted riders as scouts, but they were not used in battle.[56] With the exception of cavalry, however, the warrior pharaohs' armies of the Egyptian imperial era were in every respect modern armies capable of conducting operations in a modern manner and on a modern scale, including mounting seaborne invasions and using naval forces in conjunction with ground forces for supply and logistics. In its day the army of imperial Egypt was the largest, best-equipped, and most successful fighting force in the world, and it was Thutmose III who developed it and bequeathed it to his successors.

The Mitannian Army

Most of our information concerning the military organization of the Mitanni is derived from two sources. The first and most detailed is the famous Nuzi archives. Nuzi was the capital of the province of Arrapha situated on the eastern fringe of the Mitannian Empire, which was strategically located between Assyria and Kassite Babylonia. The second source is the rendering of Mitannian chariots and troops that appears on the sides of the Thutmose IV's war chariot. The Mitannian state's political structure, noted earlier as probably an innovation of the Mitanni superimposed on the old Hurrian social order, seems to have been imposed as well on Mitannian vassal states, turning them into principalities whose governance and military administration were strongly influenced from the center. One result was a confusion of names when referring to the Mitannian state. Thus, in the Nuzi archives there are references to a "man of the lands" of Hanigalbat, Arrapha, Mitanni, and Naharin, implying that the Mitannian state was a confederacy of powerful sub-kings linked by fealty and kinship to a central great king, or that the Mitannian kingdom was made up of a central kingdom and a confederacy of foreign vassal states.[57] Usually when different names for the Mitanni are found in ancient texts, they are used by different countries and may have been derived from the regions of the Mitannian Empire with which those countries had most frequent contact. So, for example, the Assyrians called the Mitanni Hanigalbat in their own language while the Kassites of lower Babylonia referred to them as Arrapha. The Hittites called them Mitanni, and the Egyptians Naharin. If the assumption is correct, it is likely that

Arrapha's administrative structure described in the Nuzi texts was the same as found in the other provinces or vassal states of the Mitannian Empire.

The administrative structure of the Mitannian province reveals a concern for war as well as for the government. Each province was divided into districts (*halsu*), and each of these halsu possessed a fortified capital and armory. Smaller towns (*alu*) throughout the district were also walled for defense. A royal governor (*halsuhlu* or *shakin mati*) administered the province for the king. Originally these governors would have been the king's blood kin; however, later they were probably replaced by men of competence tied to the king by an oath of fealty. A mayor (*hazannu*) administered the towns of the district. The countryside was divided into large estates (*dimati*) worked by tenants (*ashshabu*) and owned by a lord (*bel dimtu*). The warrior ethos of the Mitanni is reflected again in the fact that these estates were composed of a few villages and a fortified manor house or keep for defense.[58] The hazannu appears to have had military duties as well and was responsible for the security of his district. Whether he also served as a field commander is unknown. Clearly, however, cities, towns, and estates were required to raise militia forces while the larger cities and more strategic border towns were often garrisoned by professional troops of the royal army.

The centerpiece of the Mitannian army was the warrior caste (*nakhushshu*) of military professionals who were bound by oaths of loyalty to the king and served at his bequest. The oath was called the *isharu* (literally the word of the man of arrows) or *ilku*. Soldiers were called *alik ilku,* or "those who perform the ilku duty." The elite corps of the professional army comprised the chariot warriors known as maryanna. The term *maryannu* itself means "noble chariot warrior" and derives from the Indo-European word related to Sanskrit *marya,* meaning "youth" or "hero."[59] As one might expect in a country of fortified feudal fiefdoms, the elite chariot warriors held large estates granted by the king in return for their military service (not unlike the later European feudal system), although some maryannu seem to have had a hereditary claim to these estates. There seems to have been more than one rank of maryannu status tied to military service, and one suspects that a system of subvassals pledged to the high lord by oaths of military service sometimes were referred to as maryannu as well.

The term seems also to have been applied to both chariot and nonchariot warriors and to professional and militia troops.

The organization of the Mitannian army remains unclear. We are certain that the king possessed a bodyguard of chariotry known as *shepi sharri* (literally, the feet of the king), consisting of ten chariots. This bodyguard originally had its roots in the coterie of the tribal chief's best warriors who accompanied him in battle. Later, however, it probably comprised the country's leading nobles and advisers rather than necessarily its best warriors. Much of the army was made up of charioteers, known as *alik seri* (campaigners). There must also have been a central force of maryannu chariotry, for we read of such units being sent to four towns to reinforce local garrisons. Infantry units (*shukuthlu*) made up of both spearmen and archers equipped with swords, daggers, leather armor, and helmets existed, but we know nothing of their organization or quality except that the ashshabu were also permitted to serve in their ranks.

Chariot units (*emanti*) of five or ten vehicles were commanded by an officer called an *emanthuhlu*. These units could be grouped into larger units based on multiples of six (the old Sumerian-Assyrian system) and commanded by a "chief" emanthuhlu, who was also responsible for supplying rations to his men. One of these chiefs is also described as commanding a garrison, so it is possible that the emanthuhlu applied to infantry commanders as well. Other texts refer to officers called *rab* with the decimal number of men under their command appearing next to the title. Thus, rab (5), rab (10), and rab (12) refer to officers in command of units of these respective sizes. A confusing aspect of the Mitannian military organization is that it appears to have used no consistent numerical system as its base. Thus there are textual references to 3,000 *alik ilki* (perhaps combined units of chariots and archers), 536 charioteers, 82 archers, 55 bowmen, and so on.

There are references to "tablets of the left" and "brothers of the right," suggesting that the army had right and left wings, but such a conclusion is speculation.[60] Further compounding the problem of organizational definition is that estates, towns, and cities were required to raise levies of militia troops at the king's request. If the feudal period of later Europe is any guide, these numbers became meaningless in a practical sense in that the strength and organization of militia units were rarely standard or recorded. That the Mitannian army was well organized can be deduced from the fact that all its armor, helmets, and weapons were manufactured in royal arsenals as state industries and issued to the troops in a systematic manner. When military equipment was worn out or broken, it was turned in and replaced and repaired at royal expense.[61]

With the Mitannian army's chariot corps composed of nobility and established as the combat arm of decision, it is not surprising that the Nuzi texts provide more information on this branch of the army than on any other. Regarding the Mitannian chariot, for instance, the texts say it was constructed of light wood and hides. One text notes that twelve goatskins were required to cover a chariot frame and between nine and eleven sheepskins to cover the floor. This detail suggests, albeit roughly, that the Mitannian chariot was somewhat larger and heavier than the Egyptian machine but not as large as the Hittite chariot. Seals depict the Mitannian chariot with wheels of four, six, and even eight spokes, again suggesting that some Mitannian machines were quite heavy.[62] It was also regular practice to oil the spokes to prevent the wheels from warping. A particularly interesting aspect of the Mitannian chariot was that some of them appear to have been armored with metal scales (*sariam*). One inventory mentions a unit of a hundred chariots equipped with scale armor protection. The depiction of the Mitannian chariots taken from the cab of Thutmose IV's war chariot also shows them with armored cabs.

Given that a suit of Mitannian body armor consisting of five hundred scales weighs approximately thirty-five pounds and calculating the area of a Mitannian chariot cab to be almost twice the area required to cover the human torso in scale armor, the cab armor added about seventy-five to eighty pounds to the chariot's weight. It was a Mitannian practice to armor their chariot horses as well. Horse armor (*parashshamu*) consisted of a textile coat of thickly woven felt or hair about three centimeters thick that extended from the withers of the horse to the loins. Sometimes this textile coat was covered with a leather, copper, or bronze scale overcoat. A coat of bronze horse armor would easily have weighed more than a hundred pounds. Add to the cab's weight the Mitannian chariot warrior's usual scale armor suit of approximately thirty-five to forty pounds and his bronze helmet at another eight to ten pounds, and the load on the Mitannian chariot was considerable. While the Mitannian chariot was far heavier than the Egyptian machine, it was still lighter than the Hittite vehicle.

What this point suggests is that the Mitannian machine's design might have been a compromise forced by two factors: the variable terrain in which the machine was required to operate and the multiple tactical roles it had to play depending on the capabilities of the enemy chariots, Hittite or Egyptian, it had to engage. The Mitannian Empire encompassed very different types of terrain. To the east, where the Assyrians and Kassites had to be dealt with, the ground was flat, open, and grassy—conditions that placed a premium on speed and maneuverability. To the north and northwest, in Armenia and Anatolia, the terrain was uneven, mountainous, and forested—conditions that favored the short-distance attack from an ambush position. In northern Syria as well as farther south in the Beqqa Valley and Lebanon, the terrain was mixed, requiring a machine that could serve either role depending on the circumstances. With each type of terrain came a different enemy whose own chariots reflected their respective tactical doctrines. The Hittite machine, for example, was very heavy, carried a crew of three spearmen, and was designed for short-distance ambush. The Egyptian chariot, by contrast, was fast, highly maneuverable, and perfectly suited for flat, open ground.

3.4. MITANNIAN CHARIOT

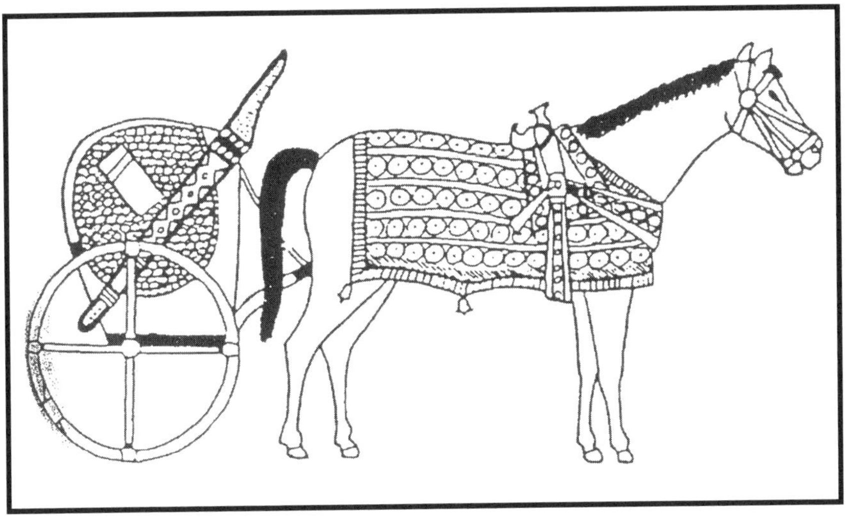

The Mitanni needed a chariot to fight in different types of terrain and to perform multiple tactical roles, resulting in a machine that was both heavy and light enough to permit it to perform adequately in all types of terrain but was probably not able to excel in any of them.

The chariot's middling performance may have been the reason why both Mitannian charioteers and their horses wore heavy armor. Their armor and weapons—two composite bows, two quivers of arrows, a shield, and a lance—suggest strongly that the tactical role of the Mitannian chariot was not to fight at close quarters as the Hittites did. Both the bow and lance were to be used either from afar, as in a movement to contact, or en passant if closely engaged. Firepower and passing engagement, then, were the two tactical roles afforded by a moderately heavy Mitannian chariot carrying a well-armored charioteer. These capabilities could be adequately employed against the heavy chariot the Hittites used as a mounted infantry platform fighting in uneven terrain. When fighting Egyptian chariots, the Mitannian machine gave its charioteer an equal capability in firepower since both the Egyptians and the Mitanni were armed with the same composite bow. While the Egyptian machine held advantages in speed and mobility, the Syrian terrain did not offer many opportunities for battle on flat, even plains. The heavier Mitannian vehicle, with its far better protected charioteer, offered greater advantages in delivering shock and increasing the archer's survivability both when engaged at close range en passant and when employed on uneven terrain, which itself could neutralize the Egyptians' advantage in speed and maneuverability.

As with any weapon of war, the trick was to employ it properly. In the hands of an able field commander the Mitannian battle chariot afforded considerable advantages against different types of enemies, provided one used the vehicle with proper consideration for the terrain upon which the battle was fought and the tactical objectives for which the machine was being employed. Some validity may be lent to the above analysis by noting that of all the people of the Canaanite-Syrian land bridge, the group whose chariot was most strongly influenced by the Mitannian design was the Canaanites. An examination of the various types of terrain in which the Canaanites had to fight suggests they chose the Mitannian design for the same reasons as the Mitanni did, that is, its ability to function well on different types of terrain.

Our knowledge of the Mitannian charioteer comes largely from the Nuzi archives, and these texts refer to the Mitannian armor as the armor of Hanigalbat. Scale and lamellar armor appear to have been a Hurrian invention of about the seventeenth century BCE, and the Mitanni and everyone else seem to have adopted them in the Near East in a relatively short time. Evidence for this theory lies in the fact that all the people of the Near East at this time used terms for armor that were derived from the Hurrian *sharyani* (coat of mail).[63] This word appeared in Akkadian as *sariam,* as *saryannni* in Hittite, *shiryon* in Hebrew, and *tiryana* in Ugaritic and Egyptian.[64]

The Mitannian charioteer's armor consisted of a mail coat with sleeves and a long skirt covered with individual bronze scale plates called *kursimetu,* after the Akkadian *kursindu* (snake), an analogy to the reptile's overlapping scales. The scaled coat and skirt required almost a thousand scales to fabricate, with the sleeves of the coat requiring another two hundred scales. Two hundred smaller scales sewed over a leather cap served as a helmet (*gurpisu*). Sometimes these helmets had a crest of plaited leather. The most common helmet found among the Mitanni and throughout the Near East was the bronze helmet (*gurpisu siparri*). Sometimes charioteers shaved their heads and wore a linen or leather cap beneath the helmet to tighten the fit. The most elaborate helmets were the great bronze scale helmets (*gurpisu siparri kursimetu*), which offered more protection than either the leather or sheet bronze models did.[65] The charioteer's neck was protected by a high, thick bronze or leather collar, a typical feature of the suits of armor of this period. A thick leather belt protected the charioteer's abdomen and helped him bear the armor's weight. The charioteer carried a long dagger (*patru*) in his belt for self-defense should he be forced from his machine.

In contrast to both Hittite and Egyptian practice, the Mitannian chariot driver was equally well equipped with scale armor and helmet. The driver carried a small shield (*aritu*) made of wood and sometimes covered with beaten bronze. Chariot shields seem to have had a double grip—one could be held in the hand, and another consisted of a pair of leather straps through which the driver could slip his arms, permitting him some protection while guiding the horses.

3.5. MITANNIAN CHARIOT ARCHER

Chariot horses were prized and expensive military assets, and there was an organized system for acquiring, breeding, and training horses, a surmise supported by the fact that the term for reserve horses (*matru*) has come down to us. Horses began training with the chariot when they were a year old and began pulling chariots by their third year. By their fourth year they became proper chariot horses and served until they were nine or ten years old.[66] Cavalry was unknown, but there is some evidence that messengers (*mar shipri*) traveled by horseback. The term for "horseman"

was *rakib susi*, suggesting at least that riding horses was not entirely unknown. There is no evidence, however, of horsemen having been put to military use.

We know next to nothing about the Mitannian infantry. We can be fairly certain that there were shukuthlu infantry units and units of archers and spearmen as well. Beyond that, we can say only that the infantry was equipped with swords or long dirks for protection and that they wore leather helmets. We have no idea how they were tactically employed. The chariot's primary role in Mitannian tactical doctrine suggests that the Mitanni may have employed their infantry in a manner similar to that of the Hittites; that is, they were primarily used as a platform of maneuver designed to engage the enemy and fix his position until the chariotry could strike him at a vulnerable point. As in other armies of the period, archer units provided covering fire for the infantry during its movement to contact and, once the infantry was engaged, played a supporting role by directing plunging arrow fire against the enemy's rear formations or flanks. Beyond these obvious and general observations, little else is known about Mitannian infantry tactical doctrine.

Although the Mitannian Empire was short lived, its innovations in warfare were significant. Most important was its introduction, if not the invention, of the horse-drawn war chariot to the other armies of the Near East and, perhaps, the first use of the spoked wheel in war. Mounting an archer on the chariot gave new flexibility and lethality to a weapon whose impact to this point had been only marginal. The chariot's range, mobility, and speed wrought a revolution in tactical thinking in the Near East. One has only to recall, for example, the devastating defeats the chariot-equipped Hyksos had inflicted on the Egyptian army to appreciate the quantum leap in tactics and lethality that the Mitannian war chariot generated. Within a few short years, however, every major power of the region had equipped its armed forces with this latest weapon, and a new era of mobile warfare commenced.

The Armies of the Canaanites

In Thutmose's day, the military capabilities of the Canaanite city-states' armies were substantial. Each city-state raised and trained its own armed forces, most of which were similar in weapons and organization. There was no unified national command because no high king ruled over all Canaan. But in time of war, the city-states were capable of acting in concert and coordinating the movement and deployment of their forces, as they did when such a coalition fought Thutmose at Megiddo. The term *resuti* (subordinate ally) has come down to us from the Ugarit texts, suggesting that within the military coalitions, princes permitted their forces to act under the command of a central commander. The king of the Ugarit city-state usually took the field as commander in chief, but it was not unusual for military command to be delegated to trusted generals. Regular, fully equipped troops (*sabu nagib*) were distinguished from militia or irregulars, and the term was applied to both infantry and chariotry, suggesting that regular infantry units existed. Field commanders were called *muru-u*, but we do not know the size of the units they commanded. It is likely, however, that the decimal system of unit strength was employed just as it commonly was elsewhere. Ugarit was among the largest, richest, and most powerful Canaanite states, and its military organization was probably typical of the other states' forces.

The primary striking arm of the Canaanite armies was the elite chariot corps manned by the social elite of feudal nobles called maryanna (chariot warriors). Each maryannu was a professional warrior who, at least originally, maintained his chariot, horses, grooms, driver, runners, and equipment at his own expense. The maryannu's wealth was derived from his holding of a fief, which, although the king originally conferred it, seems over time to have become hereditary.[67] Among the general warrior caste of maryanna was an inner elite of "picked men"(*na'arun*). These elite units comprised infantry as well as chariotry, with the latter commanded by a chief of chariotry (*akil narkabti*). A smaller battle guard called the Maryanna of the King also existed.

The Canaanite chariot, much like the Mitannian chariot, was heavier than the Egyptian vehicle but lighter than the Hittite machine. Yigael Yadin suggests that this variation was a result of the increased Egyptian influence in Canaanite affairs,[68] but this explanation is unconvincing. Both the Egyptian chariot's mission and the terrain upon which it maneuvered were quite different from what the Canaanites had to consider when developing their vehicle. Canaan offered few smooth plains, where the opportunity for wide-ranging maneuver and speed provided dividends.

Instead, its terrain was similar to that of northern Syria and the land of the Mitanni and featured rocky ground, hills and mountains, forests and glens—conditions that put a premium on surprise, ambush, and shock. The Canaanite chariot was heavier than the Egyptian model because of its four- or six-spoked wheels. Also, after moving the axle to the center of the platform to take the weight off the animals, it accommodated a larger carrying platform whose floor was fashioned of wood for strength. This increased weight caused the machine to lose a good part of its maneuverability in a turn and compromised the animals' endurance to some degree.[69]

The Canaanite chariot warrior, like his Mitannian counterpart, was heavily protected by a mail coat of scale armor. His horse, too, wore a textile or bronze scale coat. These devices were designed to protect the horse and crew from the enemies' arrows as they closed to engage. There is no hard evidence that the driver wore armor, but given the Mitannian influence on Canaanite chariotry, it is likely that he did. The primary weapons of the Canaanite charioteer were the composite bow, a heavy spear, and a club, the latter to be used only in the direst emergency should the warrior find himself afoot.[70] Depending on the tactical mission, the Canaanite chariot was capable of carrying a three-man crew, a fact suggested by the

3.6. CANAANITE CHARIOT

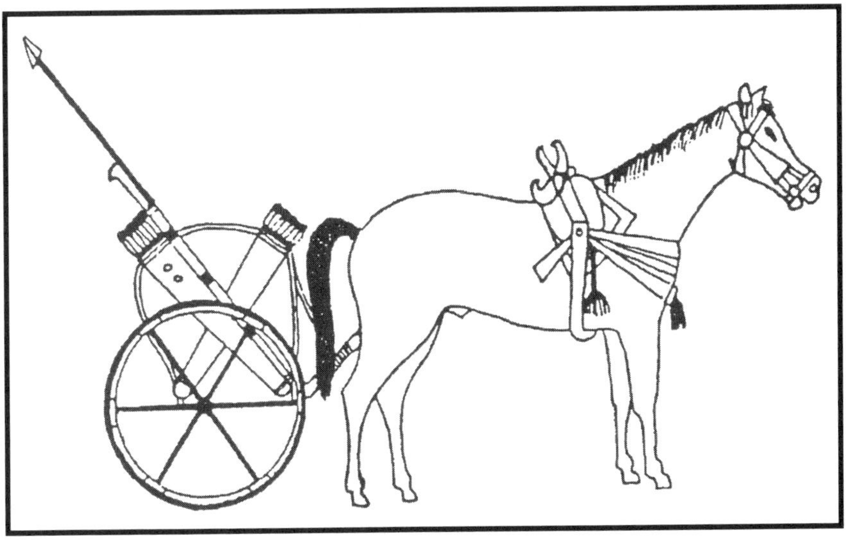

portrayal of the machine with javelin cases. Michael Grant believes that Canaanite chariots had leather tires and, perhaps, cab armor fashioned of bronze scales.[71]

Canaanite infantry (*hupshu*) was made up of both militia and regular units. Most of the infantry were semi-trained militia (*khepetj*) or conscripted and corvée peasantry, who were lightly armed with bows and spears. Canaanite tradition dating from tribal days dictated that the infantrymen supplied their own equipment, but we are uncertain if this tradition persisted into biblical times. The Amarna letters refer to different types of infantry distinguished by their weapons, namely, bows and spears.[72] Canaanite regular infantry were probably well-trained professionals who were heavily armed. These units wore armored corselets and helmets and carried a sword, a shield, and the socket ax. The Canaanite infantry's shield used a Hittite design. Shaped like a figure eight with a narrow waist, this shield allowed the soldier to have a greater field of view of his opponent in close combat and to wield the sickle-sword or ax more flexibly. With the Sea People's arrival in the twelfth century, the Canaanites adopted the round shield and outfitted their infantry with the spear. At the same time, however, the Canaanites replaced the sickle-sword with the straight sword. Scale armor for the regular infantry also became commonplace.[73]

The king chose elite units of heavy infantry for their loyalty and bravery to serve as the palace guard of the Canaanite kings. The Ugaritic texts mention these na'arun as composing an inner elite of the general maryannu warrior caste. Most likely there were special elite chariot units as well. At the battle of Kadesh in 1274 BCE, Ramses II was rescued in the nick of time by a unit of these elite shock troops, which fell upon the Hittite flank and broke the encirclement. These particular na'arun were Canaanite mercenaries in the service of the Egyptians. A relief of the battle portrays the Canaanites attacking in phalanx formation—line abreast in ten rows, ten men deep—and armed with spears and shields, suggesting that they were elite heavy infantry.[74]

The Canaanite kings supplemented their forces with hired freebooters called *Apiru*. This class of outcasts, debtors, outlaws, and restless nomads formed wandering groups of raiders and often hired themselves out to princes and kings as mercenaries. Often called bandits (*habbatu*) or

3.7. THREE TYPES OF CANAANITE INFANTRY

Dusty Ones, these wandering brigands posed a serious threat and often had to be brought to heel by the Canaanite princes by force of arms. One of Israel's great generals, David, was an Apiru whose reputation as a soldier brought him to the attention of King Saul. When forced to leave Saul's court, David returned to his old mercenary occupation by raising a force of six hundred "discontented men" and hiring his soldiers out to one of the Philistine kings.[75] The size and military sophistication of these brigand groups could present a considerable threat to public order. A record from Alalakh tells of a band of Apiru comprising 1,436 men, 80 of which were charioteers and 1,006 were *shananu* (probably archers). Another text records the capture of the town of Allul by a Habiru force of 2,000 Apiru.[76]

The Canaanites' military tactics were similar to those of the Mitanni in that the army relied on its chariot units to strike the enemy from ambush, catching him while still in column of march or while deploying for battle. For instance, the Canaanites' precise plan at the battle of Megiddo was to set an ambush for Thutmose III's army along the Aruna road and hit the Egyptian column as it moved onto the Plain of Esdraelon. If surprise was not possible, Canaanite generals used the chariot to deliver shock against enemy infantry formations. This tactic required that "chariot runners," or infantry, accompany the chariots. The Canaanite charioteer engaged the enemy from close range, firing his bow and hurling javelins, while relying on his heavy armor to protect him from enemy fire. In this tactical application, infantry phalanxes of spearmen supported by archers acted in support or, if on the defensive, held their positions and provided the chariots with a platform of maneuver.

The primary role of the Canaanite chariot, however, was as a strategic weapon. They were mobile, sufficiently heavy, and well-armored vehicles that could range far from their bases to protect the cities from being besieged. Defending the cities was at the center of Canaanite strategic thinking, and the chariots were the key element in achieving this mission. Chariots could intercept armies long before they reached the city walls, forcing the enemy to fight on terrain and at a time not of its choosing. Chariots were ideal for ambushing enemy patrols, harassing the enemy's route of march, keeping communication lines open, and chasing down hired mercenary Apiru. No infantry force could achieve such a mix of tactical and strategic flexibility. Chariots, of course, were expensive, and their crews required extensive training and permanent maintenance at royal expense. The expense was worth it, however, for the chariot allowed the Canaanite kings to erect a strategic defense in depth based on flexible and mobile tactics.

The system of mobile defense worked well for more than two centuries, but Canaan's wealth and strategic position made it a tempting target for the national predators who wished to control the land bridge. Over time the encroachments, immigrations, settlements, and aggressions of the Egyptians, Aramaeans, Sea People, and Israelites took their toll, with the result that by the time of King David of Israel, the Canaanites had been deprived of three-quarters of their land area and 90 percent of their grain-growing land.[77] All that remained of these proud warrior people's land was the central Phoenician coastal strip and its immediate hinterlands. But at the time of Thutmose III, the Canaanite city-states were still a formidable military force with which he had to contend frequently.

Canaan's legacy lived on into the modern era. It was the Canaanites, for example, who first performed the extraordinary feat of dissecting the sounds of human speech into thirty basic sounds, thus giving the world its first true alphabet.[78] They also were the first to set their language to music. The Canaanites, in turn, taught the Hebrews how to set their poetry to music, giving the world one of the great gifts of civilization—song.

Nubian Armies

We know very little about the armies of Nubia. From the Middle Kingdom through Kamose's intervention in Nubia during the Hyksos period, the weaponry and organization of Nubian military units appear indistinguishable from that found in Egypt at the same time.[79] Nubian soldiers portrayed in tomb models, paintings, and bas reliefs are armed with the mace and short throwing javelins with either stone or copper tips, and they carried hide-covered, pointed-top shields, the same weapons found in contemporary Egyptian armies. The Nubians did not appear to use the long infantry spear, however. The archers of both armies carried the same recurved bow and fired arrows with sharpened fire-hardened tips. There is no evidence that either army had bronze swords, arrowheads, or socketed spear blades. While Nubia had copper, it lacked tin to manufacture bronze weapons and armor. No mention of the horse in Nubian warfare is found.[80]

The Egyptian incursions that followed the expulsion of the Hyksos produced some leakage in Egyptian military technology to Nubia. The famed Medjay desert tribes had fought on the Egyptians' side during the Nubian incursion into Upper Egypt in support of the Hyksos, and the Medjay became loyal Egyptian allies for years. They were later constituted into elite units in service to the pharaoh. Reliefs from this period show the Medjay armed with bronze penetrating axes. Other loyal Nubian units are shown equipped with the long infantry spear with socketed, bronze spear blades. Beyond this example, however, there is no evidence of the widespread use of bronze weapons or their technical manufacture in Nubia. Having acquired the new bronze weapons from the Hyksos, the Egyptians seem to have copied the Hyksos policy of denying bronze technology to others and applied it to Nubia by blocking the export of tin to the country.[81] The result was that the lethal bronze weaponry never became widely available in Nubia.

From time to time, Nubian rebels could still raise sufficient manpower and carry out raids against Egyptian towns and forts using obsolete weapons. But in a set-piece battle, Nubian rebels always found themselves at a significant disadvantage. With the Egyptian army's incorporation of the chariot and composite bow, the disparity in weapons and their lethality between the Egyptian occupiers and the Nubian rebels increased. By Thutmose III's reign, the occasional rebellions in Upper Nubia ceased to be a problem. Egyptian troops dealt with them easily.

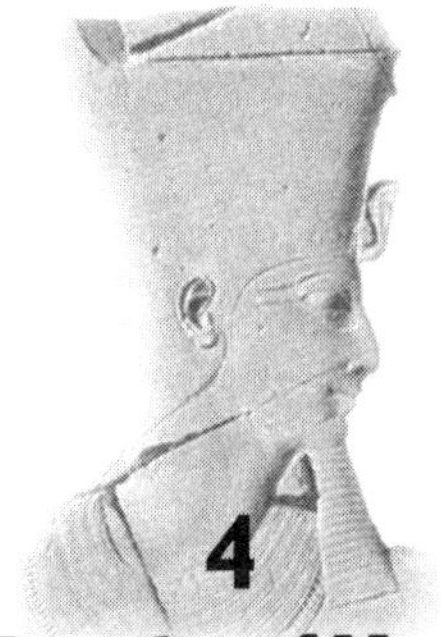

4 The Battle of Megiddo

The battle of Megiddo is the first battle in history for which we have a name and a sufficient account of events from which to reconstruct a portrait of the strategy and tactics employed by the antagonists. In this sense it can be said that the battle of Megiddo is the starting point for the study of military history. Moreover, Megiddo was one of the most important battles of antiquity. In the same way that Scipio Africanus's victory at Zama set Rome on the path to empire, Thutmose III's victory at Megiddo was the first step in the creation of an Egyptian empire that lasted for half a millennium. Thutmose III's establishment of that empire marks him as one of the greatest military commanders in history.

The conflict between Egypt and a coalition of Asiatic kingdoms that occurred at Megiddo in May 1481 BCE had its roots in a strategic power shift that was taking place further to the north on the Great Bend of the Euphrates River.[1] For a century prior to the battle, Indo-European invaders had been consolidating their hold on the former territory of Hurri-Land, transforming it into a new warrior kingdom called Mitanni. The period of Queen Hatshepsut and Thutmose III's joint rule in Egypt coincided with this period of Mitannian consolidation and expansion into northern Syria. The city-sate of Kadesh on the Orontes River rose rapidly under Mitannian protection and gained influence over the states of Canaan as far south as the city of Megiddo that controlled the Esdraelon Plain in the Galilee.[2] At the same time another Mitannian ally, the city of Tunip, increased its power by establishing control of the vital Eleutheros Valley connecting coastal Syria with the interior.[3]

Queen Hatshepsut seems to have been less than resolute in protecting Egyptian influence in Canaan and lower Syria and resisting Mitanni encroachments there. The lack of Egyptian response encouraged the Mitanni and their allies to press their influence farther south,[4] and Egyptian troops were forced to suppress revolts instigated by Asiatic enticements in Sharuhen and Gaza. In the winter of 1482 Queen Hatshepsut may have died, and the throne fell to Thutmose in his own right. Thutmose regarded the new Mitannian power configuration and its extension into Canaan as a strategic threat aimed at Egypt. Since the expulsion of the Hyksos, the Egyptians had regarded the Syrians and Canaanites as the heirs of these dreaded invaders. Thutmose saw the Syrian-Mitannian alliance as the prelude to an invasion of Egypt itself.[5]

Hatshepsut's death probably accelerated Asiatic plans for the invasion. Gathering an army of troop contingents from thirty-one Asiatic chiefdoms, some from as far away as the Euphrates and others "from as far away as Naharin" (the Egyptian name for Mitanni), suggests that the purpose of this large force was not to deal with some local concern.[6] The enormous harvests obtainable around Megiddo were needed to sustain the invasion force on its march to Egypt.[7] The commander of the Asiatic coalition was the chief of Kadesh.

Egyptian defenses against such an invasion force were less than ideal. If the Asiatics crossed the Carmel Ridge from Megiddo and gained the southern Canaanite plain, few Egyptian forces were there to stop them before they reached Gaza and Sharuhen.[8] Once beyond Gaza, there were no natural fortifications from which Egyptian troops could mount a defense of the Egyptian homeland. Thutmose concluded that the only way to defend Egypt was to prevent the Asiatic coalition from marching on Egypt in the first place and bring battle to it before it could cross the Carmel Mountains. To this end, he assembled his army and prepared to advance into Canaan, cross the Carmel Mountains, and attack the Asiatics at their marshaling point at Megiddo.

Thutmose used the winter to plan his campaign and assemble his troops at a base in Sile. Located some ten kilometers north-northeast of modern Qantara, Sile was on the coastal road near the mouth of the Pelusiac branch of the Nile. Called the Wall of Princes, the area had been fortified since Middle Kingdom times. The original fortifications were a series of forts that controlled the roads to Canaan and south to Sinai. These fortresses were rectangular enclosures of mud brick surrounded by moat ditches. Entry to the forts was through a single narrow gate, and the high walls were equipped with watchtowers.[9] The forts were manned by archers and spear infantry who were capable of mounting only a static defense.

Under the New Kingdom, perhaps beginning with Thutmose I, the design of these forts changed. The Egyptians enlarged them, making them some three hundred meters on a side, with walls sloping backward from the front toward the interior like a trapezoid. The front and side walls were nine meters high while the back walls were only about four meters. They replaced the single narrow front gate with two wider side gates, each of which was nine meters across. The design of these New Kingdom fortresses reflected their changed tactical role after the chariot emerged as an important combat arm in Egyptian armies. The old forts were designed to ward off infantry attacks while the new ones were large cantonments containing maneuverable chariot units that could engage in an elastic defense. The high walls remained a formidable obstacle to infantry assault, and the large side gates allowed two chariots abreast to rush through and engage enemy infantry on open ground. The enemy might even be allowed to commit against the front walls, at which point chariots rushed from the side gates and crushed the enemy against the wall. It is unknown if the forts at Taru, for instance, were all of this later type by Thutmose's time, but it is probable that at least some of them were.

Thutmose's Army

Nowhere in the *Annals* are we told the size of Thutmose's army when it left Sile.[10] Estimates range from as many as 20,000 to as few as 5,000 or 6,000 troops.[11] This said, a fair guess might still be ventured. The *Annals* of the battle tell us that as the Egyptian army's van reached the battlefield over a narrow road through the Carmel Mountains, its rearguard was still in camp. The road distance between the camp and the van was 9 miles. If these facts are true, it is possible to estimate the size of the Egyptian army. The proportion of troops to animals in the armies of antiquity was about the same as for a U.S. Army infantry brigade during World War I, or on average 1 donkey or mule for every 5 men. An American infantry brigade comprised 6,310 men and 1,021 animals and occupied a road space of 8,385 yards, or approximately 4.8 miles.[12] Thus, an Egyptian army occupying a road space of 9 miles would have numbered in the neighborhood of 12,000 men.

If the estimate is correct, then the Egyptian army comprised two combined-arms corps with each having 5,000 infantry and a chariot brigade of 500 vehicles that could be tailored into units of 10-vehicle platoons, 25-vehicle companies, or 50-vehicle battalions depending on their tactical requirements. The references to horses in the *Annals* make clear that Thutmose's army had its chariots at Megiddo. Thutmose would have known that Asiatic armies possessed large complements of chariots as a matter of course and that Megiddo was located on the Esdraelon Plain, ideal chariot country. It is unlikely, then, that Thutmose would have left his chariots behind, and there is no reason to believe that the Egyptian chariot brigades were at other than full strength.

The report of an Egyptian officer named Henu, who led an expedition to Punt (Somalia) during the Middle Kingdom, left us a description of the Egyptian infantryman's military kit. Henu says, "I went forth with an army of 3,000. I made a river and the Red Land a stretch of field, for I gave a leathern bottle, a carrying pole, jars of water, and twenty loaves to each among them every day. The asses were laden with sandals." The leathern bottles are water canteens, and the carrying pole was a forked stick carried over the shoulder hobo-style to which other equipment and weapons were lashed. This military equipment was still in use during the New Kingdom. The "loaves" were flat unleavened bread similar to naan or pita bread and common throughout the Middle East. An example of a military field pack has survived,[13] but it is unclear if it was carried over the shoulder with straps or, like the Roman soldier's pack, lashed to a carrying pole. Tents made of linen or leather seemed to have been reserved for officers,[14] while common soldiers slept on reed mats that could be rolled up and tied atop the field pack. The Egyptian soldier's spear was lashed to the carrying pole while his sword was stuck under his broad leather belt. Reliefs show Egyptian soldiers carrying ox hide shields on their backs that were strapped over their shoulders. By Thutmose's day, the old sandals of woven reed soles appear to have given way to much sturdier leather-soled sandals. Later, a strap was added that held the heel to the sole, making it possible for the soldier to run without losing his footgear. The importance of the new footgear to the army's military capability can be implied from the fact that Thutmose was the first pharaoh to have himself portrayed wearing sandals in his statues and reliefs.

Protecting the soldier from heat and sun was vital to keeping the army in fighting trim. The Egyptian soldier wore a short kilt (*shendo'ot*) and a sleeveless upper body shirt to protect him from the sun. Because of the heat, the bronze helmet the Asiatics and Mitanni favored was never widely used in Egypt. Instead, soldiers wore *nemes*, or a folded cloth of heavy breathable linen that could be soaked with water to cool the head. Other tighter-fitting caps of leather or cloth were also worn, probably depending on the climate where the soldiers were stationed. Later, a military-style wig came into use. The hair beneath all these head coverings was worn short. The Egyptian soldier used vegetable and animal oil to keep his skin moist and to prevent sunburn. Just as modern soldiers do, Egyptian troops used a wet cloth tied around the mouth and nose to protect against dust inhalation in the desert environment.

The staple of the Egyptian military diet was emmer cereal grain fashioned into a flat thin bread.[15] A ten-day supply of bread, eighty small loaves, could easily be carried in the soldier's backpack. It could also be baked on the march. Flattened into a patty, the moist dough stuck to the side of a three-foot, heated, cone-shaped stove, which was made of dried mud, and fell off the stove's side when fully baked. Supplying an army with firewood to cook rations was a major logistical problem for all armies of antiquity,[16] but the Egyptians did not use firewood for cooking. Instead, they used dried animal dung—cow dung for civilian use and horse and mule dung in the military camp—as their basic fuel.[17] The animals in the baggage train kept the army sufficiently supplied with cooking fuel while on the march. Egyptian field rations included smoked goose flesh, beef jerky, and smoked or salted fish. A favorite staple of the Egyptian soldier was beer, often provided by traveling breweries. Milk was sometimes provided, and in one account a recruit complains that all he was given to eat was sour milk, salted fish, and hard bread. Egyptian soldiers ate onions, cucumbers, beans, lentils, chickpeas, and cabbage, along with their bread. They also commonly ate radishes since they were believed to prevent stomach illness.[18]

Rations and equipment not carried by the soldier himself were transported in the logistics train.[19] Egyptian armies of the period used mules and donkeys equipped with panniers to transport food and equipment. Human porters also provided a significant proportion of the army's transport capacity. The four-wheeled cart was unknown in Egypt during Thutmose's day. All carts portrayed in reliefs are two-wheeled vehicles, little more than covered chariots pulled by donkeys and mules. The Egyptian armies did not use the ox-drawn cart until Ramses II introduced it. Even then this cart had only two wheels and seems to have been identical to the large two-wheeled oxcart of the Hittites and Philistines.

Supplying the Egyptian army with water while it crossed the Sinai presented a problem. The wells along the coastal route of march were weak and sometimes brackish. While they sufficed for small garrisons, they were inadequate to supply Thutmose's large army.[20] Thus, the Egyptians had to store water at several points along the route. In the desert environment, a soldier needs eight to nine pints of water a day to survive, with the animals requiring considerably more. Once the army reached Gaza, however, supplying it with water would have been less of a problem. Gaza and other coastal cities of Canaan depended mostly on cisterns for their water supply. By mid-May, the winter rains would have already filled these cisterns to capacity. April and May are also the months when the harvest is ready in Egypt and southern Canaan, so the granaries of the cities and towns along Thutmose's route would also have been full and able to supply the army's needs.

Under the best of conditions, however, an ancient army on the march was a medical disaster. An army of 10,000 men could expect to lose 3 to 4 percent of its force, or about 400 men, to heatstroke, exhaustion, dust inhalation, and other respiratory problems. Another 1,700 men, or 17 percent of the force, were lost to routine injuries: broken limbs, sprains, cuts, falls, and accidents.[21] As soldiers marched in column, dust choked their lungs, dried out their sinuses, produced chronic coughing, blinding headaches, severe nosebleeds, and eye irritations. Many soldiers suffered injuries to their feet, which were unprotected except for the sole of the sandal. Without arch or side support, ankle injuries were common. The animals accompanying the army also caused damage by kicking or stepping on soldiers, and accidents with wheeled vehicles led to broken bones and other serious wounds. Blisters, lacerations, and abrasions were endemic.[22] The incidence of these injuries increased when an army moved quickly and with little rest or when it moved over irregular terrain, as did Thutmose's army once it left Egypt.

The Advance to Yehem

In April 1481 BCE the Egyptian army marched out of Sile along the coastal road toward Gaza. Its advance to Megiddo was divided into four operational phases, each influenced by time, terrain, and the enemy's reaction. First, Thutmose had to move his army from Egypt to Gaza. The army covered the 125 miles from Sile to Gaza in ten days, a rate of march of about 12 miles a day.[23] It is of great importance that Thutmose reached Gaza on the anniversary of his accession to the throne, that is, on the first day of the new regnal year. This day was normally an occasion of great celebration and feasting, but he had no celebration that year. Thutmose remained in Gaza only overnight, ordering the army back on the march the next day.[24]

The second phase required traversing the terrain from Gaza to Yehem (modern Yemma), a distance of eighty miles, much of it across the open southern Sharon Plain, perfect terrain for an Asiatic chariot attack. Yehem was a key road junction controlling the entrance to the Wadi Ara and the Aruna (iron) road that led over the Carmel Mountains to Megiddo and the Esdraelon Plain, the classical Greek name for the Jezreel Valley. The danger in the army's movement from Gaza to Yehem lay in the possibility of discovery by Asiatic reconnaissance units or even a collision with the advance units of the Asiatic main force making its way across the Sharon Plain en route to attack Egypt. Under these circumstances, security of the Egyptian force was paramount, and Thutmose covered the eighty miles in about nine days, a slower rate of march than his journey to Gaza took. When the Egyptian army arrived at Yehem, it had been on the march for nineteen straight days.[25]

The third phase required the army to move over the Carmel Mountains and gain the open plain next to the ridge upon which Megiddo sat without being attacked, worn down by enemy harassment along the way, or, worse, ambushed as it exited the mountains and moved to the plain.

4.1. THUTMOSE'S ROUTE TO MEGIDDO

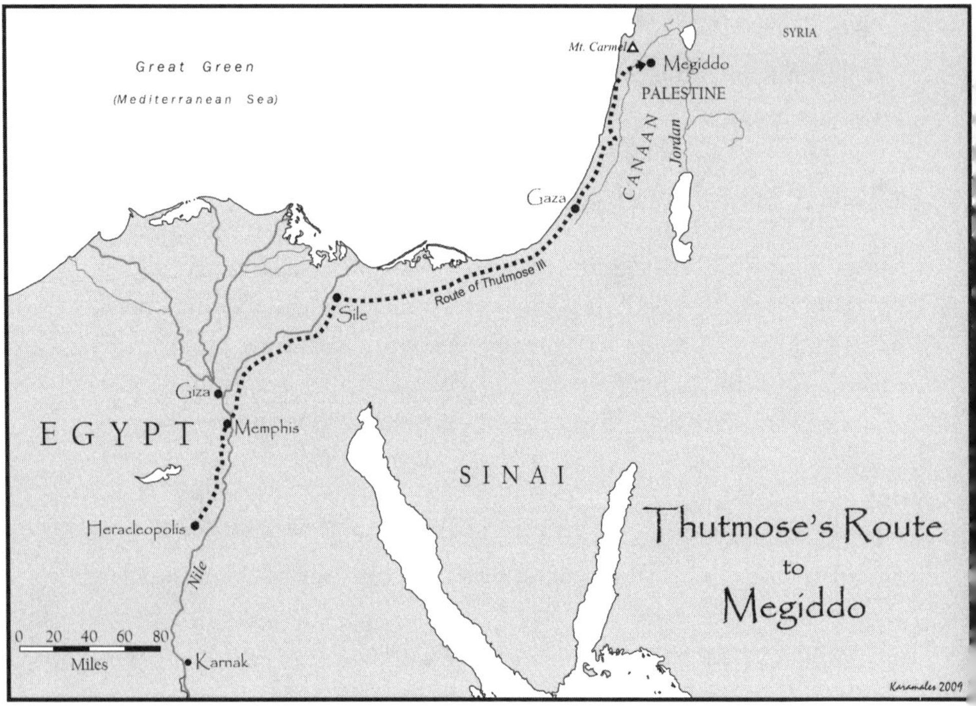

Only after Thutmose's army forced the exits and gained the Esdraelon Plain could it bring the enemy to battle in phase four.

The logical point of Asiatic resistance to the Egyptian advance would have been to engage Thutmose south of Gaza, where the terrain favored the Asiatic chariots and provided no natural defenses for the Egyptians. At a minimum, medium-size chariot forces could have been used to harass the Egyptians as they marched from Gaza to Yehem. Had this been done, the Asiatics could have maintained contact with Thutmose's army and remained aware of its location as it moved toward the Carmel Mountains. Even a small screening force falling back before the Egyptians' advance could have accomplished this basic mission. Knowing where the Egyptian army was at all times would have permitted the Asiatics to deploy forces at points of resistance south of the Carmel range. Asiatic infantry could have been easily blocked the entrance to the mountains at Wadi Ara, but the Asiatic commander undertook none of these operations. Instead, he allowed Thutmose's army to move unhindered into the Carmel Mountains, where it could attempt the crossing to reach Megiddo itself.

The failure of the Asiatic commander to discover Thutmose's army, monitor its movements, and prevent its seizing the Wadi Ara appears to be a case of gross military incompetence. But the charge is not completely warranted. The armies of the Canaanite and Syrian principalities were made up mostly of professional warriors led by a professional warrior elite. Their commanders were battle-hardened veterans for whom war was a profession and an obligation of their social status. Why, then did the Asiatic commander make such obvious tactical errors? The answer is that the Asiatics were so strategically focused on preparing for the coming offensive against Egypt that the possibility of a preemptive attack by the Egyptians was beyond their imagination. They entirely neglected the possibility of an Egyptian preemptive strike.

The Asiatic armies assembling at Megiddo were instead preparing to invade Egypt.[26] There was no other event or set of circumstances that would have otherwise justified the military cooperation of more than thirty-one leaders of different kingdoms, including the leaders of kingdoms as far away as northern Syria and Mitanni. An invasion of Egypt would require a very large force, somewhere in the vicinity of fifteen thousand to twenty thousand men and numerous chariot squadrons. This military capability was quite beyond the capacity of any single state and was possible only by assembling a large coalition. An invasion of Egypt made sound strategic sense in the eyes of the Mitanni, whose policy of *drang nach süden* (to the south) aimed at weakening Egypt and gaining influence in Canaan.

Megiddo was a logical place to assemble the invasion force. It controlled the Esdraelon Plain and sat astride the highways connecting southern Canaan and the coastal plain to Egypt. Megiddo also influenced the trade along the coastal plain to the north, since this trade flowed around Mount Carmel, down through the valley, and up the road to Damascus and on to the Euphrates River. Twenty miles behind Megiddo lay the fortress of Hazor, blocking the route to the Euphrates. Command of Megiddo was vital to controlling the communications routes through Canaan and was the strategic key to Egyptian influence in the Syrian zone. Without Megiddo, Egypt lost the ability to mount preemptory operations against the northern Asiatic states and to monitor and prevent the emergence of hostile political and military coalitions in an area defined as strategically vital to Egypt's defense.

Megiddo was also the most important fortified city in central Canaan. When Thutmose exhorted his troops to fight well against the city, he said, "The taking of Megiddo was the taking of a thousand towns." He was giving voice to the strategic truth that Megiddo's location was the key to further Egyptian expansion beyond the coastlands of southern Canaan and into the areas of Phoenicia, Syria, and, ultimately, beyond the Euphrates.[27] The strategic importance of the area around Megiddo, then and now, is evident in that over the last four thousand years, at least thirty-four battles have been fought in this small valley, with the last having occurred in 1967.

The city's walls were 325 meters long by 230 meters wide, enclosing an area of approximately 13 square acres and accommodating a population of approximately 3,100 residents.[28] The city's walls were 10 meters high and 6 meters thick and had only one gate to the south. Located on a steep hill overlooking the Esdraelon Plain, the steepness of the slope itself made an approach from the north, east, and west difficult. Although Megiddo had no moat, it had a long sloping glacis facing south to compensate for the shallowness of the hill's grade there that reduced the height of the walls.[29] The glacis was designed to prevent the use of scaling ladders. This description of Megiddo's fortifications must be accepted with some caution, however. It is not completely clear which of the twenty settlements layered one on top of the other at the excavation site belong to the period when Thutmose besieged and captured the city. There is also no evidence for the existence of a massive city wall around Megiddo at this time. It is possible, but not certain, that the earlier walls constructed during the Middle Bronze Age period were still in use when Thutmose attacked the city, and it its these walls that archaeologists have measured.[30]

The chief of Megiddo was an important person, and scores of smaller towns and hamlets depended on him for protection and commerce. Megiddo had an abundant water supply connected by an underground tunnel to a spring outside the walls. But its greatest asset for supporting an invasion of Egypt was its control of vast agricultural fields near and beyond the city that produced enormous harvests of grain. This harvest was needed to feed the invasion force as it moved over the Carmel Mountains, to the Canaanite plain, and attacked Egypt.

Unlike Egypt and southern Canaan, where the harvest is ready in mid-April to early May, the harvest at Megiddo is not ready until June.[31] Accordingly, the Asiatic invasion force could not assemble at Megiddo until at least mid-June, when the harvest would be available to feed and supply the armies for the march across the Carmel Ridge. Until then, the bulk of the Asiatic army had to remain in their home garrisons within their respective kingdoms. Harold Nelson walked the ground at Megiddo at the same time of year that Thutmose arrived and offers a description of what he, and possibly the Egyptian troops, observed at the plain around Megiddo: "What they saw before them was the wide expanse of level land, probably covered with ripening harvests, stretching for half a mile to the banks of the Kina."[32] The description of the harvests as "ripening" confirms that the crops would still have been in the field and not ready for harvesting for at least another three to four weeks. If so, then the Asiatic army could not have been already assembled in force at Megiddo when Thutmose arrived because there would have been no way to feed it.

The terrain in the Esdraelon Valley around Megiddo also made it unlikely that the Asiatic armies were already assembled at the city when Thutmose arrived. The Kishon River and its many tributaries crisscross the valley floor and its environs. From the winter rains the surrounding mountains give rise to numerous streams that empty upon the valley floor. Poor drainage further contributes to the swampy conditions in the flat plain around Megiddo for much of the year. Except for the driest summer months, beginning in June, the area is a muddy morass that would hinder troop movement.[33] Many of the Asiatic contingents marching to Megiddo from the north would have been forced to traverse the flood plain of the Kishon River on the Acco Plain, which would have been almost impassible for months after the seasonal rains. These conditions would have made the Asiatic armies' march to Megiddo and their encampment there difficult until the ground firmed up sometime in early June. Thus, the Asiatic armies had not yet assembled around the city when Thutmose arrived because they were also still waiting for the ground to dry.

Whatever troops were at Megiddo when Thutmose arrived could not have been the fully assembled Asiatic force of 15,000 to 20,000 men and chariots needed to carry out the strategic mission of attacking Egypt. In the *Annals* we are told that after the battle Thutmose captured 924 enemy chariots, 340 prisoners of war, and 200 corselets of armor. Enemy casualties amounted to only 83 dead.[34] By contrast, Merneptah's battle against the Libyans killed 3,410 men while Ramses III's later Libyan campaign inflicted 12,000 dead. The battle at Megiddo seems to have been little more than a skirmish by comparison.[35]

This point is controversial for it has been assumed in other accounts of the battle that the Asiatic coalition was very large and already in place around Megiddo when the Egyptians arrived. Nelson's account says, "The Asiatics certainly did not outnumber the Egyptians, and we therefore place the contending forces at between 10,000 and 15,000 men each."[36] Written in 1913, Nelson's version was one of the earliest accounts of the battle. He based his analysis on having walked the ground, thus lending his work great import. His description of the battle became a basic source document that was incorporated into later accounts, often without critical analysis. No evidence supports Nelson's or anyone else's estimate of the size of the Asiatic force at Megiddo. The only information available to us is circumstantial, and what appears in the *Annals* are lists of the numbers of Asiatic prisoners and dead. The *Annals* do not give the strength of the enemy force. If there were 15,000 to 20,000 men in the Asiatic army at Megiddo, one is entitled to ask where they went after the battle.

The impression taken from the texts that the Asiatic army had already formed in large numbers at Megiddo may be the result of a textual mistranslation. Hans Goedicke suggests that the Egyptian word translated as "armies" in previous accounts should really be translated as "heavy fighters," which were the mercenaries or the personal battle guards that accompanied the chiefs of Asiatic kingdoms.[37] Goedicke discerns from the texts that three types of soldiers accompanied the chiefs to Megiddo: maryanna, or chariot warriors; "fighters," which he defines as heavy infantry; and light infantry, probably including archers.[38] What the texts describe at Megiddo, then, is not an assembling of armies but a gathering of chiefs accompanied by their personal military retinues in advance of their armies, which would arrive later, when the harvest was ready and the ground was dry. Since only the chiefs of Kadesh and Megiddo are mentioned, we might rightly infer that the remainder of the coalition chiefs had also not yet arrived.

Any attempt to determine the size of the Asiatic force is an exercise in speculation. Each of the 892 chariots captured from "the vile army" would have required a driver and a maryannu archer-charioteer. The chariot team entered battle accompanied by at least one and sometimes two runners, or infantrymen whose task it was to protect the chariot team and the horses from infantry attack. A groom also accompanied the chariot team and tended the horses. In a pinch he, too, might be pressed into service as light infantry. Taken together, then, the Asiatic chariot force of drivers, charioteers, and runners numbered some 2,676 combatants. Additional runners and the grooms might have added another 1,500 or so troops. The heavy infantry mentioned in the texts made up the chiefs' battle guards and could not have amounted to more than 150 to 300 men, depending on how many local vassals of the chief of Megiddo were present but not mentioned in the texts. Any archer contingents would, of necessity, be quite small. Perhaps another 30 to 40 archers could be added, bringing the total to approximately a maximum 4,500 combatants. The chief of Megiddo would have provided most of the men after requiring the full mobilization of the military resources available to his local vassals. Without the additional chariot runners and grooms, though, the Asiatic force would have numbered no more than 3,000 combatants.

After nineteen days on the march, on May 14 the Egyptian army arrived at Yehem, where it encamped and rested for the anticipated crossing of the Carmel Mountains. The name of the town, coming from the root meaning to watch or protect, indicates its strategic location protecting the opening to the Wadi Ara and the Aruna road running over the mountains to Megiddo.[39] Thutmose spent three days at Yehem, during which time his reconnaissance units explored the prospective routes leading to Megiddo and attempted to learn the disposition of the Asiatic force.

The Egyptian intelligence service traced its origins to the Middle Kingdom Period, when the title of Master of the Secrets of the King in the Army is first found.[40] The intelligence service had kept an analytical eye on the Canaanite-Syrian area of operations for centuries, employing spies, commercial agents, and diplomatic contacts to assess political and military developments in the area. It was probably the intelligence service that discovered the Asiatics' intention to assemble the military coalition to invade Egypt. Egypt's extensive and long-standing commercial relations with Canaan provided the intelligence service with knowledge of the terrain, routes of advance, fortifications, natural obstacles, locations of wells, villages, crop fields and their yields, and other information important to Egyptian military planners in the theater of operations. This data also covered the Aruna road leading to Megiddo. A surviving intelligence report notes that an important official serving in Canaan was expected to be familiar with the Aruna route and to know the locations on the road that were conducive to setting ambushes.[41] It is likely, then, that as part of the campaign planning process before he left Egypt, Thutmose was briefed by his intelligence officers on all the relevant information concerning the Megiddo campaign, including the terrain and routes of advance over the Carmel Mountains. This operational brief would surely have addressed the state of the Asiatic forces' mobilization and the ability of the assembly area around Megiddo to support them logistically. Only the *disposition* of the Asiatic force around Megiddo remained unknown, and Thutmose's reconnaissance units quickly determined that once they reached Wadi Ara.

On May 16 Thutmose called his field commanders together to discuss the operational plan. After noting that the chief of Kadesh and some other units were in Megiddo, Thutmose ordered his commanders, "Tell me what you think about it [the operational plan]."[42] It is important to note that Thutmose did not explain the plan to his generals before asking for their opinion. This detail suggests that all the conference participants were aware of some previous plan, perhaps the same one presented in the campaign's operational briefing before they left Egypt in which the route over the Carmel Mountains had already been discussed.

It is not unusual for a commander's subordinates to disagree with elements of his operational plan. The Egyptian generals argued that of the three roads leading to Megiddo, two of them—the one leading to Ta'anach to the south and the other to Djefty to the north—were wider and easier to negotiate than the Aruna road, which led from the village of Aruna to the Esdraelon Plain. The Aruna road was narrow and winding, forcing troops to march in single file in some places and reducing their pace. The slower rate of march would force the van of the army to exit near Megiddo

4.2. THREE ROADS TO MEGIDDO

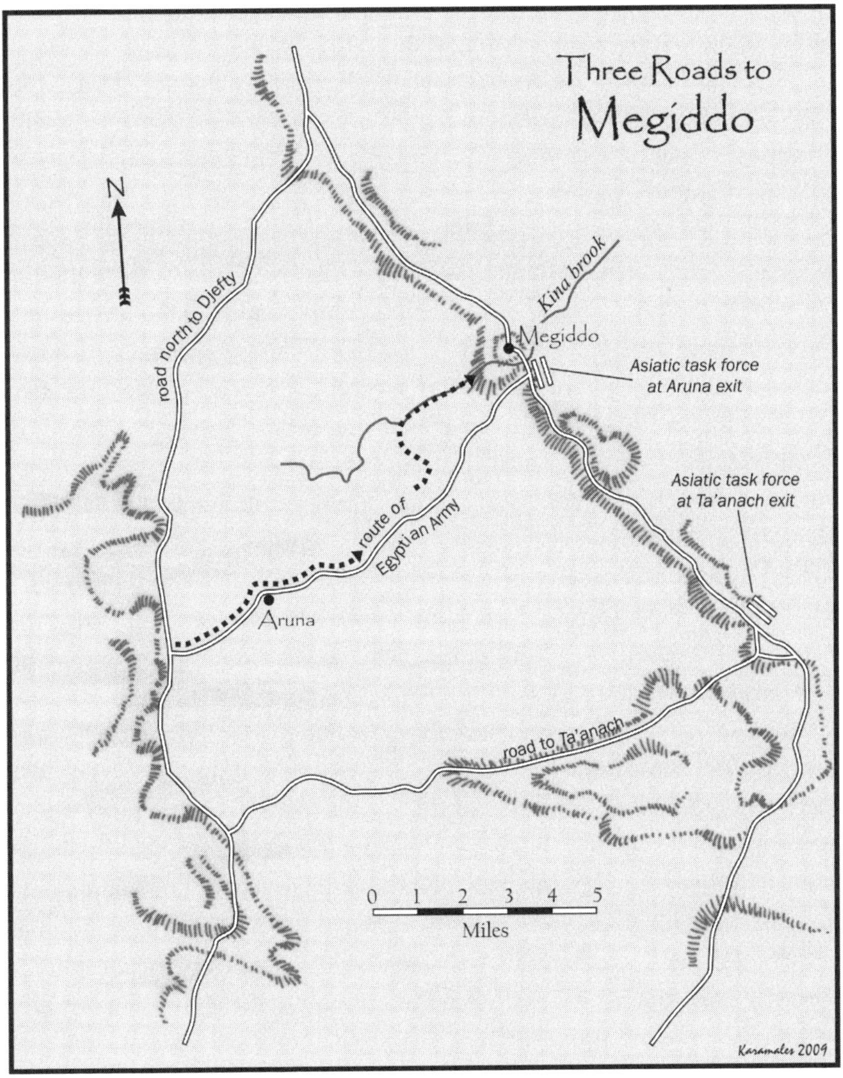

while its rearguard was still in camp at Aruna.[43] Presumably all parties to the discussion had access to whatever new information the army's reconnaissance units had obtained over the last three days of patrolling. Citing the new intelligence, the generals note that "it is reported that the enemy are standing outside [where the Aruna and Ta'anach roads exit the mountains and run to the plain] and that they have become numerous."[44]

From these reports we may surmise that the Asiatics had discovered the presence of the Egyptian army and deployed their troops to block the Ta'anach and Aruna exits leading to the Esdraelon Plain.

It is clear from the *Annals* that the Egyptian reconnaissance units had discovered the Asiatic troop dispositions before the army left Yehem. Thutmose broke camp and left Yehem on May 18. On that day, the annalist tells us, "Now they [the Asiatics] were already drawn up in numerous squadrons but the enemy was isolated: their southern flank was at Ta'anach in the hills, the northern flank was at the southern corner of the valley of Qina."[45] Nelson suggests that the Asiatic units guarding the Aruna and Ta'anach exits were detached force components and that the Asiatics had deployed the bulk of their army as a central reserve between the two blocking forces.[46] This reasonable conclusion is based on the assumption that the Asiatic army was at full combat strength when it took the field, but, as I have tried to show, that proposition is questionable. No evidence supports Nelson's assertion. Nor does his argument address why the Asiatic commander failed to cover the exit at Djefty.

The *Annals* inform us that Thutmose decided to proceed down the Aruna road but tell us nothing about why he chose that route. It may be that he decided to keep to the original plan he made before leaving Egypt. It may also be that his reconnaissance units had discovered another route leading from the Aruna road to Megiddo that exited the mountains at a place where his army could avoid the Asiatic force blocking the exit, and for the time being he may have kept this knowledge to himself. We cannot know Thutmose's reasoning, but we can summarize what he knew at the time he made his decision to cross the Carmel Ridge. Thus, he knew that both the Ta'anach road and the Aruna road debouched from the mountains onto the open plains around Megiddo. He understood that the Asiatics had already moved units to block both roads' exits. He was aware that the northern road to Djefty, the longest of the three, joined the road to Megiddo about five kilometers northwest of the city and that apparently the Djefty exit was unguarded.[47] Thutmose realized that the Aruna road offered the shortest distance to the objective, but because of its narrow and winding nature, it would take longer to traverse than the Ta'anach road. Thutmose also determined that the Asiatic force waiting for him was of only marginal strength and that the Egyptian army outnumbered it in infantry while being relatively equal in chariots.[48] Given this knowledge, it is difficult to discern what military advantage Thutmose might have seen in taking the Aruna route.

Thutmose also knew that a Syrian-Canaanite army would be chariot heavy and light on infantry. The Egyptian army had its normal complement of two chariot brigades of five hundred vehicles each. The rest of the army, or some ten thousand men, was infantry, the Egyptian combat arm of decision. If Thutmose entered the plain at either Djefty or Ta'anach, both about five kilometers from the city, his infantry would have had to force the pass and suffer considerable casualties at the hands of the maryannu chariot archers. After accomplishing this step, he would have still had to fight a chariot battle on the open plain in order to advance on Megiddo itself. The result would have been a battle that played to the Asiatic strength. To avoid this battle Thutmose planned not to use the Aruna road exit and move straight at Megiddo, exiting the mountains closer to the city on ground favorable to his infantry. But where was this area, and how did Thutmose get there?

The March to Megiddo

On May 18, Thutmose's army left Yehem, entered the Wadi Ara connecting to the Aruna road, marched the thirteen miles to the village of Aruna, and encamped.[49] Nelson's review of the land in 1910 found it to have adequate space and water to accommodate the large army.[50] Aruna sits on the southern side of the Carmel Ridge, some three miles short of the highest elevation at Mismus. The distance from Aruna to Megiddo is seven miles; from Mismus to Megiddo is four miles. Camping below the highest point of the ridge effectively concealed the army and its cooking fires and prevented patrols covering the Aruna exit or camped on the Esdraelon Plain from discovering it.

Much is made in the *Annals* about the narrowness of the Aruna road and the need for the army to go "horse after horse"—that is, in single file—with all that implies for the army's rate of march.[51] In fact, the Aruna road was no mere path but one of the main commercial roads over the Carmel Mountains, and it is difficult to believe that a much traveled road over the mountains would be so narrow as to require an army to move in single file. Marching four abreast in column requires a space of only four meters across. A commercial road unable to accommodate at least this distance would have been useless. When the comments in the texts concerning the Aruna road are examined in context, it is clear that the concern of Thutmose's generals was not about the narrowness of the road and its impact on the army's rate of march. The generals were apprehensive about the narrowness of the road's *exit* to the Esdraelon Plain. Thus, they asked Pharaoh, "In what fashion shall we go forth from this path, which tends to be narrow?"[52] The generals were concerned that if the army could not assemble into battle units before entering upon the plain, the chariot forces waiting at the exits would massacre them.

The Aruna road was a perfectly usable military road, and the annalist might have emphasized its narrowness in the texts for dramatic effect. Thus, we are told that the army moved in single file from Yehem to Aruna when there was no geographic need to do so. Again, it reads, "And then His Majesty caused that to go forth in front. His army itself was caused that it spreads out in its order of marching single file, while His majesty was the first of his army." Pharaoh usually is presented as riding his war chariot. Was Thutmose in his chariot when he led the army down the Aruna road? If so, how narrow could it have been?

The problem with the Aruna road from a tactical perspective was not that it was narrow and slowed the army's rate of march but that it led to a death trap. An Asiatic chariot task force of perhaps three hundred vehicles covered the Aruna exit to the Esdraelon Plain while a larger force of perhaps six hundred to seven hundred chariots guarded the exit from Ta'anach.[53] The two forces were only four miles apart and could quickly come to one another's support once Thutmose's army appeared at one of the exits. There was no place large enough near the Aruna exit in which the Egyptian army could assemble *before* it came out of the pass. If Thutmose attempted to force the narrow exit by means of his superior numbers, he would be forced to feed his infantry piecemeal onto the open plain, and his men would not be in their battle formations. Moreover, the Egyptian infantry could not expect any support from their chariots once exposed because the chariots had been disassembled and carried by porters on the march through the mountains. The chariot teams would need time and a place to reassemble their vehicles and get themselves in fighting condition, but the exit from the Aruna road did not have the necessary space.

Thus, if Thutmose had tried to force the Aruna exit, he would have had to fight without his chariots against a professional force of maryannu chariot warriors deployed on an open plain that provided no defensive terrain for the Egyptian infantry to cling to. Otherwise, he would have had to try to assemble his vehicles and horse teams on the open plain while under attack from the northern task force. If the southern task force had rushed to join the battle, it would have caught Thutmose's army in the rear, trapping it between the two forces. It was an impossible tactical situation and one in which the Egyptian army might easily have been destroyed.

Various accounts of the battle have attempted to explain away the military realities surrounding Thutmose's exit from the Aruna road and have offered solutions that are largely unconvincing. It has been argued, for example, that battles in antiquity were arranged in advance as to time and place, so the Asiatic chariot units deployed at the road exits were there only to determine that the Egyptians had arrived on the battlefield and not to bring them to battle.[54] Another argument holds that the Asiatics were simply "too supine" to attempt an attack, even though they possessed all the advantages for successfully accomplishing it.[55] Still another explanation asserts the chariot force guarding the Aruna exit had been transferred to the task force protecting the Ta'anach exit before Thutmose arrived at the Aruna exit.[56] And finally, another claims the Asiatic commander must have been incompetent in not taking full advantage of his military forces to attack the Egyptians at the Aruna exit.[57] The *Annals* do not support any of these explanations, and all violate the most basic rules of tactics. What these accounts have in common, however, is their failure to consider the obvious—that is, Thutmose and his army did not exit the Carmel Mountains through the Aruna road and indeed had taken another route.

The assumption that Thutmose exited at the Aruna pass is not supported by the texts. The *Annals* tell us that Thutmose's army came out of the mountains not at the Aruna exit, but at a place called the Kina Valley. We are told, "Lo, the rear of the army of His Majesty had come out from the mountain of Aruna [the highest elevation on the Aruna road] while the vanguard had come forth towards the Valley of Kina—and after they filled the plain of this valley."[58] Referring to the arrival of the Egyptian army, the texts say that "the vanguard had come forth toward the Valley of Kina."[59] The texts also tell us that Thutmose himself "arrived at the south of Megiddo at the edge of the Kina valley, when the 7th hour was turning in the day."[60] And finally, "behold, now that his Majesty has come forth together with his troop of *nhtw* [elite troops, or probably Pharaoh's battle guard] and they have seized the valley."[61] The Kina Valley, therefore, should be distinguished from the Esdraelon Plain upon which the Aruna road exits. There does not appear to be a text reference that supports the assumption that the Egyptian army debouched from the Aruna road on to the Esdraelon Plain. The evidence points instead to Thutmose and his army arriving at the Kina Valley.

Illustration 4.3 depicts the important terrain features around Megiddo relevant to our understanding of Thutmose's movements to the battlefield. The Kina Valley is a narrow strip of flat flood plain approximately 254 meters at its widest and 82 meters at its narrowest point. It begins at the mountains' edge in the south, runs north a little longer than a mile, and ends in an exit on the plateau sitting about a mile in front of Megiddo. The area within the valley affords sufficient space to accommodate an army of ten thousand men.[62] From its source in the mountains the Kina brook runs the length of the valley to the flat land, where it crosses the top edge of the Esdraelon Plain and eventually empties into the Kishon River. Low forested hills run along both sides of the valley, presenting an obstacle to attack from the flanks. The Asiatic chariot task force blocking the Aruna exit would have had at least one mile of hills and forest between them and the Kina Valley route, making it impossible to see, hear, or intercept the Egyptian army moving toward Megiddo through the valley.

Approaching the Megiddo plateau along this route, the Egyptian army could have easily moved straight ahead, crossed the Kina brook, and deployed on the plateau. When Nelson reconnoitered the terrain, he found the stream at the Kina bend to be fifteen to twenty feet deep and enclosed by almost perpendicular banks.[63] The Egyptian army did not, therefore, cross at the Kina bend but at a place a short distance back down the valley, where the valley floor was separated from the raised plateau by a shoe-shaped low hill. Crossing over the "instep" of the shoe, the Egyptian army could have gained the plateau in front of Megiddo with little effort. Advancing through the Kina Valley, Thutmose would have

4.3. MEGIDDO AND ITS ENVIRONS

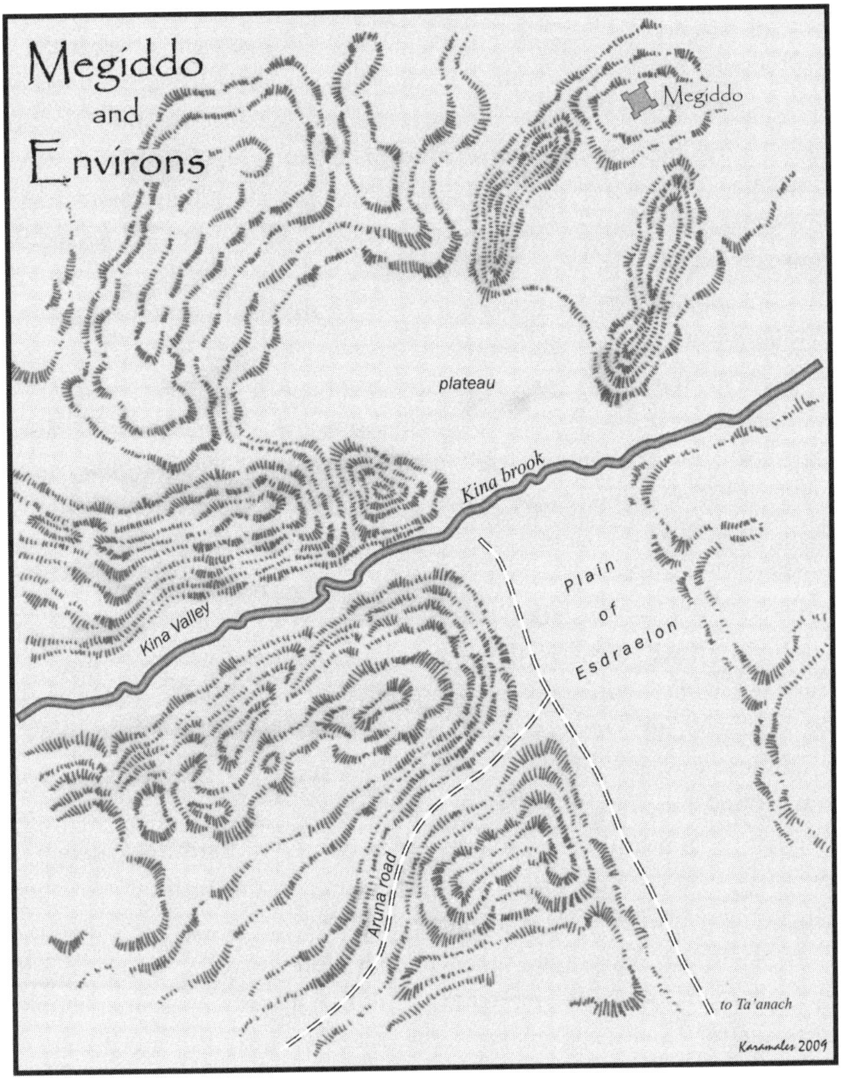

arrived behind both chariot task forces guarding the road exits at Ta'anach and Aruna and could have assembled his army on the plateau without opposition.

Before outlining Thutmose's route to the Kina Valley, a word of caution is in order. The locations of roads in antiquity, especially roads that traversed plains and agricultural areas, usually cannot be determined with any confidence. These roads' locations shifted over time, mostly in response to the rise and fall of new towns and changes in commerce. Only those roads that traversed mountains might be located with some certainty. Roads that crossed mountains in antiquity followed courses marked out by nature, and the wadis and passes that existed then still exist.[64] In determining the route Thutmose used to cross the mountains and arrive at the Kina Valley, we may be fairly certain that he followed the wadis and paths that may be found today with the aid of aerial and satellite photographs.[65]

By rejoining Thutmose at his camp at Aruna in the middle of the Carmel Mountains, we may trace his route to the Kina Valley. The highest point on the Aruna road is at modern Mismus, or about three miles' distance from the Egyptian camp at Aruna. At Mismus, a wide wadi branches off to the left and may be followed for less than a mile before it branches into another wadi that debouches on the banks of the far southern end of the Kina brook. The distance from this intersection to the Kina brook is about a half mile. The total distance from Mismus to the Kina brook is two miles, and when added to the distance from the Egyptian camp to Mismus, the total distance from the Aruna camp to the brook is about five miles. The drop in elevation from Mismus (944 feet) to the Kina brook (650 feet) is such that most of the journey is downhill. The width of the wadi varies from 18 to 22 feet, sufficient to accommodate a troop column moving four abreast at route step. The route along the Kina brook to the Kina Valley's southern end varies in width from 45 meters to 88 meters, and with the brook running through it, the troops were forced to march along the flood plain on either side of the stream.[66] The distance from where the army first gained the Kina brook to the valley's south end, where Thutmose assembled his army, is just a little more than a mile. Thus, the total marching distance from the Aruna camp to the assembly area in the Kina Valley is approximately six miles. At a rate of two miles an hour downhill, it would have taken the Egyptian army about three hours to cover the distance.

The texts tell us that Pharaoh was awakened early on the morning of May 19, suggesting that the army also began its march very early in the day.[67] Sometime around 9:00 a.m., with Thutmose leading it, the Egyptian army's advanced guard arrived at the Kina Valley's far southern end.

4.4. THUTMOSE'S ROUTE TO THE KINA VALLEY

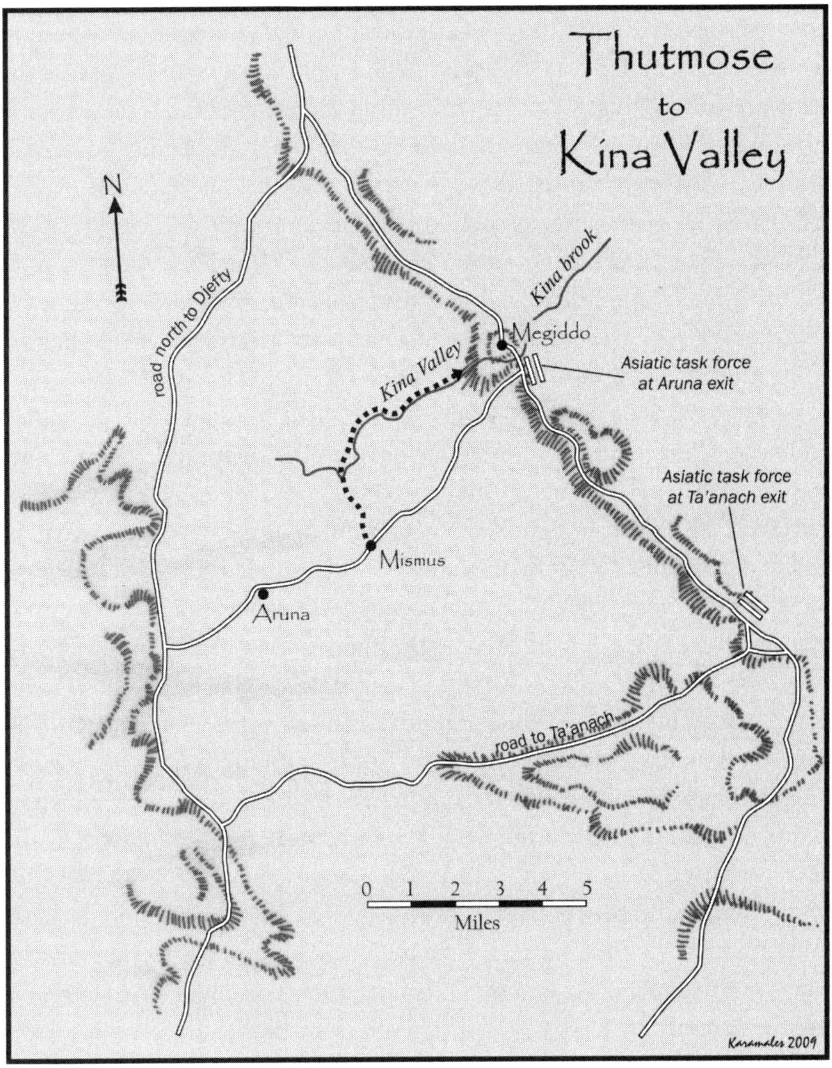

"Behold, now that his Majesty has come forth together with his troop of *nhtw* and they have seized the valley."[68] The rest of the army was still on the road "bound for the path of Aruna while the vanguard had come forth toward the valley of Kina."[69] The reference to the path of Aruna seems not to be to the Aruna road but to the path that led from the road to the Kina brook.

When the army's units began arriving at the southern end of the valley, Thutmose's generals became concerned that the king might move precipitously and enter the plateau in front of Megiddo before the entire army was assembled. They pleaded with him to wait until the rest of the army arrived.[70] Thus, "lo . . . he [Pharaoh] sat on a stool there awaiting the last of his troops."[71] The texts are precise as to when the army's rearguard completed the march and reached the assembly area. The texts tell us, "Lo, the last of the arrears was coming forth from this path when the shadow turned."[72] The reference is to the shadow clock the Egyptians used to tell time, and the reference to the turning of the shadow is to the noon meridian, or high noon. The rear of the army arrived in the Kina Valley six hours after the vanguard began its march.

By noon of May 19, Thutmose's army had reached the Kina Valley undetected and was only a mile away from the opening leading to the Megiddo plateau. Thutmose must have begun preparing his army for battle in case he had to fight his way onto the plateau. The texts are silent on the details, but certainly he would have assembled his army into their combat formations. He would also have directed some of his chariot units to screen the army's movement onto the plateau. Elite heavy infantry units, either the King's Braves or the strong-arm boys, probably led the column to protect against attack. None of this movement should have taken more than a few hours, so that by 3:00 p.m. Thutmose would have been ready to cover the last mile from the assembly area to the plateau upon which he planned to debouch his army, establish his camp, and fight the battle the next morning.

That Thutmose gained the plateau without opposition is clear from the texts: "At the coming forth by His Majesty [against that enemy] who was readied with numerous battle units, he did not find a single enemy. Behold, the [Asiatic] southern attack force was [still] at Ta'anach, while the northern attack force was stationed at the southern shoulder [corner] of the territory of Megiddo." Although the northern task force had anchored its flank on the southern corner of the brook, it failed to detect Thutmose's passage onto the plateau. It probably missed him because when the Egyptians crossed the "instep" of the low hills farther down the valley from its opening near the brook, the hills and thick forest screened his route from the Asiatic position. Moreover, the Kina brook ran between the plateau and the Esdraelon Plain. Its depth and steep banks at the southern corner effectively turned the stream into an obstacle to chariot movement from the plain to the plateau. Had the Egyptians been discovered debouching upon the plateau, the northern task force would not have been able to mount an attack.

Thutmose established his camp on the plateau about a mile from the city.[73] He had more than three hours of daylight to arrange his camp and make his preparations for the following day.[74] The Egyptian armies of the New Kingdom regularly established a fortified camp on campaign and especially so on the eve of battle. The Egyptian camp was rectangular in shape and surrounded by a ditch deep enough to disrupt a chariot attack. Entry to the camp was over a bridge traversing the ditch and ran through a single gate. The earth from the ditch was piled up to form a berm upon which a wall of the infantry's shields was constructed.[75] The shields were strapped to the soldiers' spears or held to the spears by passing the shafts through the shields' handgrips.[76] The spear was then driven into the ground, holding the shield upright. Since disarmed soldiers are of little use in warding off an attack, each soldier slept on his reed mat behind his shield and spear so he could react quickly in the event of an attack. Inside the wall, the camp was arranged around Pharaoh's war tent, which was located in the middle of the compound.[77] The tent's entrance was oriented to the east, the direction of the rising sun god, Ra. Pharaoh's chariot and elite infantry battle guard surrounded the king's tent. All other units, animals, tents, and other equipment were positioned for handy access.

The texts do not tell us when the Asiatics became aware of the Egyptians' presence, but it must have been shortly after they began to debouch on the plateau. There is no information concerning the Asiatics' reaction. One can reasonably imagine, however, that messengers were dispatched to the units guarding the Ta'anach exit with orders to redeploy to Megiddo. The units guarding the Aruna exit must have redeployed as well. There is no evidence of any contact between the opposing forces; however, it is reasonable to assume that the Asiatics conducted reconnaissance. The Asiatic forces reassembled at their battle camp located close to the walls on the city's south side. It was dark by the time all the Asiatic forces and commanders could be gathered together in the camp, and the evening must have been spent deliberating how to deal with the formidable Egyptian army that sat on the plateau only a mile from Megiddo's gate.

Although he had achieved strategic surprise, Thutmose's position was by no means free of danger. His army was tired, and the falling darkness raised the specter of a night attack. Although he held the numerical advantage, Thutmose had no way of knowing if other Asiatic chiefs and their armed contingents were closing on Megiddo to join the planned invasion force. If they were en route and arrived soon, Thutmose would lose his advantage and be forced to fight against a numerically superior foe. The only way to reduce this risk was to attack quickly before additional Asiatic forces arrived. As darkness enveloped the Egyptian camp, Thutmose ordered his troops to be fed and provided food from his own stores for his men. The officers were treated to a mess dinner with their commander. Sentries were posted around the camp and ordered to be steadfast and watchful. The officers went through the ranks, ordering the men, "Prepare yourself! Ready your weapons!" They had to be ready to fight in the morning.[78]

The Battle

The texts do not provide a complete account of the battle. Thus, the historian is forced to glean clues from an analysis of the terrain, the nature of the combatants, and the basic principles of tactics the armies used during the period. This said, it is still possible to construct a reasonable account of the battle consistent with all the information available.

The battle took place on May 20, the twenty-eighth day after the Egyptian army set out from its base at Sile and the day after completing its crossing of the Carmel Mountains. Thutmose was awakened early, and his commanders immediately briefed him. Pharaoh was told that "the desert is well, and that the northern and southern troops are safe also."[79] This report has led some to suggest that the two wings of the Egyptian army had already been deployed during the night and had established their forward battle positions to the north and south of Megiddo. Moving large bodies of troops in the dark, however, would have been unprecedented for armies of the period and is not plausible. More probably, Thutmose's officers told him that the army had not suffered any attacks during the night and was safe in camp. The phrase "the desert is well" is probably best rendered as "all is well" or even "we have the good ground." The king was assured the army was in good shape and ready to be deployed for battle.

Thutmose gave "instructions for the entire army to be spread out for fighting, while His Majesty will proceed on a chariot of fine gold furnished with his battle-gear, like Horus strong-of-arms." The army was ordered to break camp and assemble in two wings, which they called horns, and to begin moving into position for the attack. "The southern wing of the army of His Majesty [is deployed] towards the southeastern tower over the edge of the Kina; the northern wing towards the northeast of Megiddo."[80] Pharaoh himself led the chariot force in the center.[81] "And then His Majesty was entirely powerful at the head of his army."[82] From this point forward, the *Annals* offer no further details about the battle.

Thutmose's goal of capturing Megiddo could not have been achieved without first defeating the Asiatic army defending it. In antiquity, two factors largely determined tactical deployment: the relative numbers of the combatants and the terrain upon which the battle was fought. By gathering his forces beneath the city's walls, the Asiatic commander had already chosen the terrain for the battle. Once his plan to stop the Egyptians at the Aruna and Ta'anach passes had failed and the Egyptian army had deployed on the plateau, the Asiatic commander had no choice but to pull his forces back and assume a defensive position. The Asiatic armies' strength and composition also influenced its tactical deployment. The Asiatic force was chariot heavy and supported by chariot runners and small contingents of infantry. As noted earlier, this force comprised some 1,000 chariots, about the same number of chariot runners, and 150 to 300 or so heavy infantrymen. The chariot grooms could also have been pressed into service, but they would have been largely ineffective in battle. The Egyptian army numbered between 10,000 and 12,000 trained troops, including archers, light and heavy infantry, and two 500-vehicle chariot brigades. Although the chariot forces of both combatants were equal, the Egyptians possessed an advantage in infantry. Whereas the Asiatic army's combat arm of decision was chariotry, the Egyptians' arm of decision was infantry. It was to be expected, then, that Thutmose would rely heavily on his infantry while the Asiatic commander relied on his chariotry.

Considering that chariots are unstable when used on uneven ground and useless in steep or wooded terrain, the terrain around Megiddo severely limited the Asiatic commander's tactical options. Megiddo lies at the far end of a south-north elongated ridge. The terrain to the city's rear and east is very steep. While the terrain is less steep to the west, it is still too steep for chariots.[83] Chariots can be usefully employed on only one place on the ridge, and that is to the south along the gently sloping ground leading down from the ridge to the plateau upon which the Egyptian army was encamped. The distance from the city to where the lip of the plateau reaches the beginning of the incline is approximately one mile. The slight downward slope, for a drop of thirty-three yards over one mile, provided a small advantage to the Asiatic chariots in that it forced the Egyptians to fight uphill.

The battle was fought within a tactical box approximately one mile long from north to south and 460 yards wide from west to east. The western edge of the battlefield was bordered by a row of low hills. Two hills marked the boundary to the east, but they presented no obstacle to infantry maneuver. Along the battlefield's eastern edge, beginning on the lower plateau and running farther to the east, was the Kina brook. An infantry force moving north along the eastern boundary of the tactical box could sweep its flank along the brook for a few hundred yards before the brook meandered away from the battlefield and became useless as a tactical obstacle.

A 460-yard-wide tactical box becomes a very small place when attempting to deploy 2,000 chariots and 8,000 infantry within it. Two chariots arranged abreast attacking in line occupy 9 yards of space. Thus, 100 chariots arranged in line would have required 900 yards, or twice the width of the Megiddo battlefield. This does not take into account the space required for the Egyptian infantry to occupy both flanks. The Asiatic camp, therefore, was forced close to the city's walls out of necessity. There was little space to place it anywhere else. The battle space at Megiddo was so small that it deprived both commanders of any ability to maneuver tactically. The battle must have quickly turned into an intense, close-order chariot-infantry melee. In this kind of combat, numbers convey an advantage and the intensity of the battle can quickly overwhelm the soldiers' psychological endurance, leading to rapid collapse and a rout.

The terrain and the Asiatic troop deployment forced Thutmose to deploy his chariots in the center and his two infantry wings on the flanks. It is possible that the Egyptians shortened their infantry line by thickening the depth of their formations, thereby gaining greater room to maneuver to their front. Thutmose would have sent chariot units to act in concert with his infantry to counter the arrow fire of the Asiatic chariots operating laterally across the Egyptian infantry's front. Chariot tactics are often misunderstood. It is commonly believed that they attacked in long lines, almost wheel to hub, with the purpose of delivering shock by colliding with the opposing chariot line or with infantry formations. This was rarely if ever the case.[84]

The chariot's combat speed was no faster than a trot or canter. Anything faster risked exhausting the horses and overturning the vehicle. Chariots usually attacked in small packets or squadrons of ten to fifty vehicles, depending on the tactical circumstances. Against enemy chariots, the idea was to get close to the enemy vehicle and take down the horse, driver, or archer with bows or javelins as the vehicles moved en passant. Once the chariot lines passed through each other, they wheeled about and engaged in individual combats. Thus, a chariot attack resembled a polo match in which the horses trotted to the point of contact and then wheeled about, putting on great bursts of speed for short distances to gain an advantage on the adversary.[85] Chariots could not shatter infantry formations by crashing into them. Horses will not drive headlong into a body of troops, especially when the troops are pointing their spears or shields at the animals' eyes. Instead, chariots attacked infantry formations by riding parallel to them at a safe distance, twenty or thirty yards, while placing aimed-shot arrow fire into the infantry's ranks. Infantry archers returned fire while the ranks moved forward to close the gap between them and the chariots and used their spears to strike the charioteers or horses or to thrust between the spokes of the chariot wheels. Once the infantry closed with the chariots, a melee ensued as the chariot runners tried to defend their vehicles and animals and the charioteers dismounted to join the fight.

Given the confines of the battle space and his numerical disadvantage, the Asiatic commander probably divided his chariot force into three elements, using the greatest number of machines to contain the Egyptian

4.5. TACTICAL DISPOSITION OF FORCES AT MEGIDDO

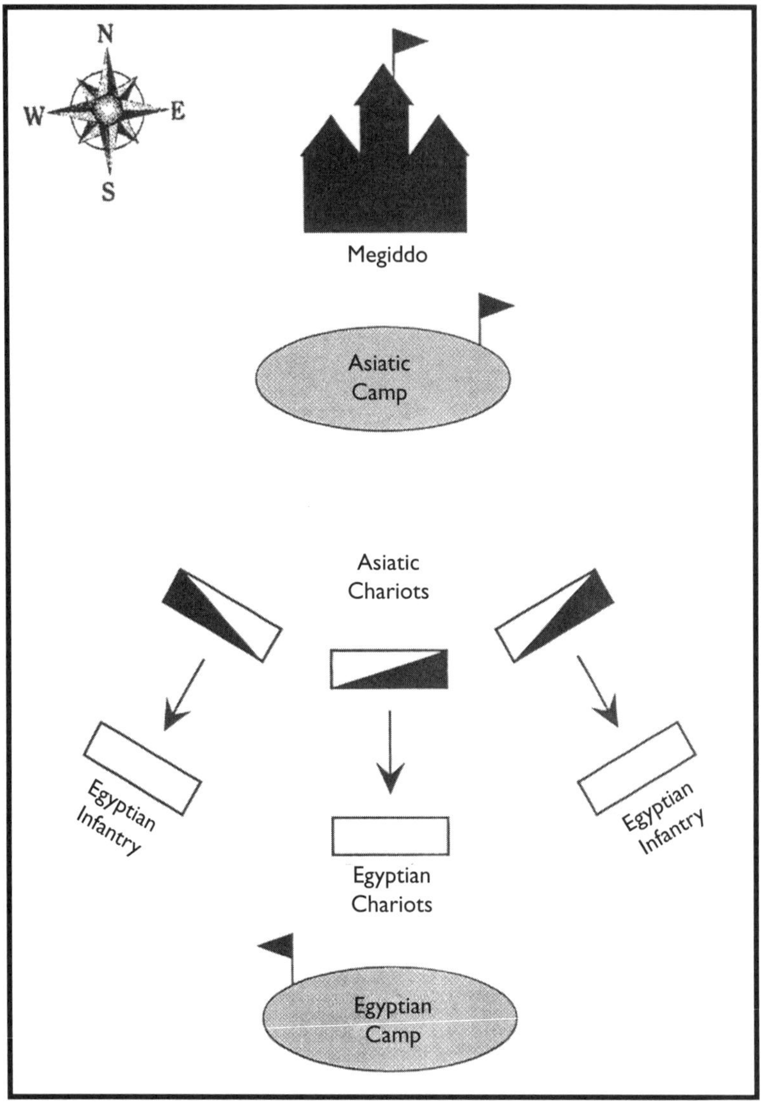

infantry. The narrowness of the tactical box meant, however, that only one side could deploy a small number of chariots along the center axis at one time, giving neither force a numerical advantage. If we assume that a third of the Asiatic chariot force, or some three hundred vehicles, was deployed to the front, some six hundred vehicles could be employed against the

Egyptian infantry. All things considered, the Egyptian infantry was the greater menace because of its numbers and position on the flanks, where it threatened to envelop the Asiatic chariots attacking in the center.

The tactical challenge for the Asiatic commander was how to stop the Egyptian infantry from moving inward in the battle space and gradually compressing the area in which the Asiatic chariots could operate. Three hundred machines in, say, companies of fifty each employed against the Egyptian infantry on each flank were capable of delivering continuous withering arrow fire against the enemy only as long as the chariots remained at a safe distance as they rode, company after company, across the Egyptian front. If the Egyptian infantry advanced too far into the tactical box, the distance between the infantry and chariots diminished on both sides of the battle space until the chariots were unable to maneuver and found themselves awash in a sea of Egyptian spear and ax-carrying infantry.

Thutmose sent some squadrons of chariots to support his infantry wings. The mission of these detached units was to engage the Asiatic chariots attacking the infantry and disrupt the rhythm of their attack, thus allowing the Egyptian infantry to advance deeper into the battle space. Like the Asiatic commander, Thutmose could deploy only a limited number of chariots along the central front at one time. He could, however, hold some in reserve, a capability the Asiatic commander did not have because of his smaller numbers. As the battle space contracted, the Asiatic chariot units in the center risked being cut off as the infantry closed in behind them. Unable to contain the infantry advance, the Asiatic charioteers attacking in the center would have been forced to turn back to save themselves, creating an opportunity for Thutmose to increase the pressure on the Asiatic front by committing his reserve chariots to the fight.

It is not difficult to imagine that when the Asiatic charioteers, struggling to hold the flanks, saw their comrades racing to the rear, they broke contact and attempted to flee to the safety of the city. Goedicke's rendering of the texts suggests that the Asiatic force commanders became overwhelmed and took flight first, abandoning their troops.[86] He argues that the commanders must have panicked because they left such valuable items as their horses and chariots behind.[87]

With the enemy falling back, Thutmose had an opportunity for great slaughter. The charioteers who fled to the northwest had to make their way down the steep banks behind the city. This terrain was so steep that they were forced to abandon their chariots and horses and make their way on foot. Others fled directly west into the valley and safety. Those who retreated toward the city were trapped between the Egyptians and the city walls. The Egyptians might have made quick and deadly work of them had they not stopped to plunder the Asiatic camp.[88] This looting allowed the fleeing troops time to be lifted to safety by the city's inhabitants, who pulled them up on the glacis that protected the city's southern approaches. By the time Egyptian troop discipline was restored, the remnants of the Asiatic army had reached safety, and the chance to crush the enemy on the battlefield was lost. The small numbers of dead (83) and captured (340) suggest that the battle, while intense owing to the disparity in numbers and the small battle space, did not last long and that most of the charioteers escaped. Many of the dead were probably infantry, and the 83 killed in action amounted to almost one-third of the engaged infantry troops.[89]

The Siege

Thutmose was furious at having been denied a battlefield victory because his professionally trained and led army suffered a lack of discipline. Without capturing Megiddo, the strategic situation in Canaan remained unchanged insofar as Egypt had not established itself as the dominant power in Canaan. Thutmose knew his failure to bring the rebels to heel would further lay bare Egypt's weakness and tempt the Mitanni to encourage other insurrections among the Canaanite principalities. If the Egyptian military effort was going to be a strategic success, Megiddo had to be taken. Thutmose tells us his reasons for wanting to capture the city: "Lo . . . all the rebellious chiefs of all the northern towns are in it and the capture of a thousand towns is the capture of Megiddo."[90]

Why not storm the city then? The Egyptians had already taken cities by storm during the wars against the Hyksos and constructed and demolished fortifications in Nubia. Egyptian pry bars and primitive battering rams worked well enough against mud brick walls, and Egyptian soldiers, with their shields strapped to their backs like turtle shells for protection, knew how to overcome walls with scaling ladders.[91] But Megiddo's casement walls were faced with stone, rendering the Egyptians' tools useless. The city's geography also made an assault difficult. Megiddo was located on an elongated ridge that narrowed at its northern end to a point totally occupied by the city. The west, east, and north sides of the city sat directly over the steep slopes of the ridge, forming an additional natural defense. The city could be assaulted only from the open flat plain to the south.

The key to storming a city successfully is having the numerically superior attacking force mount simultaneous assaults against the city's walls at multiple points, making it impossible for the defender to quickly shift sufficient forces against the many points of attack. Megiddo's geography permitted an assault only against the southern wall, thereby negating the Egyptian attackers' numerical advantage. To capture Megiddo, Thutmose would have to do it by siege.

Laying siege to Megiddo made sense on other grounds as well. First, Megiddo was a rich city in a strategic location and held several vassal towns in its orbit. Destroying it would only require the Egyptians to rebuild it later and would weaken its hold on the vassal towns. Better to take it intact and thus preserve its political influence along with its fortifications. Second, Megiddo's harvest was still in the fields, so the city's inhabitants were forced to live off the diminished stores left over from winter. Thutmose could, therefore, reasonably plan on the siege being short, as indeed it turned out to last only thirty-seven days.[92] Third, Megiddo's formidable geography could be turned against it. The city's high walls, built closely on the steep drops on three sides, made it unlikely that the city's defenders could escape or mount combat sorties from any direction except through the south gate. There was no need then to waste the army's time and hard physical labor in constructing a wall around the entire city. Thutmose had only to build a wall to seal off the southern gate. The small effort needed to isolate the city gave the army time to confiscate the harvest, terrorize nearby towns into submission, and take sheep, cattle, goats, and horses as war booty from the surrounding vassal towns. Finally, Thutmose had no way of knowing if an Asiatic relief force was converging on Megiddo. With only a small part of his army needed to enforce the siege, he had sufficient manpower remaining to conduct reconnaissance and deal with any relief force that appeared.

While the siege continued, Thutmose and some troop contingents pillaged three other towns in the area whose chiefs had supported the chief of Megiddo. The *Annals* identify the towns as Yenoam, Nuges, and Herenkeru, but their locations cannot be identified with certainty.[93] The *Annals* do not record any fighting in capturing these towns, and it is likely that with Megiddo's fate all but sealed, they threw open their gates to the Egyptians. Thutmose's troops took what they wished, and he personally received oaths of loyalty from the chiefs of all the towns. The Egyptians imposed a system in which the towns were to supply tribute to Egypt on a regular basis. "Now the arable land was made into fields and entrusted to controllers of the king's house to reap their harvest." Pharaoh's bailiffs would oversee the lands and give a portion of the harvest to Egypt each year. This or some similar system of oversight was imposed on Megiddo's former vassals, who were now vassals to Pharaoh. The Egyptian army recorded the grain and livestock it took from Megiddo and its vassal towns. The list of captured items includes 2,250 horses, 1,929 head of cattle, 2,000 small goats, and 20,500 sheep along with 27,500 sacks of grain.[94] The army consumed much of these items during its forty-day operation in and around Megiddo.

Megiddo surrendered on June 27, sixty-six days after the Egyptian army had left its base at Sile. Besides the chief of Megiddo, the surrender mentions only a specific group of people called "the hill-dwellers of Retenu." Retenu (not to be confused with Retjenu) is the Egyptian name for the Canaanite hinterlands, probably including the upper part of the Jordan Valley but not the Beqqa Valley.[95] These chiefs were the minor vassals of Megiddo's chief and surely not the powerful chiefs of the major principalities of Syria and their large troop contingents who had not yet arrived when Thutmose attacked Megiddo. The minor status of these vassals is further indicated by the fact that after pledging their loyalty to Thutmose, they were permitted to return to their old positions and lands.[96] The texts do not mention what happened to the chief of Kadesh, except that some royal furniture ostensibly belonging to him was confiscated. If the leader of such a powerful city-state as Kadesh had been taken prisoner, it would have been a major event that would surely have been recorded in the official *Annals*. If the enemy chief had been captured, he would have been shipped back to Egypt as a great prize of war and, in due course, executed. Thus, just as the other powerful Syrian chiefs, apparently the chief of Kadesh had not arrived at Megiddo in time to take part in the battle.

Local vassals approached Thutmose before he left Megiddo and begged him to establish a garrison in the area "to control the nomads." The most likely place for a garrison near Megiddo to quell the desert nomads' raids was at Beth Shean. This town later became the strategic linchpin to Egypt's control of the Galilee and the King's Highway interior road to Syria. It was probably Thutmose who first established this important town as an Egyptian garrison.[97]

The capture of Megiddo placed authority over the key communications routes from Egypt to Canaan, Syria, and Mesopotamia firmly in Egyptian hands. The victory also resulted in the submission of other towns in the Syrian-Canaanite zone. Thus, Kadesh and Tunip had to be concerned about the presence of Egyptian power within striking range of their cities. By extending the frontier of the Egyptian sphere of influence northward and by demonstrating Egypt's willingness to use force to insure its interests, Thutmose III tied the towns of southern Canaan more closely to Egyptian security interests, just as they once had been during the Thutmose I's reign. There would be no more revolts in Sharuhen or Gaza.

Thutmose's defeat of the incipient coalition of would-be invaders at Megiddo was the first step in reversing the serious decline in Egypt's influence and prestige that had taken place during the reigns of Thutmose II and Queen Hatshepsut. The new Egyptian king had served notice to the Syrian princes and their Mitannian masters that Egypt considered Canaan to be within its own proper sphere of influence and that it intended to remain the dominant power on the Canaanite-Syrian land bridge. The Egyptian hold on Canaan was still tenuous, however, and Egypt had much to do before it could safely turn its back on its new vassals. The Mitannian attempt to extend its influence within the Egyptian security zone had been prevented, but Egypt remained on the strategic defensive for the time being.

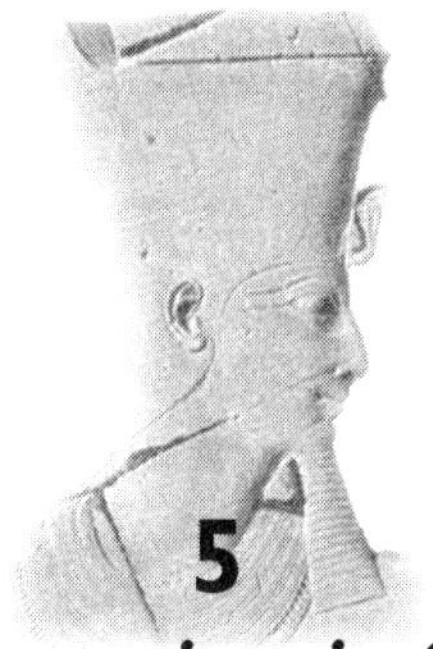

5
The Campaign in Canaan

The surrender of Megiddo in June found Thutmose's army healthy, undiminished by casualties or hard labor, and in fighting condition. Much of the campaign season was still available for further military operations. The foodstuffs taken as booty after the battle were more than sufficient to sustain the army for weeks. The harvest was now available in northern Canaan and southern Lebanon, so logistically the Egyptians could easily support any extension of the Megiddo campaign by living off the land. Moreover, because Megiddo's harvest was vital to feeding the Canaanite cities, which were not usually agriculturally self-sufficient, Thutmose could seize the harvest and be in a position to starve the recalcitrant towns into submission once winter set in.[1] Thutmose possessed the right military instrument in the right place at precisely the right time to continue the war against his enemies. He did exactly that.

Thutmose was an excellent strategist, and he realized that the insurgencies the Syrian chiefs and their Mitannian supporters instigated would not end with his victory at Megiddo. An immediate Egyptian withdrawal from Canaan would only allow the antagonists to fill the vacuum and encourage more rebellions. The former Canaanite vassals of Megiddo who had sworn their loyalty to Thutmose were weak reeds and could not yet be depended upon to resist renewed pressure from the Syrian city-states once the Egyptians left. Finally, numerous Canaanite chiefs who had supported the Syrian cause still had to be convinced that their interests lay with a new loyalty to Egypt. Whatever Thutmose chose to do, the one thing he could not do was to return to Egypt.

Thutmose was facing these problems because of Egypt's past strategic failures. Thutmose I, the king's grandfather, had once succeeded in establishing Egyptian influence all the way to the Euphrates River, where he defeated a Mitannian army and erected a victory stela on the banks of the great river. But the king had failed to establish garrisons in the newly acquired areas. Instead, he left commercial agents to represent Egyptian power. During his successors' reigns, Thutmose II and Hatshepsut paid little attention to maintaining Egyptian power and prestige in Canaan and Syria. Those Canaanite chiefs who remained loyal to Thebes saw their entreaties for help against Syrian encroachments go ignored. As the new Mitannian state grew in power, it gradually pressed its influence southward, using the Syrian city-states as cat's-paws and finally precipitating the crisis with which Thutmose III was then forced to deal. The young king did not intend to make the same mistake his grandfather had. Egypt had once more come to the land of Canaan. This time, however, it intended to stay.

From Megiddo, Thutmose turned his army northwest and marched on upper Canaan and southern Lebanon, the land of Retjenu. He covered seventy-five miles in a week and approached the seaward bend of the Litani River and the southern border of ancient Phoenicia.[2] The Litani River's headwaters arise west of the city of Baalbek in the fertile Beqqa Valley, where they are fed by mountain springs. As the Orontes River flows north from the nearby great springs of Labweh on the east side of the Beqqa, the Litani flows south, trapped in a deep gorge along the eastern ridge of the Lebanon Mountains, until it suddenly turns due west at right angles and pours into the sea some eighty-five miles from its source. It was at the westward bend that Thutmose aimed his army. At key points along the river bend sat the towns of Yenoam, Nuges, and Herenkeru.[3] The towns formed a *tripolis*, or a group of three towns under the control of a single chief. Thutmose hurled the might of his army at them and overwhelmed them all.

Their geographical location may have recommended them to Thutmose as targets. The towns were clustered within ten miles of the key port of Tyre. While Tyre was not an ally of Egypt's and had to play a cagey game to keep the Syrians and Mitanni at a distance, the city had long been a friendly trading partner of Egypt's. Its port was a valuable place to land troops should that be necessary in the future. By striking at the three towns,

5.1. ZONE OF EGYPTIAN OPERATIONS IN SYRIA

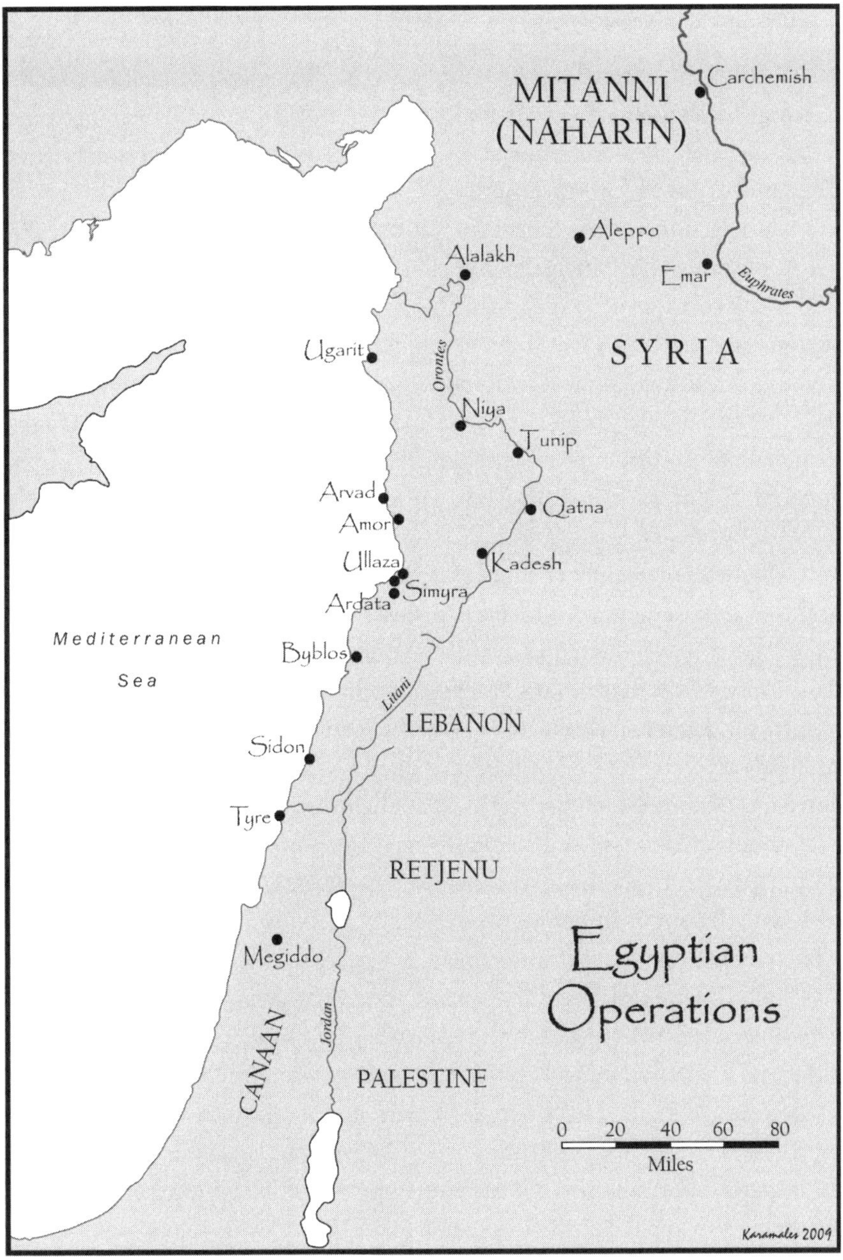

Thutmose was also weakening the city of Kadesh's influence in the area. The towns were within the city's orbit to the north and had supported the Syrian adventure at Megiddo. In addition, the narrow, swift branch of the Litani River that flows west to the sea constitutes a significant obstacle to troop movement. By controlling the bend of the river, Thutmose also controlled the river crossings and the axis of advance leading north from Canaan to Tyre, Sidon, and Byblos.

No account of the battle for the three towns has survived, but the list of plunder taken includes the chief's furniture, suggesting that there was some resistance. The *Annals* tell us that some "non-combatants who surrendered because of famine" were also taken, which suggests a siege.[4] Perhaps one or two of the less defended towns were overtaken quickly, and the chief and nobility held out longer in the capital. In all, 2,505 individuals, including 87 children of the chief and the nobility, were taken.[5] In a quick encore to Megiddo, Thutmose had struck at some of Kadesh's allies in its own backyard. Kadesh could not have failed to receive the message.

To make his point even more clearly, Thutmose established a "fortress in the land of Retjenu . . . which his majesty built in his victories among the chiefs of Lebanon, the name of which is: Menkeheperre [Thutmose III]-is-the-Binder-of-the-Barbarians."[6] The Egyptians had regularly applied this title to the Hyksos. The location of this fortress is uncertain, but it was probably close to Tyre or Sidon.[7] We have no information concerning the garrisons Thutmose left behind at Beth Shean and Megiddo, but they were probably similar to those he established later throughout the empire and patterned after those the Egyptians used to control Nubia. These garrisons were usually small and sometimes doubled as supply depots. The troops within them often had commercial representatives, scribes, and, we may be sure, intelligence officers living among them. The garrisons were primarily listening posts and symbols of Egypt's willingness to come to their troops' aid if attacked, for they lacked the manpower to defend themselves against a concerted assault. These kinds of permanent garrisons had permitted Egypt to turn its sphere of influence in Nubia into something resembling an imperial administrative structure responsible for collecting taxes and enforcing the loyalty of the local chiefs to Egypt.[8]

The Egyptians kept a firm grip on the political structure of the occupied chiefdoms in which the garrisons were located. Some of the local rulers were permitted to retain their title of kings, and others were called only village chiefs or headmen. Upon the death of a local ruler, a successor was chosen from the royal house, and Pharaoh sent the oil of anointing or a ring confirming his investiture of the new chief. A council of elders hemmed in the local chief's authority. An Egyptian official called a resident often played the council off against the chief while keeping all local officials in check. The resident also fixed the annual tax owed to Pharaoh and acted as a court of appeal in settling local disputes. His chief duty, however, was to see to it that the chiefs remained loyal and responsive to Egyptian wishes.[9] The resident had the support of the local Egyptian troop garrison. With garrisons established on the bend of the Litani River, at Megiddo, and at Beth Shean, Thutmose had created a trip wire extending from the sea to the Jordan Valley. Staffed by observers, overseers, military officers, and messengers, the garrisons' personnel could keep a close eye on the danger to the north and provide a warning of any Syrian or Mitannian movement.

It is evident from later events that Thutmose intended to implement a new strategic doctrine as part of an innovative Egyptian national defense strategy aimed at securing the Egyptian homeland by controlling political and military events far to the north in the Syrian zone of operations. In Thutmose's view, the defense of the Nile began at least at the Litani River and, as events developed, even at the west bank of the Euphrates River. Egypt had pursued commercial interests in the Syrian zone for centuries, mostly through trade. For most of its history, Egyptian imperialism had been confined to expansion in Nubia, with Asia remaining only of commercial concern. The Egyptians' view changed with the Hyksos invasion. Expelling the Hyksos in the early Eighteenth Dynasty forced Egypt to be concerned with events in Asia. Thutmose I had expressed this concern in an aggressive foreign policy of military operations and punitive expeditions into Syria and as far north as the Mitannian border on the Euphrates. His successors discontinued this policy, however, with almost catastrophic results for Egyptian security. Now, Thutmose III had revived and extended the thrust of his grandfather's policy in a new national security doctrine.

His strategic paradigm was rooted in the same assumptions that underpinned Thutmose I's strategic doctrine. The first premise was Egypt's need to develop a capacity to maintain and deploy large military forces over long distances. Thutmose I first recognized that Egypt required a larger and more professional army in the wake of the Hyksos expulsion. Thus, once those improvements were made, Thutmose I himself led the army on a long-distance expedition to Asia and marched six hundred miles to the banks of the Euphrates. Thutmose I also introduced the strategic concept of projecting Egyptian national power over great distances. The second premise of Thutmose I's security doctrine was its articulation of Egypt's main national security threat as originating from Mitanni and Syria, both new areas of strategic concern for Egypt. The consolidation of Mitannian power on the Euphrates and its extension southward became the dominant strategic rationale for defining Egyptian security interests and determining Egypt's responses in Asia. Egypt's view of the Mitanni was not dissimilar to how the United States came to see the Soviet Union as the main threat to its national security during the Cold War.

Thutmose I abandoned the old, defensive national security doctrine in favor of a new, proactive emphasis on expanding Egyptian influence and power far beyond the frontiers of Egypt itself as a means of preventing the formation of Syrian-Mitannian strategic threats in the Asian theater of operations. While Thutmose I saw the need for expanding Egypt's borders to the east, he did not live to carry it out. His successors neglected to follow through on the new strategy, permitting Egypt to once more rely on its old defensive doctrine of national security policy.

After Megiddo, and perhaps even before he became king in his own right,[10] Thutmose III was determined to pursue his grandfather's strategic vision and be successful. He adopted the same strategic template and introduced new methods for executing it. Once a city or town had been taken, Thutmose might replace the chief with someone more compliant or permit the chief to remain, requiring of him a public oath of submission. The oath required the chief to renounce his previous loyalty and make a "request for breath" in which the chief swore a new oath of loyalty in return for which Pharaoh presumably granted him his life.[11] Part of the ceremony involved delivering the chief's children before Pharaoh, who then chose the chief's sons and other important relatives for deportation to Egypt, where they were held as hostages.

The first example of this practice appears in an inscription in the temple at Karnak that lists the cities Thutmose captured in Retjenu during his first campaign.[12] The practice of hostage taking is not mentioned in the account of the battle of Megiddo, and it is probable that the inscriptions relate to the early campaigns in southern Lebanon undertaken immediately after Megiddo. Thus, taking children as hostages may have first occurred when Thutmose captured the three towns on the Litani River, although we cannot be certain.[13] Later in the *Annals* we are told the purpose of this practice: "Behold, the children of the chiefs and their brothers were brought to be in strongholds in Egypt. Now, whosoever died among these chiefs, his majesty would cause his son to stand in his place."[14] It is important to note that Thutmose took the chief's brothers as well as his sons, both of which represented the family pool out of which future chiefs might come. As long as Thutmose controlled this pool of royal heirs, there was little chance of hostile governance except by outright insurrection.[15]

As to whether the hostages were kept in strongholds or castles in Egypt, clearly there would have been no point in replacing a dead, executed, or recalcitrant chief with a son or brother who had been maltreated while in Egypt. Part of the purpose of holding the sons in Egypt was to expose them to the superior Egyptian culture and convince them of the benefits of remaining loyal to Pharaoh. It does not help our understanding, however, that the Egyptian hieroglyph used in the texts to identify where the hostage sons were kept is *Swhn m Y p't*, which can mean either a castle or a prison![16] In whatever manner it was accomplished, the taking of hostages clearly indicated that Thutmose was thinking strategically about how the townspeople's loyalty might be secured over the long term. Thutmose's victories were the means to the greater goal of establishing a permanent Egyptian presence in the lands he conquered.

Mindful of his grandfather's failure to adequately demonstrate the Egyptians' presence, power, and prestige by willingly resorting to force when necessary, Thutmose undertook regular inspection tours of his holdings in Canaan and Syria. At first these tours were conducted with Pharaoh himself in command of a military contingent that could be used to discipline a recalcitrant chief or punish any failure to comply with Egyptian wishes. Once Egyptian resolve was established, however, these demonstrations of Egyptian presence became an annual routine in which a senior officer and a small armed contingent made the rounds. One function of these tours was also to ensure that Pharaoh's annual tribute was paid completely and on time.

One of Thutmose's more innovative methods of controlling the subdued population was to extend the tax system that the Egyptians had established in Nubia to Egyptian possessions in Asia. Egyptian accountants established regular tax payments that had to be delivered to Egyptian agents on a scheduled basis. Much of this in-kind payment went to support the army, the administrative structure, and the local garrisons, and the rest was sent to Egypt. At the height of Egyptian rule, the area of Retjenu alone paid nearly nine thousand pounds of gold annually into the Egyptian treasury.[17] Metalworkers, shipwrights, artisans, wheelwrights, carpenters, and other skilled craftsmen were also deported to Egypt, where they found work in military or temple workshops.

Most onerous for the conquered people was the tribute in men. At the end of each campaign, large numbers of captives were brought back to Egypt, where they were set to work as corvée laborers in Thutmose's prodigious building programs. Thutmose III carried off more than 7,300 Canaanite captives. It is no coincidence that the peak of Thutmose's public works building program coincided with his military victories.[18]

The Second, Third, and Fourth Expeditions

By October, Thutmose and the army were back in Thebes, where a great celebration and feast was held to commemorate Pharaoh's victory at Megiddo. The situation in Canaan and southern Lebanon remained unstable, and in the spring (regnal year 24) Thutmose undertook a second campaign in Canaan and Syria.[19] That Thutmose had to put down rebellions in Gaza and Sharuhen before marching to Megiddo suggests that many of the Canaanite chiefs had supported the Syrian adventure or at least were prepared to join it had it shown signs of succeeding. Egypt had to reestablish control over these disloyal chiefdoms before it could turn its attention to Syria proper. In the spring of 1480 BCE, Thutmose and his army marched through Canaan and southern Lebanon in a show of force and to deal with the disloyal chiefs.

The *Annals* do not tell us the size of Pharaoh's army, but we might reasonably surmise that it was considerable. Not knowing what he might find, Thutmose probably erred on the side of caution in order to deal with any eventuality that might arise. A combined-arms division of five thousand men and a brigade of five hundred chariots would probably have been sufficient. There is only scant evidence of fighting. But in at least one instance Thutmose may have fought a set-piece battle against a people called the Fenkhu in which he "overthrew the foreigners."[20] Evidence also shows that Thutmose dismantled some towns' fortifications.[21] The Egyptians would have destroyed the most formidable fortifications, particularly those situated in the highlands and those that controlled strategic passes. There is considerable evidence that this destruction was widespread and forced the Canaanite population out of the hills and into the valleys and settlements on the coast.[22] This was a traditional method of rendering a fortified town vulnerable to future punishment. For the most part, however, it is likely that the Canaanite chiefs saw an opportunity to switch sides and retain their kingdoms by opening the gates of their cities and pledging loyalty to Egypt.

The price of Egyptian "protection" did not come cheap, however. Thutmose levied a heavy burden of tribute upon the chiefs. The campaign's records show that "the tribute of the chiefs of Retjenu" amounted to "103 horses, 5 chariots, wrought with gold with poles of gold; 5 chariots wrought with electrum, with poles of gold; total 10; 45 bullocks and calves, 749 bulls, 5,703 small cattle [sheep]; flat dishes of gold; flat dishes of silver . . . 823 jars of incense; 1,718 jars of honeyed wine."[23] The gold- and electrum-covered chariots were the prized personal transports of the chiefs, and taking them was no doubt fraught with symbolism regarding who was to be master in the future. Thutmose may have left small garrisons in the larger towns along with scribes and accountants to enforce the new Egyptian tax system. Some of these towns were turned into supply depots so that the Egyptian army might draw on them whenever it was required to take the field in the area.

For each of the following two years Thutmose and an Egyptian military contingent marched through Canaan and southern Lebanon, reinforcing the Egyptian presence and bringing other chiefs under Egyptian control. There are no detailed records of his third (regnal year 25) and fourth (regnal year 26) campaigns. That problems continued to arise seems evident from the texts, which note, "His Majesty proceeded to Upper Retjenu to subdue all the countries according to the command of his father, Amun, who put them beneath his sandals."[24] Yet other areas of Canaan were sufficiently secure so that Thutmose could entrust the task of leading the military contingent and collecting the annual tribute to others rather than lead it himself.[25] Still, it is significant that Pharaoh is described as leading these campaigns in person, a clear indication of their importance to the cause of Egyptian security.

It seems to have required three years of successive demonstrations of wielding military power and threats, dismantling fortifications, taking hostages, levying heavy tributes, and instituting enforced loyalty oaths for Thutmose to bring all of Canaan and parts of southern Lebanon under effective Egyptian control following the victory at Megiddo. Over the next two years the new system of Egyptian hegemony was reinforced by regular military visits—albeit with generals, not Pharaoh, leading smaller contingents—and the imposition of small military and commercial garrisons that oversaw the operation of the tax system. That such an effort was required over five years to pacify Canaan and southern Lebanon implies that many of the Canaanite chiefs had been in league with the Syrians and accomplices in their attempt to invade Egypt. This broad support also indicates how weak the Egyptians' influence had become in Canaan during Hatshepsut's reign. With substantial support from the Canaanite chiefs, the attempt to conquer Egypt might well have succeeded had not Thutmose III clearly grasped the grave nature of the threat and moved quickly to destroy it at Megiddo.

The Fifth Campaign

The *Annals* are silent on Thutmose's activities from regnal years 26 through 28, but it is reasonably certain that he continued to strengthen Egypt's hold on Canaan. As we shall see, Egypt was also occupied with building its first seagoing navy, which was to play such an important role in Thutmose's later campaigns. In regnal year 29, Thutmose embarked on a major military expedition deep into Lebanon, the first advance beyond the northern limits of the initial campaign at Megiddo. The years of effort to win over the cities and towns of Canaan now paid dividends in that

Thutmose could move north with little concern about revolts occurring across his line of communications. Moreover, the newly established supply depots made it possible to support the army logistically on its long march from Egypt to southern Lebanon, a distance of more than three hundred miles. Troop contingents from the garrisons stationed in Canaan were added to the army as it marched toward its objective. The size of Thutmose's expeditionary force is not recorded, but it must have been considerable. The expedition took Egyptian forces deep into Retjenu and engaged allies of the Mitanni—namely, Kadesh and Tunip—that were of particular concern since they maintained substantial forces and were close to Thutmose's zone of operations in Retjenu. It is unlikely that Thutmose would have risked an operation in such a hostile environment without substantial forces at his disposal. The Egyptian army may well have numbered around ten thousand troops.

The immediate cause of the Egyptian incursion was a change in the status quo in the vicinity of Byblos, a major port on the Lebanon coast. The *Annals* portray the events as a revolt against Egypt occurring in Zahi, the Egyptian name for coastal Lebanon.[26] In Egyptian thinking, any sort of disorder anywhere was considered a revolt against Pharaoh, who, as the divine son of Amun, was responsible for keeping order in the universe.[27] In fact, Egypt did not control the coastal plain, and the revolt was nothing of the sort. The crisis arose when the city-state of Tunip, located inland from the coast and just west of the Orontes River, sent troops to establish garrisons at Wahlia and Ullaza, two towns located at the western mouth of the Eleutheros Valley north of Tripoli and about thirty miles north of Byblos. In addition, Tunip concluded an agreement with the local Apiru to serve as mercenaries in support of these garrisons.[28] The result was that Tunip was now in a position to control the coastal entrance to the Eleutheros Valley. Its coastal garrisons were daggers pointed at the key port of Byblos.

Byblos had been an important strategic port for Egypt since at least the Middle Kingdom and perhaps before. It was an absolutely vital commercial source of Egypt's strategic materials. It was through Byblos that Egypt secured the Lebanese cedar and Syrian pine that it needed for its ships, chariots, temples, and fortresses, and Byblos was the main source of imported tin, the all-important strategic metal needed to manufacture

5.2. LOCATIONS AND DISTANCES IN THE CANAANITE-SYRIAN ZONE OF EGYPTIAN MILITARY OPERATIONS

Sile to Megiddo:	230	miles
Sile to Gaza:	125	miles
Gaza to Yehem:	80	miles
Yehem to Canaan Border:	43	miles
Canaan Border to Tyre:	14	miles
Tyre to Sidon:	22	miles
Sidon to Beirut:	25	miles
Canaan Border to Byblos:	82	miles
Byblos to Eleutheros Valley:	30	miles
Ullaza/Simyra: Controls Western Mouth of Eleutheros Valley		
Arvad:	62	miles north of Byblos
Arka Plain to Kadesh:	40	miles
Tunip to Arka Plain:	30	miles

bronze weapons. The port was also a key diplomatic and commercial listening post from which Egypt could keep watch on the city-states of Kadesh, Tunip, Qatna, and the Mitanni to the north.

Also of important strategic and commercial concern was that the Eleutheros Valley connected the interior trade and military routes along the Orontes to the Lebanon coast.[29] Through this valley ran the Great River (the modern Nahr al-Kabir, or the Eleutheros River of classical times) that began as a tributary of the Orontes and exited in the sea between Ullaza and Simyra on the coast. The Great River ran through the Arka Plain, watering one of the most fertile agricultural areas of Lebanon and providing an avenue upon which to transport the plain's agricultural products to the coastal ports.[30] Without access to the Eleutheros Valley, Egypt was cut off from its supply of cedar, which grew in abundance in the Lebanon Mountains. Moreover, the valley offered an ideal route for the armies of Kadesh, Tunip, and Mitanni to quickly reach the coast from the interior, threatening Egyptian interests in the area.

In the event of war with the Mitanni, Egyptian avenues of advance through the interior of Lebanon were already hindered by Kadesh, which controlled the exit from the Beqqa Valley along with the routes leading north from Canaan to the Euphrates. Before the Egyptian victory at Megiddo, Kadesh had controlled this route from its base on the Upper Orontes as far south as the Esdraelon Valley in Canaan. The Egyptian victory at Megiddo had reopened the land route through the Beqqa Valley, but it was blocked farther north by the fortress city of Kadesh itself. This situation placed a premium on the route that ran along the Lebanon coast and connected to the Syrian interior via the Eleutheros Valley, whose eastern exit debouched close to Kadesh. Tunip's deployment of troops to Ullaza and Wahlia had effectively blocked access to both the coastal road and the Eleutheros Valley and brought the Arka Plain and its enormous agricultural production under Tunip's influence. The forward deployment of Tunip's troops along the coast also threatened Byblos itself. These circumstances constituted a significant shift in the strategic power equation on the Lebanon coast, one that Egypt could not accept. In the spring of Thutmose's twenty-ninth regnal year, he led his army out of Egypt toward southern Lebanon with the goal of reversing the situation.

Thutmose's expedition was fraught with risk. Ullaza and Wahlia were closely tied to Tunip, and Tunip and Kadesh were allied with the Mitanni, who had a significant interest in keeping Egypt out of Syria and Lebanon. Thutmose was forced to gamble that his confrontation with the Mitannian client-states would not provoke a larger confrontation with the Mitanni themselves. If he was wrong, the young king would find himself caught at the end of a long supply line in a battle with a major power. Thutmose proved to be a gambler and moved to protect Byblos and

Egyptian interests on the Lebanon coast. He accepted the risk of engaging the Mitanni and pressed ahead daringly.

Once more we have no idea what size army Thutmose employed, but again it was probably considerable given the strength of the forces it might be forced to confront if Kadesh, Tunip, or even the Mitanni became involved. The 330-mile journey from Egypt to Byblos at 10 miles a day—and they stopped every seventh day to rest the animals and prevent injury to their backs and to permit them to graze—took the Egyptian army thirty-eight days to complete.[31] The Egyptians moved up the coastal road along the Way of Horus. The road was easily traveled until they reached the area south of modern Caesarea. There, five small rivers flowed onto the Sharon Plain,[32] creating a great swamp and forcing the army to move inland and climb the ridge near modern Zichron Ya'kov to bypass the obstacle.[33] Once back on the coastal road, the route passed the ancient city of Dor and around the Antelope's Nose, where the Carmel Mountains drop precipitously toward the sea, leaving a passage barely a hundred meters wide between the water and the mountains. From there the road rises toward Lebanon, crosses the border at a place the Bible calls Jacob's Ladder, and finally gains the plateau near the Litani River. The Egyptian garrison at the tripolis controlled the narrow Litani River crossing, which the army traversed with little difficulty. It marched the remaining 75 miles to Byblos without incident.

Thutmose's objective was to capture Wahlia and Ullaza, the two towns guarding the mouth of the Eleutheros Valley 30 miles north of Byblos. Between Byblos and the objective, however, was the town of Ardata guarding the Cold River crossing. The *Annals* are confusing in that they portray the attack on Wahlia and Ullaza as occurring before Thutmose attacked a town called Arvad.[34] A scribe who was unfamiliar with the area's geography may have made this error and confused Arvad with Thutmose's other goal, Ardata. Arvad lies 62 miles north of Byblos and is a small port obstructed by a series of offshore reefs; therefore, it cannot be the rich agricultural area that the texts described as having been pillaged by Thutmose's army.[35] With this confusion out of the way, we may now attempt to reconstruct Thutmose's campaign on the Lebanon coast.

Having replenished and rested his army at Byblos, Thutmose moved straight at Ardata, seizing it and the Cold River crossing. It was harvesttime, and "behold, there were found [the products] of all Zahi [coastal Lebanon]. Their gardens were filled with their fruit, their wines were found remaining in their presses as water flows, their grain on the terraces [which] was more plentiful than the sand of the shore."[36] For whatever reason Thutmose decided to punish Ardata. The texts tell us that he ordered "the cutting down of all its pleasant [fruit-bearing] trees . . . and the army was overwhelmed with their portions. . . . Behold, the army of his Majesty was drunk and anointed with oil every day as at a feast in Egypt."[37] One can only imagine what outrages may have been committed against the civilian population by the Egyptian army when it was allowed to run amok in the town. Thutmose could hardly leave Ardata across his line of communication as he moved north, and perhaps the town's punishment and the Egyptian garrison left behind were designed to ensure that Ardata would present no difficulties once the Egyptian army moved on.

Thutmose now moved against his primary objective, the two towns that contained Tunip troop garrisons and controlled the western mouth of the Eleutheros Valley. The garrisons comprised troops from Tunip itself ("the infantry of that foe of Tunip"),[38] local Apiru who had cast their lot with Tunip,[39] and what the texts describe as *T-h-r* warriors, or Hittite mercenaries.[40] Thus, the Egyptians encountered largely professional enemy soldiers. It is difficult to believe that the towns were taken without fierce resistance, although no account of the fighting is preserved in the *Annals*. A. T. Olmstead, relying on a restored lacuna in the inscriptions, suggests that in the capture of Wahlia, "its chief and 329 inhabitants [troops?] were taken and sacrifices offered to Amun."[41] Whatever the level of resistance, Thutmose succeeded in capturing the two towns and their troops' garrisons.

The Arka Plain is one of the most productive agricultural areas in all Lebanon. Thutmose ordered the entire harvest and much of the livestock seized. Thus, we are told that the loot included "51 slaves, male and female; 30 horses; 10 flat dishes of silver; incense oil, 470 jars of honey, 6,428 jars of wine, copper, lead, lapis lazuli, green feldspar, 616 large cattle, 3,636 small cattle [sheep]."[42] Most significant was that all the "clean grain in kernel and ground" (raw cereals and those already milled) was confiscated.[43] Once again, "the army of his Majesty was drunk." Whatever of the booty the army did not consume while it sat in Lebanon or was needed for supplies on its return march was loaded on ships confiscated in either the port of Simyra or Byblos and sent back to Egypt. Pharaoh took ship and sailed for home as well. That Thutmose could entrust his army to a subordinate to lead it safely back to Egypt reveals how much the Egyptian policy had pacified southern Lebanon and Canaan. The Egyptians no longer had anything to fear from disloyal chiefs.

Thutmose's gamble had paid off. Neither Kadesh nor the Mitanni had come to Tunip's aid, and Tunip accepted the defeat of its proxy forces without any reaction. Thutmose had enjoyed six years of military successes; however, he had yet to engage a major military opponent. But the Egyptian military expeditions were costly, took up much of each year's campaign season, and wore the army, its equipment, and its animals to the nub. Egypt's most dangerous enemy, the Mitanni, lay behind the Euphrates, safely beyond the Egyptian army's operational reach. Even expeditions against the heavily fortified cities of Kadesh, Tunip, and Qatna could not be undertaken except at the end of a very long and easily disrupted supply line. Either Thutmose would have to find some way to extend the range over which his army could project force without inordinate risk, or he would have to abandon the strategic objective of weakening the Mitanni and creating an Egyptian strategic buffer zone in Syria.

Two capabilities were required to increase the Egyptian army's operational range. First, it needed a large forward logistics base that could sustain the army in the field as it conducted operations in the interior zone of Syria and, eventually, several hundred miles farther northeast against the Mitanni on the west bank of the Euphrates. The situation was similar to what the Romans and Scipio Africanus later faced in their campaign against the Carthaginians in Spain during the Second Punic War (218–201 BCE). Rome easily reduced Carthaginian power north of the Ebro River but could not strike at Carthage's center of gravity in Spain without first obtaining a large logistics base to support Roman operations farther south and in the interior. Scipio Africanus solved the problem by attacking New Carthage, the largest Carthaginian logistics base in all Spain. With New Carthage in his hands, Scipio launched a series of offensives to the south that eventually drove the Carthaginians from the country.

Thutmose's coastal campaign had driven Tunip from the mouth of the Eleutheros Valley, opening the invasion route from the coast to the interior. Of greater importance, the Egyptians' success had gained them access to the Arka Plain. Full of fertile fields, small towns, and livestock and situated close to port facilities, the Arka Plain could provide all the logistics support the Egyptian army required to conduct sustained operations in the Syrian interior and north to the Euphrates. When the Egyptians returned to the land of Retjenu, the first thing they did was seize the Arka Plain and turn it into a huge supply depot.

But inadequate logistics were only part of Thutmose's problem. To engage the Mitanni near the Euphrates required a march of more than five hundred miles from Egypt. Even assuming sufficient logistics, the wear and tear on the army could considerably reduce its combat power by the time it had to go into action against the enemy. At ten miles a day with the required rest stops for the animals, the Egyptian army would need at least sixty days to reach the Euphrates. It would be impossible for the Egyptians to achieve strategic or tactical surprise, and they would have only a short time for campaigning before the army would have to turn for home in order to arrive before the season ended. All along the way, the army would be exposed to insurgent attacks by Mitannian allies and Apiru mercenaries. Thutmose needed a faster, cheaper, and more efficient way of transporting his army into the area of operations. His solution was the Egyptian navy.

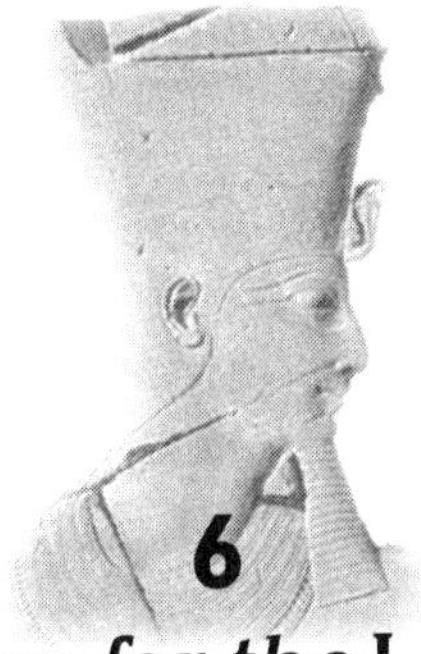

6
The Campaign for the Lebanon Coast

From the time of Thutmose I, Egyptian national security policy in Asia was concerned with two geographic areas, Canaan and Syria. Egyptian interests in Canaan were centered about the country's proximity to Egypt and potential use as a strategic platform for invasion. Although Canaan possessed few goods or materials that Egypt required, the trade routes that ran through the country were important to Egyptian commerce. Even before the Hyksos invasion, Egypt had undertaken periodic raids into Canaan to disrupt the formation of Canaanite coalitions that might prove hostile to Egypt. These raids were preemptive or punitive search-and-destroy expeditions, and the Egyptians made no attempt to garrison Canaan or to bring it within their political-economic orbit. With regard to Syria, particularly coastal Syria (modern Lebanon), Egyptian concerns were largely economic insofar as the coastal ports were the sources of important strategic materials (cedar, various woods, and tin) and outlets for Egyptian goods.[1] No pharaoh before Thutmose I had regarded Syria as a strategic threat to Egypt itself. But the rise of the Mitanni and their continued interference and growing influence in Syria forced Egypt for the first time to regard Syria as a danger.

The Sixth Campaign

Thutmose III came to the throne determined to reduce the danger of the Asian threat by imposing Egyptian political and economic control on Canaan and bringing the full weight of Egyptian military power to bear against those Syrian states he regarded as dangerous to Egyptian security interests. He spent almost six years imposing Egyptian control on Canaan. That done, in his twenty-ninth regnal year he took an army to the Lebanon coast to protect Egypt's supplies of strategic raw materials and keep open the ports and ground routes to the Syrian interior. This campaign served as a valuable reconnaissance in preparation for his next move. Thutmose was then prepared to deal with the Syrian threat in earnest. In his thirtieth regnal year, he attacked the Lebanon coast with the goal of transforming the area west of the Lebanon Mountains into a strategic platform for conducting further military operations.

Several tasks had to be accomplished before coastal Lebanon could be turned into an Egyptian strategic platform. First, Thutmose intended to come by sea to avoid the debilitating land march across Canaan. Thus, he would need a seagoing navy and control of Canaan's and Lebanon's ports for use as stopping points along the way. The Lebanon ports had to be captured and garrisoned to ensure their availability to Egyptian seaborne armies. Second, he had to establish political control over the Arka Plain and the coastal agricultural regions to obtain the necessary food and supplies to support the army's operations in the interior. Once taken, the ports and towns along the coast had to be transformed into supply depots. Third, Thutmose had to gain control of the Eleutheros Valley, the vital land route from the coast through the Lebanon Mountains to the Syrian interior. This attempt would inevitably bring Egypt into conflict with the powerful city-state of Kadesh, which guarded the valley's eastern exit. It also risked engaging Tunip and Qatna and, eventually, the Mitanni.

Capturing the coastal agricultural towns presented few difficulties for the large Egyptian army. The residents of these towns were commercial and trading people whom history would later come to know as the Phoenicians. They were unlike the fierce warrior people who populated Syria's interior. The agricultural towns were not well fortified, and their social structures were made up of farmers and merchants who lacked a warrior tradition and experience in war. The governing structure was weak and constructed around small palace economies.[2] The governments comprised a headman or chief, a council of advisers, a semi-free peasantry, and a small military contingent, which often represented only a handful of professional maryannu mercenaries who served as the chief's personal bodyguards.[3] Neither the leadership nor the citizenry were likely to mount much resistance to an Egyptian invasion, especially since only their political loyalty and not their existence, trade, or freedom was at stake.

The ports were also vulnerable to a determined Egyptian attack. In antiquity, few harbors possessed any notable port facilities. Piers and artificial breakwaters were rare.[4] Instead, ships pulled up to open stretches of beach on the shore, and men unloaded their cargoes in the surf. All the Lebanon coastal towns had areas of open shoreline where an amphibious force could easily come ashore and seize the port. Most of the port towns were unfortified, and only a few possessed a defensive citadel of sorts. Once an invading army was ashore, it readily controlled the key assets of the town, that is, the landing area itself and the nearby storage facilities. Under these circumstances, the town had little left to defend, and surrender and some sort of accommodation usually followed.

Thutmose's army could not expect to have such an easy time, however, when it came to capturing the towns in the interior of Syria. The inland city-states had long been occupied and controlled by a fierce warrior people who were, perhaps, the same people who had once invaded Egypt and whom the Egyptians called the Hyksos. Certainly in Egyptian eyes they were the same people. The interior towns were larger than the coastal towns, had larger populations, and were governed by a nobility of professional maryannu warriors whose skill and experience at war was surely equal to that of the Egyptians and probably greater. These towns were like fortified camps, and warrior nobility originally constructed some of them as military camps to control the local inhabitants and the countryside.[5]

Qatna provides a typical example. Qatna lay three days' journey from Kadesh, about halfway between Aleppo and Damascus, and was one of the largest Bronze Age cities in Syria. Constructed on a small stream that flowed into the nearby Orontes River, its rectangular defensive enclosure measured longer than a thousand yards on each side. A three-hundred-foot-wide ditch surrounded the town. The distance from the bottom of the ditch to the top of the walls was sixty-five feet. Each of the four walls had a fortified tower protecting a wide main gate through which chariot forces could sally forth to engage an attacking enemy. The gates themselves and the surrounding walls were made of limestone blocks. A single narrow bridge crossed the moat ditch and passed below projecting walls from which defenders could sweep the bridge with arrow fire.[6] These fortified Syrian cities were almost impossible for the Egyptians to take by storm. If they were to be taken at all, it would have to be by siege. Given the Egyptians' lack of siege machinery that could defeat stone walls, any siege would amount to little more than a campaign of waiting until the defenders' food ran out and forcing them to surrender.

The Egyptian Navy

To carry out his campaign against the Lebanon coast, Thutmose introduced one of the most remarkable innovations in warfare and became the first commander in history to conduct large-scale amphibious operations on the open sea.[7] Egypt was a river state, and its only practical way of transporting troops and supplies was by boat on the Nile. By the Third Dynasty, Egyptians were building boats that were 100 cubits long (1 cubit=1.7 feet) and 30 cubits wide[8] and capable of carrying eighty to a hundred tons of cargo.[9] The Egyptians first used their navy in support of ground operations in the Fifth Dynasty (2480 BCE), when Pharaoh Sahure transported troops to the Syrian coast. In the Sixth Dynasty (2340 BCE) a troop commander, Weni, conveyed Egyptian troops in "travel ships" to the Antelope's Nose (at the end of the Carmel Mountain ridge) near Haifa to deal with a revolt of the Sand People.[10] These naval operations on the open sea were small expeditions in support of raids and not sustained campaigns. Further, they were not repeated until Thutmose III conducted the "first great amphibious operations in history."[11]

Egyptian naval operations had been traditionally confined to the Nile, where they played an important role in the wars of liberation against the Hyksos. Kamose's victory stela tells us how he transported his army aboard ship to battle with the occupiers. The king sailed up and down the river, using his fleet as a mobile base from which to deploy his troops. Ahmose I, his successor, used ships to bring the Hyksos capital of Avaris under siege. His attempt to retake Nubia could not have been accomplished without the river navy to transport troops and to push the southern frontier to Buhen. His successor, Amenhotep I, used the navy to extend Egyptian control farther south beyond the Second Cataract to

Semneh. Thutmose I carried his troops in ships past the Second and Third cataracts, crushing Nubian resistance as far south as Kerma. With Nubia once more under control, the Egyptians dug canals to bypass the cataracts and carry out heavy naval and commercial traffic over long distances on a regular basis.

The Egyptian navy was an integral branch of the army and not a separate military service. Its importance, however, was evident in that many naval officers were drawn from the Egyptian nobility.[12] Under Thutmose I, the focus of Egyptian military operations shifted away from Nubia toward Asia, and the need for a land warfare capability became paramount. Then the navy became an independent branch of service and was relegated to a minor role whose mission was to keep the Nile River's traffic open to Nubia. Neither Thutmose II nor Hatshepsut showed any interest in the Egyptian naval arm, and the construction of naval ships declined considerably. The once important Egyptian navy fell into decay.

Thutmose III rebuilt the Egyptian navy and ordered the construction of a large dockyard and military base on the site of the old Hyksos capital at Avaris, turning it into a major port city on the Pelusiac branch of the Nile.[13] Just when Thutmose completed the construction of the Perunefer base is unclear, but it may have been near the end of his campaigns in Canaan. It is not impossible, however, that the old dockyards at Memphis remained the main supplier of ships and the major port of military debarkation for Thutmose's earlier campaigns in Syria, and it may have been during his later campaign against the Mitanni that the new facility became fully operational. A lord of the Egyptian Admiralty, Nebamun, was appointed fairly early in Thutmose's reign, and some high-ranking army officers were transferred to naval commands, perhaps indicating that the higher ranks of the old navy had fallen into poor condition.[14] The importance that Thutmose attached to the new naval facility can be judged by his appointment of his son, Amenhotep II, to command the dockyard and troops stationed at Perunefer.[15]

With the Memphis dockyard working overtime to supply the new navy's expanded needs, Thutmose had to acquire additional skilled sailors and craftsmen from outside Egypt. Syria and the ports of Canaan were full of experienced shipwrights, rope makers, and sailors who could be hired away with the promise of steady work and Egyptian gold. Most Egyptian boat captains only had experience sailing on the Nile, and Thutmose's navy intended to sail upon the open sea. Attracting captains with seafaring experience must have been a priority. Compared to Canaan, life in Egypt was good. The country was peaceful and food plentiful, and recruiting people with the necessary skills could not have been much of a problem.

Thutmose's intention to use the navy in support of his overseas campaigns in Syria explains why he moved so rapidly in his fifth campaign in regnal year 29 to stop Tunip's encroachment on Wahlia and Ullaza and the threat it presented to Byblos. Control of the Eleutheros Valley was vital to Byblos's ability to access the cedars of the Lebanon Mountains. The straight, long-running lengths of cedar timber were essential in constructing large Egyptian transport ships. These timbers formed the long central strakes that replaced the keels of the carvel-built Egyptian ships. Cedar timbers were also needed for supporting deck beams, tall masts, and strong steering oars.[16] Any threat to Egypt's ability to obtain these cedar timber supplies jeopardized Egyptian naval power at its root. Having already decided he would use the navy to transport his armies for his next campaign in Syria, Thutmose moved quickly to reverse Tunip's encroachment and restore access to the vital timber supplies that flowed through Byblos.

Thutmose's revival of Egyptian naval power in the eastern Mediterranean reveals the broad sweep of his strategic thinking. Commercial trade among Egypt, Canaan, and Lebanon required ships to make frequent stops along the route. In daylight, ships could make between fifty and seventy miles in ten hours with favorable winds. They did not usually sail on the open sea at night, so ships put in to the beach every evening. Thus, whoever controlled the stopping points along the coast could also control commercial shipping. Thutmose must have realized the coastal Lebanon ports were vulnerable to an Egyptian assault from the sea. One of his primary reasons for rebuilding the Egyptian navy was to carry out these assaults. Once the Lebanon ports were under his control, he knew no other port cities in Lebanon or Canaan were powerful enough to mount a serious threat to Egyptian shipping. Thutmose would then be able to move his troops and supplies by sea without fear of coastal interdiction.

While a brisk commercial sea trade existed between Egypt and Syria, it is unclear how much of it was actually carried on Egyptian ships. Much of the trade seems to have been carried in Syrian hulls. If Egypt could take over the Lebanon ports, then a great deal of commercial shipping would have to be carried in Egyptian ships. As soon as Thutmose gained control of the Lebanon ports, he ordered that all shipping of cedar timber must be carried on Egyptian ships.[17] Thus, the new Egyptian navy provided commercial as well as security benefits. The major strategic consequence of Thutmose's revival of Egyptian naval power was to establish effective Egyptian control of the eastern Mediterranean coast, which Egypt would not relinquish for more than two centuries.

The ancient Egyptians were among the oldest civilized societies on the planet and were perhaps the first people to construct genuine ships. King Snefru of the Third Dynasty built ships that were 40, 60, and 100 cubits long (58, 102, and 170 feet, respectively) for use on the Nile. The first example of a seagoing ship, or *menesh* ship, in Egypt dates from the reign of King Sahure of the Fifth Dynasty circa 2480 BCE.[18] By Thutmose I's reign, ships of 100 cubits were commonplace.[19] Queen Hatshepsut had an enormous ship constructed to carry her obelisks from the quarry to Karnak. According to William Edgerton, "Mr. Francis Elgar, the Director of Naval Construction to the British Government, calculated that the two great obelisks of Karnak, each ninety-seven feet, six inches long, could be carried on a boat about 220 feet long and 69 feet of beam, upon a draft of water of about 4 feet, 6 inches, or not exceeding 5 feet."[20] Egyptian ship design, size, speed, and carrying capacity reached their peak during Hatshepsut's reign, a development that Thutmose was able to exploit in his program to expand Egypt's navy.[21]

Most ships of antiquity were built on the foundation of a keel to provide the vessel its longitudinal strength and stability. Ribs or frames sprang up and outward from the keel at close intervals to support the hull's sides, which were further strengthened by deck beams that interlocked with the ribs. Sometimes deck beams ran through the hull and were attached to the outside. Modern ships are constructed in much the same manner. Egyptian ship construction was radically different, however. Lacking long timbers for keels, ribs, and deck beams forced Egyptian shipwrights to invent a unique method of shipbuilding. Herodotus recorded that Egyptian ships were made of "thorn tree wood," or acacia, and were built "brick fashion" in the same way that one would build a wall.[22]

Egyptian ships did not have keels and were carvel built as a shell of planking attached to ribs at comparatively wide intervals. Deck beams did not interlock with the rib frames in the modern manner but were secured to the planking of the hull.[23] The deck was laid over the beams. The Egyptians had no nails or screws, so they invented an ingenious method for joining the planks of the ship's hull together with dowels along the edges where one plank joined another. The ends were similarly held together with dowels. On the inside of the hull, flat double-tongued mortices overlapped the plank edges, pulling them tightly together and giving them vertical strength. The planks of the hulls were staggered and stepped similar to how a mason would build a brick wall so that there were no continuous seams. The lateral seams of the hull planks were caulked with papyrus to make them watertight.[24]

A ship constructed without a keel in the manner described lacked sufficient longitudinal rigidity to sail upon the open sea. In a rough sea, the waves would pitch the boat up and down from bow to stern, breaking the vessel's back. To prevent this, the Egyptians invented the girt rope and hog-truss. The girt rope was a papyrus cable wrapped around the ship's bow and stern, tightly holding the ends of the hull in place. These cables also served as anchors for the hog-truss. The hog-truss was a strong cable that ran longitudinally across the entire length of the hull and was anchored at each end of the ship. The truss passed over two "crutches" near each end of the ship, raising the cable off the deck. The cable was wrapped around a stout pole located between the crutches and was tightened to maintain tension on the truss cable itself. The hog-truss provided sufficient longitudinal stability to allow the ship to sail in heavy seas without risk of breaking in two.[25]

By Thutmose's day, Egyptian seagoing ships had evolved streamlined hulls; were longer, wider, and deeper than the old Nile ships;[26] and were "comparable to a modern [i.e., present-day] racing craft" in efficiency.[27] At sea, propulsion was by sail, and huge rectangular sails, wider than they were tall, caught the wind atop masts ranging in height from six to seventeen meters depending on the size of the ship.[28] The mast was located amidships, was stepped—that is, it could be lowered—and was held in place with side supports and ropes. The thick linen sails were controlled by ropes and yards at the base of the sail that allowed the ship to reach and tack into the wind.[29] Steering was accomplished by two aft steering oars connected to a steering post attached to the loom of the oars.[30] When entering or departing harbors, the ship's oarsmen managed the propulsion. They also augmented the ship's movement in light wind. A hundred-foot-long ship might have had as many as forty oarsmen.[31] Unlike the Nile boats, seagoing ships did not have deckhouses.

The Egyptians developed a standard design and scale for constructing their seagoing vessels that called for a ship to be three times as long as its beam. Crew strengths were calculated at one crew member per cubit of length.[32] Egyptian ships were transports of various types and were not built as naval combatants to fight other ships on the open sea. That concept did not dawn on the military minds of antiquity until late in the New Kingdom. The first use of naval combatants to fight other ships occurred during the reign of Ramses III (1186–1154 BCE), who, in the eighth year of his reign, fought what appears to have been the world's first saltwater naval battle against the marauding Sea People at the mouth of the Nile.[33]

In the eastern Mediterranean Sea, the best time for sailing is from the end of May through mid-September, when the seas are undisturbed by storms and the winds are generally favorable from the north and west at not more than twenty-five knots.[34] Under these conditions a ship could make between four to six knots, or five to seven miles an hour.[35] In unfavorable conditions, the speed dropped to between two and three miles an hour.[36] In antiquity, ships put into shore each night for the crews to eat and sleep. Ports were little more than stretches of beach protected to some degree by the natural contour of the shoreline.[37] Illustration 6.1 shows the sailing distances between the ports Thutmose's invasion fleet used in transporting his army across the 340 miles of open sea between the Nile Delta and Byblos. Where an overland march would have taken almost six weeks, the sea journey required slightly more than a week to complete. A sea voyage also avoided the wear and tear on the army that inevitably accompanied an overland march, so Thutmose's army arrived reasonably rested and ready to fight.

Thutmose's Invasion Force

The logistics of transporting Thutmose's army of 10,000 infantry and a brigade of 500 chariots and their 1,000 horses plus another 250 in reserve

6.1. SAILING DISTANCES BETWEEN PORTS ON THE CANAANITE-LEBANON COASTS

Sile to Byblos:	340 miles
Sile to El Arish:	67 miles
El Arish to Gaza:	58 miles
Gaza to Yafo:	47 miles
Yafo to the Antelope's Nose (Carmel):	55 miles
Antelope's Nose to Sidon:	33 miles
Sidon to Beirut:	47 miles
Sidon to Byblos:	63 miles

are interesting. If we accept an average Egyptian transport to be 60 cubits (102 feet) long and 20 cubits (34 feet) wide, we arrive at a ship that is comparable in size, speed, cargo space, and tons burden to the average transport used in Roman Republican times.[38] These ships could carry between 80 to 100 tons of cargo and drew about 2 feet of water in draft, which was shallow enough to permit easy beaching and pushing off.[39] These ships could be configured to carry cargo, troops, or horses.[40] Using some basic calculations, we can arrive at a description of Thutmose's transports.

The average soldier in antiquity weighed about 145 pounds and was 5 feet 8 inches tall.[41] The Egyptian soldier's equipment, including ten days' rations carried in his knapsack, hide shield, spear, sickle-sword, and thick leather belt, weighed approximately 60 pounds. Thus, a troopship had to carry about 210 pounds per passenger. A 100-foot-long and 34-foot-wide ship could accommodate forty-eight benches arranged front to back like church pews with a 1-foot aisle running lengthwise between the bench rows. A bench 20 inches deep afforded sufficient room for an average soldier to sit with 5 inches of legroom to spare. Allowing a shoulder width of 24 inches left the soldier 2 inches on either side from the man next to him. Under these conditions, each bench could accommodate fifteen soldiers in the two aisles of forty-eight rows, or a total of 720 men per transport. With their knapsacks stowed beneath the benches and their equipment stored in boxes on deck, the troops and their equipment weighed 75 tons, easily within the burden capacity of the ship.

If we make allowances for somewhat more commodious accommodations and assume that each ship was required to carry only three companies of 200 men each—the size of a typical Sa, or company of Egyptian infantry—then each ship would have to carry only 600 men, leaving sufficient room for the crew, large quantities of food and water, and equipment. Under these conditions, the ship's burden would be only 63 tons. Seventeen troop transports would have been required to transport Thutmose's army of 10,000 infantrymen.

We do not know if Egyptian troop transports were decked as their usual cargo ships were or if they were open-decked barge-like boats in which men and animals were exposed to the elements during the voyage. By Roman times both types were in evidence, and the Egyptian ships' design would not have prohibited the construction of open-decked vessels. Given the short sailing distances required—no more than a day's sail between ports—both types of ships offered advantages and disadvantages. The main advantage of the open-deck barge was that it presented less difficulty in loading and off-loading horses, donkeys, and mules. While aboard ship, the small loaves of bread, beef jerky, smoked goose flesh or pork, pressed or dried fruit, cheese, onions, and radishes that the soldier carried in his knapsack were sufficient to sustain him for the seven- to ten-day voyage. Water in the soldier's canteen could be regularly replenished from the ship's water casks. As in troopships used in modern wars, the soldiers took turns being allowed on deck for fresh air and sun. In the evening, the troops had an opportunity to stretch their legs on shore, eat, and get some sleep on their reed mats. One attraction would have been plenty of beer, which was dispensed to keep the troops hydrated and happy during the voyage.[42] Military transports were sometimes accompanied by small onboard breweries to supply the troops' beverages. Except for having to use buckets for sanitary needs, the circumstances of the Egyptian soldier aboard ship were not much different from those of soldiers on troopships during World War I.

Horse transports were another matter, however. Horses need a firm, flat surface upon which to stand, so the internal deck of the horse transport had to be flat. Thus, the carpenters would have constructed an inner deck platform in the cargo hold. The obvious difficulties involved in trying to force a horse into the hold of a decked ship suggests either that the Egyptians used open-decked vessels to transport their horses or that the animals were enclosed in railed pens on the cargo ships' decks. An average horse is approximately 90 to 115 inches long and 34 inches wide and weighs about 1,000 pounds.[43] The deck or cargo space of an open-decked boat 100 feet long and 34 feet wide permitted the construction of 90 horse stalls, each 9 feet long and 3 feet wide. A rope and linen sling in each stall supported the animal and kept it from falling as the boat pitched in the sea. A rope barrier separated each stall from the one in front of it. Ninety horses weighed some 45 tons.

It is unlikely, however, that the transports carried this many animals at a time and still had sufficient space and tonnage for the crew and supplies. If we assume a load of fifty horses, these animals would have consumed 750 pounds of hay or green fodder, 275 pounds of hard fodder (barley or oats), and 375 gallons of water per day.[44] During a ten-day voyage, 7,500 pounds of hay and 2,750 pounds of hard fodder were required to feed the animals. It is unlikely that the 3,750 gallons of water (or 15 tons!) needed to sustain the animals for ten days were carried aboard ship. Certainly some water was stored aboard to meet the animals' short-term needs. But when the ships put into shore each evening, the men had to carry water from an onshore source to the animals remaining on the boat to ensure that they were sufficiently watered.

Thutmose could have transported the 1,250 horses needed to outfit his 500-vehicle chariot brigade in only twenty-five ships and even fewer if he was willing to load the ships to their full capacity. A chariot brigade of 500 vehicles included 1,000 soldiers (drivers and charioteers), 500 grooms to handle the horses, and approximately another 400 smiths and carpenters to keep the brigade fit for combat. Five ships were required to transport the disassembled chariots and the troops and technicians of the chariot brigade.[45]

The greatest danger in transporting horses, mules, and donkeys by boat was the injury incurred when the animals were being loaded and unloaded from the boat. A horse's legs are very fragile and are easily broken if the animal stumbles. Great care had to be taken, especially so when unloading the animals from a beached transport or from a transport swaying in the surf. Equal care had to be taken in off-loading the army's 2,000 mules and donkeys. The animals required thirty-three ships to transport them, the largest number of ships for any contingent of the invasion force. The Egyptians were experienced in transporting animals by ship, having moved them regularly up and down the Nile. In addition, the Egyptians' ability to transport heavy loads, such as limestone and granite for their construction projects, was unsurpassed.[46] It would have been to Thutmose's great advantage, however, to be able to assemble large numbers of these animals in the supply depots once he took possession of Lebanon's ports and avoid having to transport them for use in future campaigns.

Taken together, the invasion force that Thutmose brought against the Lebanon coast required that approximately 12,000 troops, 500 chariots, 1,250 horses, and 2,000 pack animals be transported by sea. After leaving Egypt it took some 80 ships, making eight stops along the coasts of Canaan and Lebanon, a little over a week to reach the port of Byblos 340 miles distant. Unlike Thutmose's previous incursion into Lebanon, he undertook this full-scale invasion to establish the logistics infrastructure to support further expeditions into the Syrian interior.[47]

Invasion

The previous year Thutmose had marched up the Lebanon coast to remove the threat to Byblos after Tunip seized and garrisoned Ullaza and Wahlia in an attempt to choke off Egypt's access to the Eleutheros Valley and the cedar supply. Thutmose captured both towns as well as the agricultural town of Ardata to the south. Having captured the towns' troop garrisons, Thutmose seems to have returned home without establishing his own garrisons at either Ullaza or Wahlia. This oversight proved to be a mistake.

In his thirtieth regnal year, Thutmose attacked the Lebanon coast in earnest, mounting an amphibious invasion. He left Egypt in early June and arrived in Lebanon a week later. Although the *Annals* do not tell us where he landed, the most logical place was the port city of Simyra, located about thirty miles by sea from the friendly port of Byblos. Lying just south of Ullaza, Simyra was the closest port to the mouth of the Eleutheros Valley.[48] Thutmose had to land his troops in daylight, so the staging area from which to launch the invasion's final phase had to be no more than half a day's sail from where the invasion force would eventually come ashore. Staging from Byblos at dawn, the invasion force would reach Simyra around noon or 1:00 p.m., leaving six to seven hours of daylight to off-load their ships, move inland, and establish a defensive perimeter around the beachhead. Satellite photos of the coast around Simyra reveal a long and gradually inclined coastline that must have been perfect for beaching the shallow-draft Egyptian transports. Eighty transports separated from one another by fifty yards required just more than a mile of open beach to land and discharge their cargoes. Simyra's beach provided more than the necessary landing area.

The troops were awakened early at Byblos, fed, and loaded on the transports where their weapons and equipment were distributed. As the troopships approached the beach, companies of soldiers left their benches in the ship's belly and made their way to the deck, where they could jump overboard in the surf. Others followed as quickly as they could. Once the infantry had secured the beach, the ships carrying the chariots and horses began to unload. Elite chariot units unloaded their vehicles, assembled their horse teams, and formed their units before moving inland with the infantry. The mission of these advanced units was to deal with any resistance and to locate a suitable site for establishing a field camp. The Egyptians met no resistance, and the landing and encampment went smoothly. By dark, the army was ashore and safely established behind their field camp's shield wall. The first phase of Thutmose's campaign had gone off flawlessly.

If the texts present an accurate chronology, Thutmose's first combat operation was to move against the city of Kadesh, the source of much of the troublemaking in Asia over the years. It took several days for the army to get organized before Thutmose could begin his march to Arka, the largest agricultural town in the heart of the Eleutheros Valley. There he rested and prepared his army for the march to Kadesh, which lay about five miles to the south of the far eastern end of the valley, or about forty miles or four days' march from the coast. As Thutmose's army marched through the valley, it was well supplied from the produce of the Arka Plain and the harvests from the valley's farms.

According to the *Annals*, Thutmose "arrived at the city of Kadesh, overthrew it, cut down its groves, and harvested its grain."[49] The tomb inscriptions of Amenemhab, an officer who fought in Thutmose's army during the Asiatic campaigns, support this account. Regarding the action around Kadesh, Amenemhab's inscription tells us, "Again I beheld his bravery, while I was among his followers. He [Thutmose] captured the city of Kadesh, I was not absent from the place where he was; I brought off two men, lords as living prisoners; I set them before the king, the Lord of the Two Lands, Thutmose [III], living forever. He gave to me gold because of bravery, before the whole people."[50] Amenemhab's account certainly suggests that there was a battle of some magnitude at Kadesh. His reference to his prisoners as "lords" also implies that chariots took part in the battle, for the term *lord* refers to the maryannu nobility who served as chariot warriors. That Amenemhab performed well in battle is clear from his being decorated by Pharaoh himself before the entire army ("before the whole people"). The question remains, however, whether Thutmose actually "overwhelmed" the city of Kadesh.

It does not seem likely that Kadesh fell to Egyptian arms. The city was well fortified and had a substantial population and professional warrior class to defend it. According to Olmstead's archeological research, Kadesh was located on "a tongue of land between the Orontes and an affluent, and protected on the third side by a ditch."[51] The city walls formed a square 400 yards on a side. The ramparts of the walls were nearly fifty feet high constructed with the earth taken from the surrounding ditch, which was fifteen feet deep and sixty-five feet across. Towers protected the corners of the walls.[52] The walls enclosed some thirty-four acres. Using Yadin's metric of 240 persons per square urban acre to estimate the population of Bronze Age cities, we arrive at a population of approximately 8,000 to 9,000 people for Kadesh.[53] Relying upon Yadin once more to calculate the percentage of the population that could be put to its defense, Kadesh's population could muster about 2,200 people to fend off an attack.[54] In addition, there would have been a significant contingent of maryannu chariot warriors to participate in the city's defense. Kadesh's defenders could deploy 1.3 men for every meter of wall, a more-than-adequate number to offer stiff resistance should Thutmose attempt to storm the city.[55]

To the northwest of Kadesh, where the Eleutheros Valley exits the Lebanon range, a broad open plain runs to the foot of the city itself. It was here that Thutmose's army debouched from its march. The terrain is ideal for chariots,[56] and it is likely that the battle Amenemhab described was fought here. It may have been that the enemy was surprised by the appearance of an Egyptian army almost under the walls of Kadesh itself and hastily sent forth its chariots to block Thutmose's advance. If so, it was a tactical mistake. On open ground, Thutmose's chariots supported by his large infantry contingent would have had the advantage over the maryannu charioteers, who would have had only a small number of infantry in support. If we are to believe Amenemhab, the Egyptians got the better of the fight, and several enemy charioteers were taken prisoner. When the maryanna were driven from the field, they sought refuge behind Kadesh's walls. Thutmose was then free to "punish" the city in the traditional fashion by cutting down its fruit trees and seizing its recently harvested grain.

The *Annals'* reference to Thutmose having "overthrown" Kadesh is probably to his defeat of Kadesh's maryanna and not to his having captured the city itself. Had Kadesh been taken, it could have been taken only by siege, and there is no mention of one having occurred. If we can trust Amenemhab once more, Thutmose moved north toward Tunip and Qatna almost immediately after the skirmish at Kadesh, thereby making it very unlikely that he took Kadesh under siege. Moreover, the capture of Kadesh would have been an enormous victory and would have merited much more extensive narration in the *Annals* than it received. The tribute lists would also have reflected much greater quantities of booty than they do. The capture of Kadesh would have certainly resulted in the transfer of its "vile prince" to Egypt amid great fanfare, and some record of his execution would almost certainly exist. Nevertheless, Thutmose had still been able to demonstrate that the main perpetrator of Egypt's troubles in Syria was no longer beyond the Egyptian army's operational reach.

What followed suggests that intimidation, not conquest, was the purpose of Thutmose's march into the Syrian interior. Having made his point at Kadesh, Thutmose turned north and marched up the Orontes. The *Annals* tell us that he "came to the land of Senzar."[57] Senzar is probably the Zinzar of the Amarna texts and is located on the Orontes close to modern Hamah.[58] The march took him through the territories of the powerful city-states of Qatna and Tunip, and Thutmose put on a dramatic demonstration of Egyptian military might and his willingness to confront the Syrian cities on their own ground. Thutmose was playing a psychological game.

Marching almost under the city walls of Qatna and Tunip was risky business indeed. Thutmose must have been prepared to fight if forced to and settle the issue of who would control southern Syria and the Lebanon coast then rather than later. But neither city's army sallied forth to confront Pharaoh and his army as it passed. To ensure that the Syrians understood the scope of Egyptian power and Thutmose's willingness to use it, he fell upon the town of Senzar. Located only a few miles north of Tunip, Senzar was close enough to have been one of Tunip's vassals, and Thutmose's attack was a direct challenge to Tunip to come to its aid. Amenemhab describes the battle at Senzar: "I beheld the royal victories of the King Menkheperre [Thutmose III], given life, in the country of Senzar when he made a great slaughter among them. I fought hand to hand before the king, I brought off a hand there.[59] He gave to me the gold of honor."[60] The town seems to have been destroyed, and the "great slaughter" may have been a deliberately bloody lesson to Tunip that it might meet a similar fate. Tunip made no effort to help its vassal.

Thutmose had taken the measure of the rulers of Kadesh, Qatna, and Tunip, and he found it wanting. The success of his campaign of intimidation can be seen in the fact that after the destruction of Senzar, Thutmose turned his army around and marched back down the Orontes, once more passing through the territories of the three city-states. He presented a direct challenge to them to do battle. It had been at least two weeks since Thutmose's army had passed through their territory, more than enough time for the rulers to prepare their militaries to respond. The rulers of the Syrian cities should have reasonably assumed that Thutmose would reverse his course and try to move through the Eleutheros Valley on his way home. Any other route would have required him to cross the Lebanon Mountains overland or march hundreds of miles around the mountains to gain the coast. Again the cities offered no resistance to Thutmose's return passage through their territories. He turned west into the Eleutheros Valley and marched back to his base at Simyra.[61]

The expedition had been a risky venture, but Thutmose showed a superb strategic and psychological ability to analyze his enemies and exploit their lack of resolve. The most powerful city-states in southern Syria now realized that they were no longer invulnerable to Egyptian attack. This lesson was not likely lost on the Mitanni, either, who were watching the events from a distance with growing alarm.

The Egyptian army had been on the march or conducting combat operations for almost a month by the time it returned to Simyra. After a few weeks' rest, Thutmose ordered the army back into action. This time the target was the port of Arvad, twenty-six miles north of Simyra. The *Annals* do not tell us why Thutmose moved against Arvad. Clearly Thutmose intended to control all the Lebanon ports. The ports to the south of Simyra either were already in Egyptian hands or, like Byblos, Sidon, and Tyre, had been on friendly terms with Egypt for years. To the north, Egyptian control stopped at modern Tripoli. Arvad lay north of Tripoli and was the last remaining major port in Lebanon outside Egyptian control. Sometime in late July or early August, Thutmose moved to capture Arvad.

Arvad was located in the center of a north-south line of reefs two and one-half miles offshore opposite the site of modern Tartus. The island was only a half mile long and a quarter mile wide, and its surface rose only a few feet above the waves.[62] Arvad was well protected by both natural and man-made defenses. Submerged reefs and rocks that only the local pilots could navigate surrounded the island on three sides. Walls of natural rock that had massive blocks, some as much as fifteen feet in length, enclosed the perimeter. In some places the rock itself was so large that it had been hewn to become a part of the wall. To the west and south rose a great seawall above a natural moat. The island's water supply was stored in cisterns. Only on its eastern side, that closest to the mainland coast, was Arvad vulnerable. Two semicircular harbors separated by a jetty afforded the only seaborne access to the island.[63]

Arvad could be approached only by sea, so Thutmose took it by amphibious assault. His ships and troops were assembled at Simyra, and it was but half a day's sail up the coast to Arvad. The city's small size could hardly sustain a population of more than a thousand souls, insufficient to mount significant resistance. A small contingent of five troopships carrying three thousand men would have been a sufficient force to take the island. With no other place to land, the Egyptians came ashore at the island's two eastern harbors. Resistance would have been futile, and none was recorded in the texts. The island's palatine government saw that its interest now rested with swearing allegiance to Egypt in order to keep its freedom and maintain its lucrative trade.

After capturing Arvad, Thutmose embarked on an inspection tour of all the cities and towns from Simyra north to Arvad and west past Arka and into the Eleutheros Valley to accept oaths of loyalty from the rulers who now recognized Thutmose as their sovereign and whom he accepted as vassals. The texts tell us that the rulers of thirty-six principalities swore oaths of allegiance to their new king.[64] But Thutmose was too realistic a politician to rely upon their oaths alone. As he had done in his earlier campaigns, Thutmose took some chiefs' sons as hostages. Thus, the texts say, "Behold, the children of the chiefs and their brothers were brought to be in strongholds [castles?] in Egypt."[65] As time passed and the old rulers died, their sons were returned from Egypt and succeeded them with the expectation that they would support Egyptian interests. No doubt Thutmose intended that Egypt would control the Lebanon coast for a long time.[66]

The sixth campaign had been a success. Thutmose had shown the world how to conduct a large-scale amphibious invasion, a military capability heretofore unknown in antiquity. His invasion of the Lebanon coast gave Egypt a new military advantage that greatly increased its ability to project its power throughout the Levant. The Egyptians could now respond more rapidly to any rebellion or crisis and deploy large numbers of troops in ready fighting condition hundreds of miles from Egypt's shores. He expanded on the new amphibious capability by demonstrating his ability to move inland and operate far from his coastal base. He thus overcame the strategic barrier of distance behind which the powerful city-states of Tunip, Kadesh, and Qatna had once relied for their protection against Egyptian retaliation after their mischief in Lebanon and Canaan. With their Syrian cat's-paws now vulnerable to Egyptian attack, the Mitanni must have realized that it was only a matter of time before Egyptian power would be directed at them.

Capturing the fertile Arka Plain, the western mouth of the Eleutheros Valley, and the northern port of Arvad and maintaining good relations with the major ports of Byblos, Tyre, and Sidon made establishing Egyptian garrisons possible in some of these places. The Egyptians also constructed storage facilities and filled them with food and other materials that the army would need to sustain itself during future inland operations. The tribute list for the sixth campaign is remarkable for its brevity, listing only 181 slaves, 188 horses, and 40 chariots.[67] Noticeably absent is any mention of large quantities of agricultural products to be shipped to Egypt. Instead, the in-kind tax levied upon Egypt's new vassals was retained and stored in military-controlled depots for the army's future use. A small garrison, say a typical Egyptian platoon of fifty soldiers, would have been adequate to the task of overseeing the collection and storage of the supplies for any one town. Assuming that some forty towns had submitted to Thutmose during the campaign, a stay-behind force of only two thousand soldiers would have been needed to insure the Egyptian supply base. Although the texts are silent, Thutmose would have been wise to also leave behind part of his animal pack train, which included some two thousand mules and donkeys, and to supplement their numbers from local sources. With the army's logistical capability to support ground operations now in place in Lebanon, the eighty ships Thutmose had needed to transport his Egyptian army of twelve thousand men and their equipment could be reduced to some thirty-eight ships.

Thutmose's sixth campaign in regnal year 30 was really an effort to prepare for the future. The successful Egyptian military operations had begun to transform the area of coastal Lebanon into a strategic platform for further operations. More work lay ahead for Egypt to complete the transformation, to prepare for operations against the states of the Syrian interior, and ultimately to carry Egyptian might against the Mitanni, the great power that the Egyptians saw as their ultimate strategic threat.

The Seventh Campaign

In 1473 BCE (year 31), Thutmose returned to the Lebanon coast and once more came by sea. It is not clear where he landed, but there appears no good reason why he would not have landed at Simyra, which had served him well the year before and by now had been turned into an Egyptian supply depot. Moreover, Simyra was close to Ullaza, which had broken into open revolt. Two years earlier Thutmose had attacked Ullaza and captured the garrison the prince of Tunip had installed there. Ullaza was still under Egyptian control at the end of the previous year's campaign season. But for whatever reason either an Egyptian garrison was not established there or, if it was, it was small enough to be easily overcome. Perhaps Ullaza's proximity to the large Simyra garrison made it seem unnecessary to place a garrison there.

Sometime during the winter or early spring, the prince of Tunip had sent a sizable troop contingent to seize Ullaza again, refortify it, and occupy the town. Tunip's motives are unclear, but they must have been important if he risked angering the Egyptians. The *Annals* note that the prince of Tunip's son was placed in command of the operation and remained in Ullaza to direct its occupation and defense.[68] Having suffered the humiliation of watching Egyptian troops march unopposed across its territory the year before, Tunip's ruler may have concluded that it was only a matter of time before the Egyptians attacked Tunip itself, perhaps during the present campaign season. If so, he may have seized Ullaza to use it as a base to block the Egyptians' access to the Eleutheros Valley or, alternatively, to sit astride the Egyptian line of communication and present a threat to any Egyptian march to the interior. With Ullaza in hostile hands, the Egyptians' main base at Simyra was also vulnerable. Whatever the purpose of the Ullaza garrison, it was substantial, comprising some five hundred soldiers (mostly infantry) and thirteen chariots and maryannu charioteers.[69]

Thutmose returned to the Lebanon coast to conduct an inspection tour of the ports and inland agricultural towns that had sworn loyalty to him the year before and to ensure that his garrison had made progress in establishing supply depots in some of them and collecting the necessary stores. He apparently did not plan to engage in any major military operations, so the force that he brought with him from Egypt was probably not very large, perhaps only a few thousand troops. This force could be augmented, however, from the garrisons left behind the previous year should the need arise. Thutmose probably learned about the situation in Ullaza upon his arrival, and he moved quickly to deal with it.

Two years earlier Thutmose had reduced Ullaza's fortifications, and in the short time the Tunip garrison had occupied the town, it is unlikely that the fortifications had been improved significantly. Thutmose assembled his army and moved quickly against the town. The *Annals* tell us, "Verily, his majesty captured this city in a short hour."[70] It is also interesting that the garrison seems to have been captured intact, with "some 490 living captives."[71] These circumstances suggest that the town was betrayed from within, taken by some ruse, or simply taken by surprise so suddenly that the defenders surrendered without much of a fight. The garrison's commander, who was the prince of Tunip's son, was captured alive and delivered to Pharaoh. However the town fell, Thutmose knew that the eyes of his other new vassals were upon him, anxious to see how he would deal with Ullaza's treachery. He turned the town over to his army for pillage, "and all its property was spoil." An Egyptian garrison was then stationed in the town.[72] Thutmose showed the other towns what they could expect should they break their oath to Pharaoh.

Thutmose next set out on an inspection tour of the ports' supply depots. "Now, at every harbor at which his majesty arrived was supplied with loaves and with assorted loaves, with oil, incense, wine, honey, fruit . . . abundant were they beyond everything beyond the knowledge of his majesty's army."[73] Apparently, the rulers of the vassal towns had done what was expected of them and filled their storehouses with supplies for the Egyptian army's use. That Egyptian officers were in charge of the depots is clear from the texts' statement that the supplies "remain in the daily register of the palace."[74] Thutmose seems to have sailed from port to port on his inspection tour rather than travel overland. Pharaoh was becoming accustomed to the sea, and he would resort to this mode of travel again and again to transport his troops when dealing with rebellions in Syria and northern Canaan.[75]

Not all of Thutmose's vassal towns were on the coast. Most of them were inland and were the sources of the supplies that he ordered stockpiled in the ports. The ports were chosen as storage facilities because they were the first and easiest towns for the Egyptian army to reach when coming by sea. Also, the Lebanon coastal ports were not usually attacked. The major inland states had seen it in their interest to leave them alone and continued to use them as a source of trade goods. To be sure, they may have had second thoughts as they watched Thutmose turn the coast into an enormous Egyptian logistical base, and they had few illusions that sooner or later Thutmose would use these port facilities and depots to support his armies in a campaign against them.

The inland towns were thus very important elements in Thutmose's plan, and he made a separate inspection tour of these places. He was pleased to find that "the harvest of the land of Retjenu was reported, consisting of much clean grain, grain in the kernel, barley, incense, green oil, wine, fruit, every pleasing thing of the country."[76] That a specified portion of this harvest went to the Egyptian supply depots as an impost against each town is clear from the texts.[77] During this inspection, the "princes of Retjenu came to do obeisance to the soul of his majesty in this year."[78] During this time, taxes and imposts were delivered, oaths renewed, and gifts exchanged. This visit, however, Thutmose added another requirement. Perhaps mindful of the rebellion at Ullaza and fearing future trouble across his line of communications once his armies were in the field in the interior, Thutmose ordered the vassal towns be disarmed. Thus, the chiefs of the inland towns were required to relinquish "the equipment of their weapons of war."[79] This order included "nineteen chariots wrought with silver," that is, the expensive personal chariots of the rulers themselves. Thutmose was taking no chances.

It had required three military expeditions in as many years, but Thutmose had achieved his strategic objective of controlling the Lebanon ports and transforming the coast and the immediate hinterlands into a strategic platform from which he could launch military operations into the interior of Syria. He was now prepared to confront the Mitanni, the primary strategic threat to Egyptian security. The rigor, scope, intensity, and duration of Thutmose's military operations were unprecedented for Egypt in Asia. They had, however, been directed at a traditional sphere of influence, Canaan and Lebanon, that had long been of commercial and strategic concern to Egypt. Had Thutmose stopped there, it would have been a great achievement but one accomplished along traditional lines. Only the brief foray into the territory of Kadesh, Qatna, and Tunip was a departure from the norm. It was a harbinger of what was to come.[80]

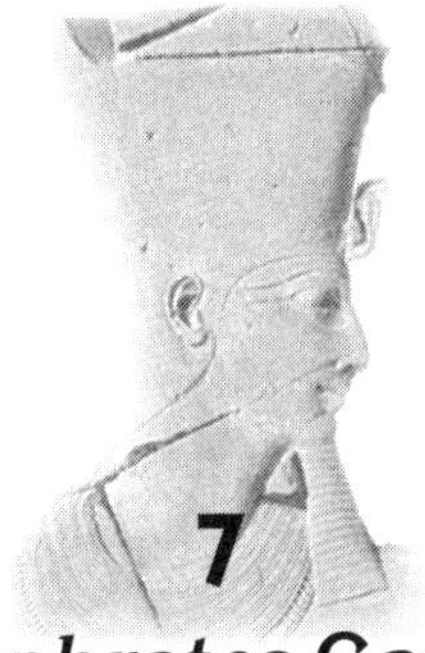

7
The Euphrates Campaign

Thutmose had spent the last decade reestablishing Egyptian control of Canaan and extending Egyptian influence to the coast of Lebanon. He led a prodigious and successful effort to reverse the half century of Egyptian decline that had occurred in those areas during the reigns of Thutmose II and Queen Hatshepsut. To achieve his objectives, Thutmose had mounted seven military expeditions in nine years, the last three coming one after another in quick and effective succession. Although restoring Egypt's power in the Levant was dramatic, in Thutmose's strategic plan the decade of military operations was only a prelude to his larger goal of confronting and defeating the Mitanni, the great power that Egypt saw as the source of its troubles in Syria and as the major strategic threat to Egyptian national security. In 1471 BCE, in his thirty-third regnal year, Thutmose was ready to deal with the Mitanni.

Thutmose returned from Lebanon in the fall of 1473 BCE after ensuring that his vassals had delivered their harvests and supplies and stored them in the port city depots. By September of his thirty-first regnal year, he was back in Egypt. Thutmose's eighth campaign began in the spring of his thirty-third regnal year, eighteen months after his previous campaign. It is intriguing to ask what Thutmose, having mounted three consecutive campaigns, did during those intervening eighteen months.

Apparently, he was rebuilding the Egyptian army and preparing for the upcoming Euphrates campaign.[1] The rigors of the previous campaigns had taken their toll on the Egyptian army, and manpower was strained by losses to casualties, disease, injury, and the expiration of conscript tours of duty. Large numbers of soldiers were needed to occupy the garrisons in Nubia and along the Egyptian borders with Libya and Asia. Thutmose's victories in Canaan and Lebanon had created new garrisons that also had to be manned. The new dockyard at Perunefer was now fully operational, and more sailors and workers were needed to staff the expanding navy. Thutmose's extensive program of public works construction was expanding, requiring more manpower for corvée labor that would otherwise have been available for military service. Thutmose needed the eighteen months to recruit, equip, and train the large number of troops he needed for his campaign against the Mitanni.

Thutmose's campaign plan required a much larger army than he had heretofore taken into the field. The only practical route of advance to his objective required the army to pass within striking distance of several powerful city-states allied with the Mitanni. These had to be dealt with in some manner before he could engage his primary adversary beyond the Euphrates. The problem's complexity lent itself to a partial solution if Thutmose could muster sufficient forces at each point of potential conflict, that is, each time he was forced to deal with a Mitannian ally along his route of march. Unlike the terrain of the earlier campaigns in Lebanon, the terrain near some of the city-states he might be forced to fight was well suited to his opponents' chariot armies. The terrain along the Euphrates was also chariot country. His own chariot arm, therefore, had to be substantial and well supported by large numbers of infantry.

His campaign plan called for the Egyptian army to deploy over a distance of six hundred miles from its base in Egypt and to maintain itself in the field for more than five months. During that time it would have to fight its way to the main objective, cross the Euphrates River, engage and defeat the Mitannian army, and then return by overland march, passing again within striking distance of the military forces of the city-states it had encountered on its way out. Only an army of significant size with well-balanced logistics and military capabilities could hope to succeed at such an effort given the forces and geographical factors arrayed against it.

The size of Thutmose's army was not recorded, but a reasonable estimate is that it required at least three infantry divisions of five thousand infantry each. At least two brigades of five hundred chariots gave the army a combat capability of a thousand vehicles. Besides its service as a combat arm, the chariots had a vital role to play in conducting reconnaissance, establishing security, and locating wells and food supplies for the army. Two chariot brigades required two thousand horses and another five hundred in reserve to compensate for losses to disease, lameness, and combat actions. Two thousand drivers and charioteers made up the combat personnel complement of the two brigades. Another thousand groomsmen were along to care for the horses. The army needed four thousand mules and donkeys to provide ground transport and six hundred smiths and carpenters for maintaining the army's equipment.[2] Another thousand or so human porters and other hangers-on who usually accompanied the armies of antiquity brought the number of personnel in Thutmose's army to almost twenty thousand and the number of animals to almost seven thousand. It was the largest army that Egypt had ever put in the field.

It is an axiom of sound military thinking that political realities determine a commander's strategic vision, that strategy determines the campaign plan, and that the campaign plan determines the operational plan that the field force will execute. Just as in modern times, this dynamic was at work in Thutmose's Euphrates campaign. The political configuration of the Mitannian system of alliances imposed significant limits on the way any Egyptian campaign could be waged against it. The Egyptians referred to the Mitanni as "the lands of the Mitanni," out of recognition of the fact that the kingdom of the Mitanni was a composite and not a national state. The lands east of the Euphrates, roughly equivalent to the geographic area of modern Kurdistan, constituted the central kingdom, and its capital was located at Washukkanni in the Khabur River Valley not far from modern Mosul. West of the Euphrates, extending into northern and west-central Syria, were "the lands of the Mitanni." These vassal states, some with Mitannian garrisons, were loyal to the king of the Mitanni. Among them was Alalakh, a prominent member of the Mitannian confederation bound by treaty to the king.[3] Two of Alalakh's subvassals, Niya and Kissuwadna, were similarly pledged. The powerful city of Aleppo to the north was also under strong Mitannian influence, as were the mid-Syrian city-states of Qatna, Tunip, and Kadesh, which controlled the Orontes River Valley.[4]

Each of these states occupied an important location, control of which could seriously hinder the Egyptian advance. Alalakh blocked the route through northern Lebanon to the Syrian interior, and Aleppo guarded the route across the steppe leading to Carchemish and the Euphrates. Of immediate importance to Thutmose's campaign plan were the cities of Qatna, Tunip, and Kadesh. The most direct route to northeast Syria ran along the Orontes River Valley, and all three cities sat directly astride the route of the Egyptians' advance. Kadesh was in a strong position to block the Egyptian advance through the Eleutheros Valley, and Qatna controlled the important ford over the Orontes River that made movement along the high east bank possible. Denied the ability to cross the river, Thutmose would be forced to make his way up the marshy west bank of the river and to pass almost under the walls of Tunip, whose resistance could be formidable.

None of these cities could be easily bypassed, and Thutmose did not have the means to take them by storm or siege and still have sufficient time in the campaign season to reach the Euphrates and engage the Mitannian main force. From a military perspective, then, Thutmose had only two options: either intimidate the cities' rulers with his army's size and power and hope they would let him pass unhindered or use his numerical advantage to quickly defeat the enemy if it chose to fight on open ground. If the enemy chose to fight and then retreat behind its walls, however, there was little Thutmose could do.

But even in antiquity, military force was often the handmaiden of politics. It seems likely that while he was preparing his army, Thutmose may have used diplomacy to attempt to reduce the threats the Syrian city-states posed. As events turned out, he seems to have been successful. Tunip's neutrality was somehow purchased, one suspects, by returning the king's son, who had been taken prisoner more than a year earlier, after the Egyptians had recaptured Ullaza. Qatna, too, found it in its interest for some reason to loosen the ties that bound it to the Mitanni. The texts tell us that "His Majesty was in the district of Qatna on the Eighth Campaign, close to the bank,"[5] and that Thutmose stopped at Qatna to visit a workshop that manufactured bows, suggesting that Qatna was already in the Egyptian camp prior to the campaign.[6] While the details of the respective bargains with Qatna and Tunip remain unknown, Thutmose seems to have achieved by diplomacy what would have required great effort to achieve by force. Diplomacy had gained him unhindered access to the Orontes River crossing as well as an unimpeded axis of advance to the north along the east bank of the river.

We do not know if Thutmose proposed a bargain with Kadesh. If he did, nothing seems to have come of it. There is no indication that Kadesh remained anything but closely tied to its Mitannian ally and hostile to Egyptian interests. Kadesh was ideally situated to block the Egyptian advance through the Eleutheros Valley by meeting the Egyptians in open battle on the plain at the valley's exit just north of the city. Alternatively, it could keep its forces in reserve and fall upon Thutmose's rear once his army turned north to reach the Orontes ford. If Thutmose permitted himself to be drawn into an attempt to storm Kadesh, he would almost certainly be forced to abandon his plans to reach the Euphrates by the end of the campaign season. His only other option was to hope that Kadesh could be intimidated by his army's size and power and think better of interfering with it on its way north. One way or another, however, Thutmose would have to deal with Kadesh.

The March to the Euphrates

Thutmose had no intention of undertaking an overland march of more than six hundred miles to reach his objective. In mid-April, a somewhat earlier-than-usual departure time that perhaps was intended to extend the campaign season by at least two weeks, the Egyptian army of 20,000 men and 6,500 animals sailed from the new port city and dockyard at Perunefer to the Lebanon coast. Thutmose needed approximately 170 ships to transport the army. The texts suggest that the invasion force landed "in the neighborhood of Byblos."[7] It would have been difficult for a single port to handle the unloading, encampment, and supply of such a large force; thus, the Egyptian ships probably landed at more than one port, most likely Simyra and Ullaza to the north, which were closer to the entrance to the Eleutheros Valley.

The texts tell us, "My Majesty sailed to the northern border of Asia."[8] This statement has led some to believe Thutmose avoided the route to the interior that ran through the Eleutheros Valley that he had taken during an earlier campaign. Instead, some have suggested, the Egyptians must have landed not at Byblos but farther north, perhaps at Arvad and Ugarit. From there, they could have crossed the Lebanon Mountains, arrived from the west outside of Qatna, and taken that city. This northern route avoided the Eleutheros Valley and the city of Kadesh entirely.[9] This explanation fails on several grounds. First, Arvad's port was too small to handle such a large fleet. Second, no evidence exists that Ugarit was within the Egyptian sphere of influence at this time, and it is not mentioned as one of the port cities that Thutmose captured and turned into supply depots. Third, no easy passage runs through the Lebanon Mountains from Arvad to Qatna. The same texts tell us that the Egyptian army was encumbered by wagons; therefore, it is unlikely that Thutmose would have chosen a much more difficult route for his army to follow than the one through the Eleutheros Valley. Fourth, the theory ignores the fact that Qatna was already within Egyptian control, if only diplomatically, and did not have to be captured to gain access to the Orontes River crossing. More likely the phrase "the northern border of Asia" is only the scribe's idea of where Lebanon was located and not the precise geographic location of where the Egyptian army landed.

Once ashore on the Lebanon coast, the texts say, "My Majesty ordered that many ships be built from cedar from the mountains of God's Land and in the neighborhood of the Mistress of Byblos. They were placed on chariots and towed by bulls. They traveled ahead of my Majesty to ferry across the river that is between this foreign land and Naharin."[10] Here is evidence of Thutmose's brilliant military mind at work. He ordered the construction of landing craft to ferry his army across the Euphrates so he could carry the battle to the Mitanni. It is operational planning at its best. The Euphrates is a formidable barrier and is almost two miles wide in some places where it touches northeastern Syria. Without boats to cross this mighty barrier, the campaign against the Mitanni would not have been possible.

What kind of boats could be built and transported 270 miles overland "on chariots towed by bulls"? Obviously a boat of sufficient size to be useful in ferrying troops would be far too heavy to be transported overland. Instead, R. O. Faulkner suggests, the boats might have been built in sections that were then transported to the Euphrates, where they were reassembled for use.[11] How these craft were constructed, disassembled, and then reassembled is not immediately clear in light of several factors, not the least of which is that the nail and screw were not in wide use (and not at all in Egypt). More likely, what Thutmose had constructed in Byblos were rafts and not proper boats as such. It would have been a far easier task to fell the long cedar logs from the Lebanon Mountains; mill them flat on one side; notch and drill the holes that would fasten them together with wooden dowels, pegs, and papyrus rope; load the prepared logs on wagons; and then assemble them when the army reached the Euphrates. A raft thirty feet long and twenty feet wide, enough to hold seventy troops and their equipment, could easily have been constructed and transported in this manner. They could even have been equipped with steering oars and small stepped masts and sails, assuming that Thutmose intended to use them to sail down the Euphrates.

How were the rafts transported overland? When the texts say, "They were placed on chariots towed by bulls," it means that the rafts were placed on wagons towed by oxen.[12] This observation is interesting since the four-wheeled wagon was unknown to the Egyptians at this time. Two-wheeled carts that resembled chariots with a carrying box where the cab was usually located were the Egyptian army's primary means of mechanical military transport. Given that it is impossible for a two-wheeled cart to carry twenty- and thirty-foot logs, it is likely that four-wheeled wagons were used to transport the rafts. Not having seen these contraptions before, the Egyptians had no word for them and called them by the familiar name of chariots, which, to some degree, they resembled. The Hittites appear to have used the four-wheeled wagon at the time, and it probably came to Syria from the north.[13] Thutmose's use of wagons during his campaign is the first use of four-wheeled wagons in Egyptian military history. Yet, Egyptian armies did appear to have adopted the vehicle generally for later military use. They are not in evidence, for example, in the camp of Ramses II at the battle of Kadesh a century later.[14]

The decision to transport the rafts overland using ox-drawn wagons had significant implications for Thutmose's rate of march. Mules, horses, and donkeys can easily march twenty miles a day with full pack loads, even while towing a two-wheeled cart. The yoke and collar used to tether oxen in antiquity pressed hard upon the animals' windpipe, increasing the rate at which the animals became exhausted.[15] Furthermore, oxen move more slowly than mules do. A mule-drawn wagon can easily make nineteen miles a day, whereas an ox-drawn wagon can average only eight to ten miles a day.[16] Unencumbered by oxcarts, the Egyptian army could have moved twelve to fifteen miles a day, covering almost a third more distance. Assuming no further impediments, however, Thutmose's army and its wagons would take thirty-five days to reach the Euphrates.

Determining Thutmose's route of march through Syria to the Euphrates is complicated by a lingering academic debate regarding the source materials. In fact, Thutmose's march route can be deduced only from a single source, Amenemhab's tomb inscriptions. They describe a series of battles and skirmishes in which he claims to have participated during the Euphrates campaign.[17] One side of the debate argues that the events Amenemhab described are arranged chronologically so that the route of march follows the sequence of events as it evolves in the tomb inscriptions. The other side suggests that the sequence is not chronological at all but thematic. Thus, the route of march cannot be deduced from the order of events portrayed in the inscriptions.[18] There is, however, a third possibility. When the events and locations described in the Amenemhab inscriptions are placed next to a map of the theater of operations, military logic and operational necessity can be used to suggest a route of march and order of events that, while it conflicts with the claims of both sides of the academic debate, seem to make practical military sense and fall within the Egyptian army's operational capabilities, namely, its rates of march, distances, human endurance, geography, logistics, and so on. Map 7.1 depicts the deductions about Thutmose's route of march.

The most direct axis of advance from the debarkation ports on the Lebanon coast to the Orontes River Valley to northeast Syria was through the Eleutheros Valley. Thutmose was already in control of the valley's entrance, the Arka Plain, and some of the inland agricultural towns in the valley itself. The Egyptian troops that landed at Simyra were closer to the valley's entrance than those units that landed at Byblos. It would have taken a few days for those troops and the log-laden wagons to cover the thirty miles from Byblos to the army's final line of departure at the mouth of the Eleutheros Valley. It is almost forty miles from the line of departure to where the valley exits the mountains five miles north of Kadesh on the open plain, or a five-day march. Assuming an eight-day journey by boat to the Lebanon coast, another twenty days to off-load the army and cut and mill the timber for the rafts, and another five days' march to the Kadesh

7.1. THUTMOSE'S ROUTE OF MARCH TO THE EUPHRATES RIVER

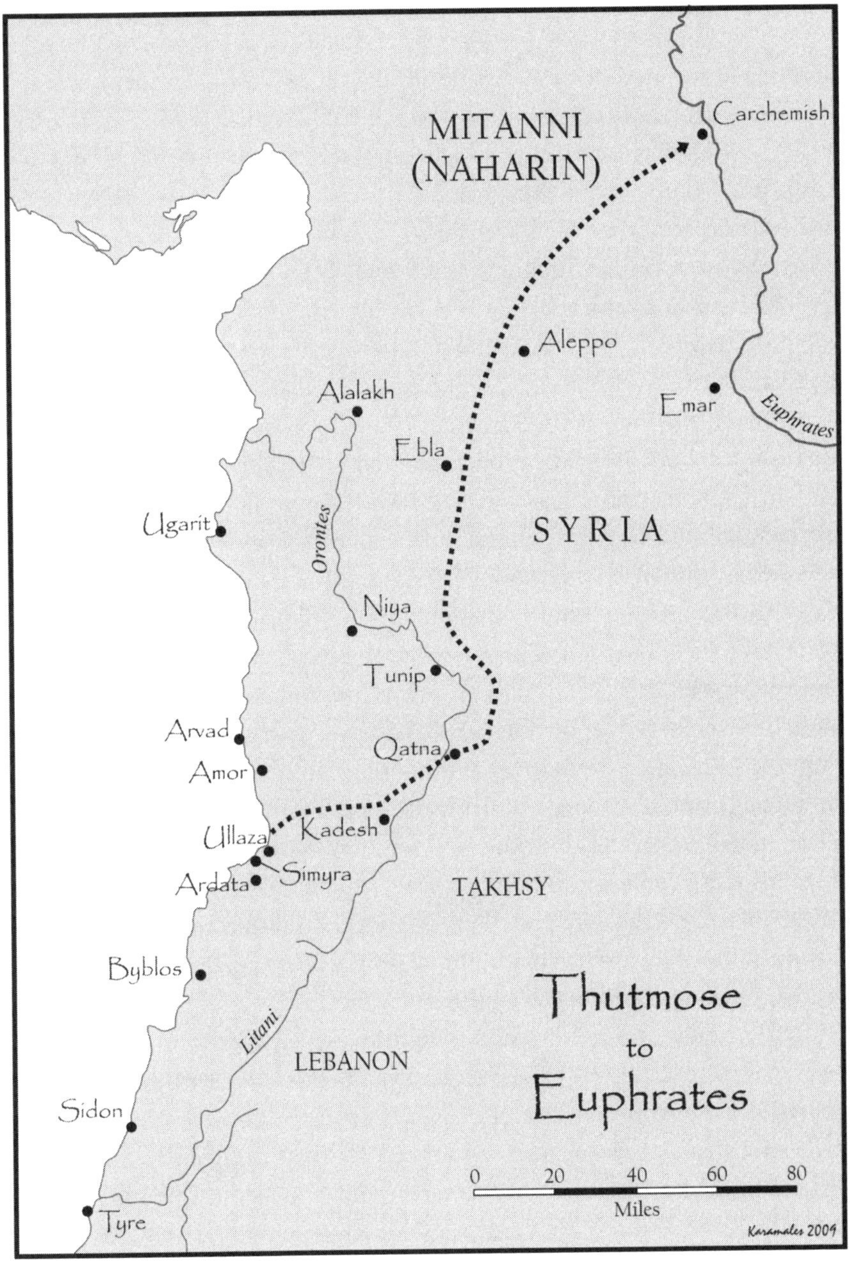

Plain, Thutmose's army had already been in the field longer than a month before he reached the Orontes Valley.

The Orontes arises in the east of the Beqqa Valley from natural springs. From there it runs due north, falling two thousand feet through a great gorge until emptying in the Lake of Homs. Beyond is a broad valley of rich farmland upon which stood the cities of Qatna, on the east bank, and Tunip, on the west bank. Farther to the north, just beyond the agricultural region of modern Hamah, stood the city of Niya, probably the Apamea of classical times. The Orontes is largely non-navigable, and the river's historical importance lies in the convenient axis of advance it has provided for armies throughout antiquity. The battles of Kadesh (1275 BCE) and Qarqar (853 BCE) were fought on its banks.

When the van of the Egyptian army approached the plain around Kadesh, its body stretched back for ten to twelve miles.[19] Thutmose had to consider the possibility that Kadesh would offer resistance to his passage and probably prepared for an attack by sending his chariot squadrons forward in considerable strength to clear the valley's exit. Only an incompetent enemy commander would not have employed his reconnaissance units to keep watch on the Egyptians as they approached the valley exit, and the Egyptian army must have been an impressive sight as it emerged upon the plain. The size of the Egyptian force was larger by several orders of magnitude than anything Kadesh could put in the field, and the silence of the texts is probably an accurate indication that the prince of Kadesh thought discretion the better part of valor and kept his main force inside the city walls. Thutmose and the grand army of Egypt passed through the plain of Kadesh and into the Orontes River Valley without incident. That night when the army camped downstream, its rearguard was still in the Eleutheros Valley.

Thutmose's route of march took him next to the vicinity of Qatna, where, if we can believe the texts, he remained for two or three days and toured a workshop that manufactured bows.[20] Qatna was located twelve miles northeast of Homs near the end of the road connecting the middle Euphrates Valley to the Mediterranean and was some thirty-five miles from the Eleutheros Valley exit, or four days' march. Three days after leaving Qatna, the Egyptian army reached Tunip, which was twenty-six miles distant from Qatna.[21] We might reasonably surmise that it was here that Thutmose returned the son of the king of Tunip whom he had captured at Ullaza. From there Thutmose marched to Aleppo sixty miles away, a journey that took eight days.

Thutmose's route of march through the Orontes Valley shows him to have been a superb logistician. The route along the river ensured his army and its large number of animals would have a sufficient supply of water. All the towns and settlements that the Egyptians passed through were located in the fertile agricultural belt of the Orontes. It was mid-June and the harvest was coming in, so the army could replenish its food stores from the agricultural towns along the route.[22] As with most later armies and those of classical antiquity, the Egyptian army could carry only enough supplies to last about ten days before the supplies had to be replenished.[23] Thutmose's line of march was planned so that each location where he could replenish the army's supplies was no more than ten days' march from the previous stop. The longest march across the steppe, from Aleppo to Carchemish, was only seventy miles or just under ten days.

By a shrewd combination of diplomacy and intimidation, Thutmose had moved his army from the Lebanon coast to Aleppo's outskirts without having to fight a single battle. Along the way his army had been well supplied with food and water, and except for the wastage of men and animals that inevitably took its toll on any army on the march, the Egyptian army was in good fighting condition.[24] It fought its first battle of the campaign at the Height of W'an just west of Aleppo.

Geography, politics, and logistics made some sort of skirmish around Aleppo inevitable. Aleppo was a key ally of the Mitanni and the last allied state between the Egyptians and the Mitannian homeland. It was also the final military obstacle to Thutmose's advance. Aleppo was on the edge of the last agricultural region before the barren steppe that separated the city from the Euphrates. An army seeking to gain the steppe from the Orontes basin had to pass almost under Aleppo's walls. Thutmose needed access to the region's food supplies to sustain his army while crossing the steppe. The Egyptians could not bypass the city to the east because close to the city the ground was marshy and wet. To avoid the marshes by marching farther east would have forced the Egyptians to march into the rocky desert and to attempt the steppe's crossing without replenishing their food supplies. Moreover, the eastern route left Aleppo on the Egyptians' flank with all the possibilities that implied for an attack. The Egyptian army had already been on the march for almost eight days since leaving Tunip, and most of their field rations were already gone. Thutmose ordered his army to march west of Aleppo, plundering the countryside for the supplies he needed to cross the steppe and march on Carchemish.

Amenemhab records that he took part in some sort of skirmish before the battle at the Height of W'an near Aleppo.[25] He tells us, "When his Majesty came to Naharin, I brought off three men from the fight there; I set them before thy Majesty as living prisoners."[26] Then later he tells us, "Again I fought hand-to-hand on that expedition in the land of the Height of W'an on the west of Aleppo. I brought off thirteen Asiatics as living prisoners; 13 men, 70 living donkeys, 13 bronze spears, the bronze was wrought with gold."[27] We learn later from Amenemhab's tomb inscriptions that he was a member of the King's Braves, an elite infantry unit.

Amenemhab's capture of living prisoners and living donkeys suggests that the action he participated in was not against Aleppo's regular forces, or one would have expected him to have produced "hands," that is, the severed hands of those he killed. Rather, it is likely that the incident Amenemhab recorded was one of scores like it that occurred when Thutmose's army began to plunder the countryside and confiscate food supplies and anything else of value the army needed. If so, the fight would have been against small contingents of militia or coteries of local vassals defending their farms. The rulers of Aleppo surely knew that the Egyptian army lacked the siege technology to overcome a city fortified with rock walls and probably sealed themselves up inside their fortifications until the Egyptian storm passed. No doubt this situation suited Thutmose well for he had no interest in attempting to overcome Aleppo. Seizing its food supply and intimidating its rulers into inaction were sufficient. Thutmose observed one of the basic principles of the operational art of war by maintaining the strategic direction of his army.

Crossing the steppe between Aleppo and Carchemish occurred without incident. Pastoral nomads sparsely settled the area, thus there were few settlements from which opposition might have been mounted. The Egyptians' next engagement occurred outside of Carchemish. Amenemhab tells us that "again I fought on that expedition in the land of Carchemish."[28] Thutmose made no attempt to attack Carchemish itself, and as with the other cities that Thutmose passed, the rulers of Carchemish closed their gates and waited for the Egyptians to pass. The engagement of which Amenemhab speaks, again, was probably no more than a skirmish, perhaps with the militia forces of some agricultural manor or town in the fertile region along the Euphrates' banks.

The Battle

The army rested a few days and replenished its supplies from the stores confiscated from the farms on the river's west bank. The four-mile-wide area around Carchemish, which the Egyptians called Karakamisha, was a rich agricultural region stretching three miles north and six miles south of the city itself on the Euphrates' west bank. A larger fertile area almost eight miles wide and running south for thirteen miles occupied the east bank of the river.[29] Carchemish guarded the place where the Euphrates narrows into two streams and is separated by a number of large islands that serve to narrow the river's width and weaken its current as well. The distance from the west bank to the largest island is only seventy-five meters. The island itself is about three hundred meters wide. The second stream on the far side of the island is one hundred meters wide. It was here, using the islands as a midpoint on the river, that Thutmose probably crossed the Euphrates.

The texts tell us, however, that Thutmose's army crossed the Euphrates at the place called the Great Bend: "Thutmose III crossed the Great Bend of Naharin with might and with victory at the head of his army."[30] The geography of the area disputes this notion. The Great Bend is some eighty miles south of Carchemish along a route that passes through rocky desert for most of the distance. Once at the Great Bend, the river cuts through limestone cliffs and ledges, creating high banks that make access to the river's edge very difficult. At the center point of the Great Bend, the width of the Euphrates is almost five miles. Most important, however, is that Thutmose had no good military reason to cross at the Great Bend. Except for the town of Emar, which seems to have been little more than a donkey caravan stop, there were insufficient food and water supplies in the area to restock his army, no agricultural settlements to draw stores from, and no enemy armies to engage. It is likely that the texts' claim that Thutmose crossed at the Great Bend is an exaggeration.

The Egyptians were a river people, and crossing the narrow streams of the Euphrates near Carchemish presented no problem. The pre-milled, predrilled, and pre-notched timbers carried on the wagons were easily assembled by driving wooden pegs into the holes and lashing the timbers together with papyrus rope. One imagines that the rafts had railings around the edges to prevent the soldiers and animals from falling overboard during the crossing. A long length of papyrus rope tied to each end of the raft and held by gangs of men on each shore allowed the raft to be floated and guided to a landing point on the opposite shore. The empty raft could then be pulled back across the river, reloaded, and floated across once more.

A raft thirty feet long and twenty feet wide could accommodate about 16,200 pounds of weight before sinking. Thus, it could safely transport seventy soldiers and their equipment across the river. It would have taken a single raft no more than three trips to transport an Egyptian infantry company of two hundred men. The same size raft could accommodate fifteen horses or thirty donkeys and mules per trip. We do not know how many rafts Thutmose hauled overland to the Euphrates, but assuming four wagons could carry a single raft, a column of only forty wagons would have easily transported ten rafts.[31] Using ten rafts to make the crossing, each raft would have had to make only 21 trips, or 214 trips total, to move the entire infantry contingent of fifteen thousand men across the river. A total of 167 trips was required to transport the 2,500 chariot horses. Since Thutmose did not intend to move deep into Mitannian territory, we may safely assume that the donkeys and mules were left on the west bank. With each raft making about twelve trips a day, Thutmose would have been able to transport his combat army across the Euphrates in about three days.

How much of the army needed to cross the river depended on Thutmose's intentions. The most likely surmise is that he intended to meet the Mitannian army in battle with the goal of destroying it. Crossing the river was designed to draw the enemy to him, forcing it to fight on the borders of its territory and distant from its supply bases. The land between the Euphrates and the cities of the Mitannian interior was sparse and afforded few opportunities for an invader to live off the land, making it unlikely that Thutmose thought driving inland and attacking the capital were possible. Thus, to fight a decisive battle, Thutmose needed his entire combat army on the east bank.

The Gebel Barkal stela tells of a great battle between the Egyptians and the Mitanni that took place on the east bank of the Euphrates in which "the numerous army of the Mitanni was cast down in one hour. They have disappeared completely as those who never were, like an end of the Devourer, by act of the arms of the great good god, strong in battle, who causes slaughter among everyone."[32] Ostensibly the battle was with the Mitannian king,[33] but the list of booty taken from the defeated army belies the claim that a great battle was fought. The booty consisted of 3 chiefs, 30 of their wives and children, 606 male and female servants and their children, and 80 men at arms.[34] These are hardly the numbers and items we would expect if a major armed force had met defeat on the plain of the Euphrates. The texts do not mention any captured arms, armor, chariots, horses, prisoners, and, above all, enemy hands. At best, the Egyptians seem to have defeated only a local garrison of Mitannian troops and certainly not the king's main army.

There must, however, have been some sort of engagement because the texts tell of Thutmose chasing an enemy force that fled before him. The *Annals* indicate that Thutmose "pursued them after for an *iter*, and not one looked behind him, but fled headlong like herds of game, for their horses bolted."[35] An iter is a measure of length or distance between two and ten kilometers long.[36] The term occurs in the inscription along with the word *Skdwt,* which means "as boats travel."[37] *Skdwt* is an idiomatic phrase properly taken to mean something similar to "as the crow flies" rather than to imply that Thutmose sailed down the Euphrates in pursuit of his enemy. To have done so would have made no military sense. Ten miles downstream from Carchemish the land turns to rocky desert with insufficient arable land to support agriculture or a retreating army. Whatever force engaged Thutmose on the east bank would have logically retreated due east toward the capital of Washukkanni about 140 miles away. The soldiers would have withdrawn farther into the interior of their homeland, where troops, garrisons, and walled towns could have come to their aid. It appears unlikely that Thutmose would have sailed downstream on the Euphrates. More likely he would have marched down the east bank through the agricultural region for about ten kilometers until he met the desert, at which point he would have turned back toward Carchemish.

The texts suggest that is exactly what happened: "Behold, his Majesty went north capturing the towns and laying waste the settlements of that foe of wretched Naharin."[38] At some point as Thutmose ravaged the countryside, a small force of hastily formed militia troops from three towns turned out to fight the Egyptians but were quickly crushed.[39] The Mitannian regulars were nowhere to be found, "having fled pell-mell, like herds of wild game."[40] The texts reveal in great detail the destruction Thutmose wrought on the land of the Mitanni:

> I destroyed his cities and his settlements and I set fire to them. My Majesty turned them into ruins, so that they could not be rebuilt. I captured all their people who were carried off as prisoners, and the cattle thereof without bound, and likewise their property. I took their grain, I tore out their barley, I felled their trees, all their fruit trees. Their region was killed, my Majesty destroyed it. It has become a burnt place where there are no trees.[41]

Years before, Thutmose's grandfather, Thutmose I, had led a military expedition to the Euphrates and later erected a victory stela on the river's east bank. Now his grandson did the same thing. According to the *Annals*, "He set up a tablet east of this water [Euphrates River]; he set up another beside the tablet of his father, the king of Upper and Lower Egypt, Okheperkere [Thutmose I]."[42] Thutmose's stela was probably set up on the heights north of Carchemish and was either inscribed on a quarried stone or on the face of a natural rock there. Just when Thutmose erected the stela remains a mystery. The Gebel Barkal stela says he erected it following the defeat and flight of the Mitannian king while the Armant stela tells us it was erected after he conducted the river crossing and plundered the river towns. The *Annals,* however, claim the stela was put in place immediately before the Egyptians left on the return march to Syria. The last alternative makes the most sense.

Placing a victory stela on the heights of Carchemish had great symbolic importance in the Egyptians' eyes. To Egyptians, the stela marked the new boundary of Egyptian influence and power. Its erection on the territory of the Mitanni signified that the Mitanni were now a client state of Egypt and subject to Pharaoh's rule.[43] In reality, of course, it was not true. Thutmose's raid had not changed the balance of power between the antagonists at all, and the Mitanni remained a great power for another fifty years. But in the Egyptians' eyes, Thutmose had utterly defeated the great power to the east.

The Euphrates campaign had an unanticipated political consequence that fell to Egypt's advantage. After Thutmose returned to Egypt, the king of the Hittites sent an emissary to Pharaoh bearing gifts of silver, wood, and precious stone. Presumably the mission's purpose was to open diplomatic relations between the two countries. In its march west of Aleppo on its way to Carchemish, the Egyptian army had passed close to the Syrian Gates, the mountain pass that led to the Hittites' territory. The size of the Egyptian army and its ability to project military force over such great distances must have caused the Hittites to worry that one day Egyptian power would be aimed at them. And, indeed, they were right. Over the next century, the area of northwest Syria and the Syrian Gates, the area the Hittites called the land of Amaru, became the arena of conflict between the two powers. Thutmose's demonstration of Egyptian military might led the Hittites to conclude that they should open diplomatic contacts with Egypt. The mention of the Hittite diplomatic mission in Egyptian texts is the first appearance of the Hittites in the historical record.[44]

The Attack on Kadesh

Thutmose and his army did not linger for more than a week or so while replenishing their supplies from the agricultural area around Carchemish to sustain them on their return march. A recently discovered inscribed block in the Egyptian Museum of Cairo tells the story of Thutmose's return march through the steppe between Aleppo and the Euphrates: "My Majesty commanded to bring it outside for me. Then in order to tread the roads of this country . . . His Majesty commanded to have organized . . . Then His Majesty dispatched the army and the chariotry to plunder this settlement. Then . . . these towns were set afire."[45] The term *town* used in the inscription indicates rural settlements, the type commonly found on the steppe, and not fortified urban centers. This description suggests that Thutmose was destroying those settlements in the region that were allied with Aleppo and the Mitanni.[46] Presumably Thutmose had left these settlements unmolested on his outward march in order to save time and to conserve his army's combat power and had planned to deal with them on his return.

One of the objectives of the Euphrates campaign was to place under Egyptian control the area south and west of Aleppo and the Orontes Valley as far south as the river's headwaters at modern Baalbek. Egyptian diplomacy had neutralized the power of Tunip and Qatna, if only temporarily, and the march to the Euphrates had isolated Aleppo. The Egyptians had demonstrated how the latter's agricultural regions could be ravaged at will even though the city itself had not been captured. Kadesh was now the only remaining obstacle to Egyptian success. The Egyptian army had been in the field for almost three months, and if Thutmose had plans to deal with Kadesh he first had to rest and replenish his army. After a march of more than a hundred miles from the Euphrates' banks, the Egyptian army had arrived at Niya, where it rested to regain its strength.

The *Annals* do not offer any record of Thutmose's return march; instead, they jump from setting up the boundary stela directly to marking the king's arrival at the town of Niya. "His Majesty arrived at the city of Niya, going southward, when his Majesty returned [from the Euphrates] having set up his tablet in Naharin, extending the boundaries of Egypt."[47] Niya was probably located on the west bank of the Orontes overlooking the Ghab Valley, some thirty miles northwest of modern Hamah, and between Aleppo to the north and Kadesh to the south. It is probably the biblical Shepham and the Apamea of classical times. The area affords good supplies of food and water.

Thutmose rested the army at Niya for only a week or so, during which time he took part in an elephant hunt. His grandfather had stopped once at Niya too and had hunted elephants while returning from his Euphrates campaign. His grandfather's example seems to have been very much in Thutmose's mind. He tells us, "He granted me another brave deed by the sea of Niya. He made me drive together a herd of elephants. My Majesty fought them, they being a herd of 120 elephants."[48]

Amenemhab's account of the elephant hunt is more dramatic:

7.2. THUTMOSE'S RETURN ROUTE FROM CARCHEMISH TO EGYPT

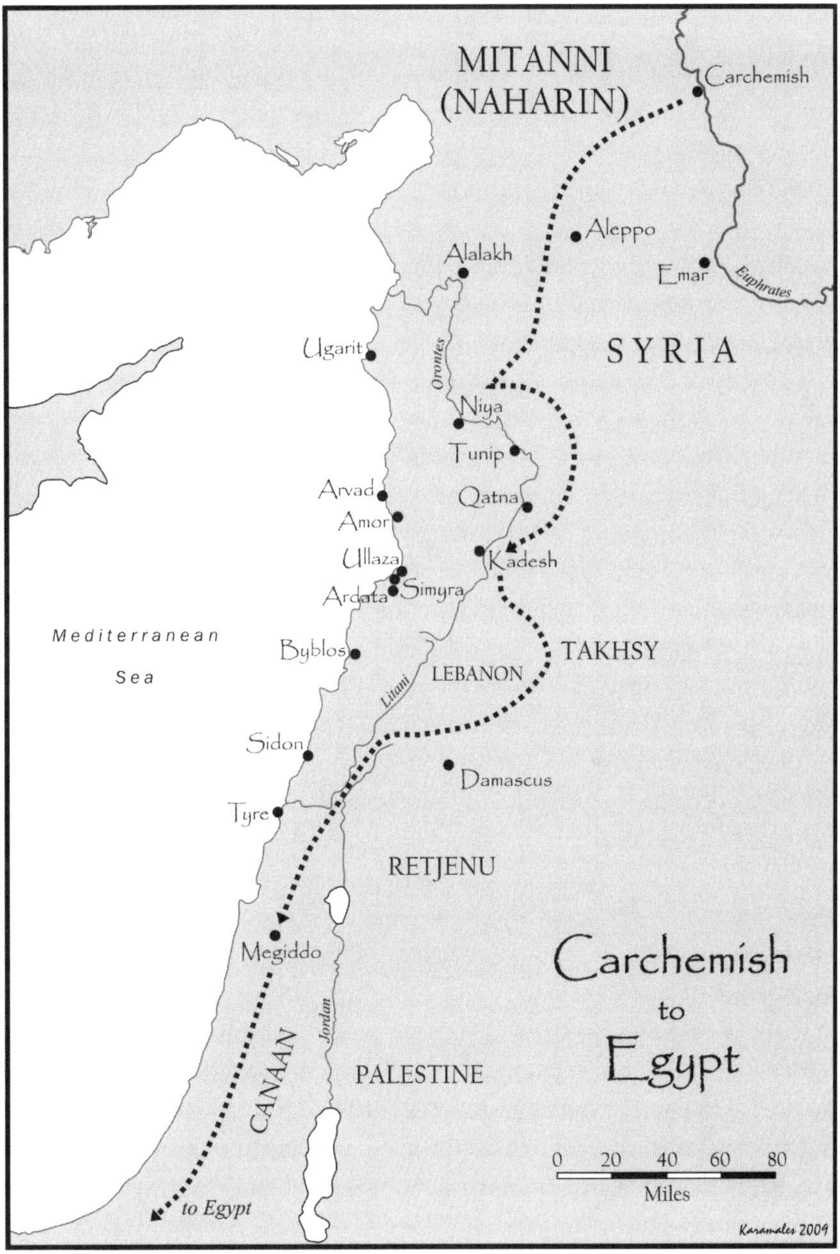

> Again I beheld another excellent deed which the Lord of the Two Lands did in Niya. He hunted 120 elephants, for the sake of their tusks and . . . I engaged the largest which was among them, which fought against his Majesty; I cut off his hand [the animal's trunk] while he was alive before his Majesty, while I stood in the water between the rocks. He gave me joy, it filled my body with rejoicing, he endued my limbs.[49]

An elephant hunt was no doubt dangerous business, and Amenemhab is not shy about screaming his own praises in his tomb inscriptions, which were meant to last for eternity.[50]

With the army now replenished, Thutmose ordered it to move south toward Kadesh, sixty-five miles away. His route took him back over the Orontes River and to the hard ground of the east bank. Traveling on the east bank permitted Thutmose to bypass Tunip and avoid disrupting the fragile relationship he had arranged a few months earlier by returning the king's captured son. The Egyptians arrived at Qatna, where they remained for a day or two to prepare the army for its assault on Kadesh.

The *Annals* are silent about the attack on Kadesh, forcing an uncomfortable reliance once more on the venerable Amenemhab's account. Even here, however, we have a problem. Amenemhab records a chariot battle and an attack on Kadesh's walls. The question is whether the events are part of the same campaign or, as Henry James Breasted believes, are parts of two separate campaigns against Kadesh. If Donald B. Redford is correct that Thutmose never captured Kadesh either in this campaign or later in regnal year 42, we might reasonably see the two tales as different phases of the same campaign against Kadesh, first a battle of chariots in the open field and then an Egyptian infantry attempt to storm the city.

It must have been early August when Thutmose moved against Kadesh, allowing himself about a month to contend with it before he had to turn for home. The march from Kadesh to Egypt would take some thirty-seven days, bringing Thutmose back to Egypt around late September or early October. Consequently, Thutmose did not have enough time to overcome Kadesh by siege, which, given the Egyptians' lack of siege technology, meant starving out the defenders in any case. The harvest was already in, and the city's stores were sufficient to last the winter.

If Thutmose was going to capture Kadesh, he would have to entice its defenders into a battle on open ground or take the city by storm.

The terrain around the city is ideal chariot country, and it seems likely that some sort of chariot battle or at least a skirmish took place there. Kadesh's army was a chariot-heavy force of maryannu warriors, and logically they would have tried to engage the Egyptian chariots on familiar ground. Amenemhab's tomb inscriptions begin by noting, "The prince of Kadesh sent forth a mare before the army; in order to [disrupt] them, she entered among the army."[51] The implication is that two chariot forces were arrayed before each other in a set-piece battle. Amenemhab goes on to tell how he "pursued after her on foot, with my sword, and I ripped open her belly; I cut off her tail, I set it before the king; while there was thanksgiving to god for it!"[52] Amenemhab seems to be taking credit for saving the army from disorganization by killing the mare before its scent could excite the Egyptian chariot horses to unruly behavior. Unfortunately, he tells us nothing more about the battle.

The tale of the mare leads one to suspect that Amenemhab, an infantry officer and not a chariot officer, knew little about horses. Chariot horses were not stallions but geldings and would not have been interested in the scent of a mare in season.[53] Stallions, which are fiercely competitive with other stallions, are castrated because geldings possess a calmer temperament that allows trainers to work them together and stable them side by side.[54] Egyptian booty lists often make distinctions between captured horses and stallions, suggesting that stallions were not usually used as war horses but kept for stud.[55] The ancients were well aware of the association of stallions with traits of courage and virility, and kings were eager to associate themselves with these characteristics. It is not impossible, then, that the horses of the king and other high-ranking officers might have been stallions. Certainly the war art of Egypt and other countries in the Bronze Age seems to have gone to great lengths to convince people that their leaders' horses were stallions. Scores of bas reliefs and other portrayals of warhorses show them as animals with intact genitalia. A closer examination of these portrayals, however, reveals that the placement of the genitalia is anatomically incorrect, that is, located farther toward the center of the horse than normal in order to make them more visible than they would appear in reality.[56] In this way, kings portrayed their gelded war horses as true stallions.

Amenemhab's tale is questionable on other counts. First, it is unclear how he would have caught up with the mare on foot. Second, his claim that "with my sword I ripped open her belly; I cut off her tail" seems disingenuous. The basic weapon of the Egyptian infantry was the curved sickle-sword, a weapon completely unsuited for stabbing. Even assuming Amenemhab could muster the force a somewhat dull bronze blade would require to bring down a horse, it is unclear how he would have landed the blow on an animal that was quite a bit taller than he was. Killing a horse is no easy matter. A thousand-pound horse has some one hundred pints of blood; it can lose 30 percent of it and live. Horses have excellent hemostatic systems that cause blood vessels to retract into the tissues and seal themselves off. Even when an artery is cut, a horse takes hours to bleed to death.[57] The only certain way he could have brought down the horse was to strike it between the eyes with an ax. Finally, Amenemhab's paucity of knowledge of horses is revealed further in that killing the mare would not have eliminated her scent or its effects on the stallions. Since the mare's scent would have affected the horses of Kadesh as well as those of the Egyptians, presumably the noses of the Canaanite stallions were swabbed with some potent-smelling salve to mask the mare's smell.[58]

Whatever skirmish or battle was fought on the plain of Kadesh, it must have been inconclusive, with the maryanna retiring behind the safety of the city's walls. Thutmose then mounted an attack on the city by storm. Given the Egyptians' advantage in manpower, the most appropriate method of attack was for the archers to lay down heavy covering fire to keep the defenders off the battlements while assault troops rushed the walls and tried to reach the top using scaling ladders. Thutmose's elite infantry, the King's Braves, of which Amenemhab was a member, was renowned for being the first to attack a city's walls. The Egyptian shield, with the shoulder strap attached to its inner surface, was well suited to the task of protecting the soldiers during the assault. Slung over the soldier's back in the fashion of a turtle's shell, it protected his body while leaving his hands free to make the climb and fight once over the walls.

Simultaneous with the attack on the walls, other troops attacked the gates. With their shields covering their backs, assault troops armed with axes hacked at the gate's bolts and hinges in order to bring it down. Both of these operations required brave and disciplined troops. Amenemhab numbered himself among them. He tells us, "His Majesty sent forth every valiant man of his army, in order to pierce the wall for the first time, which Kadesh had made. I was the one who pierced it, being the first of all the valiant; no other before me did it. I went forth, I brought off [captured] two men as prisoners."[59] Amenemhab's use of the word *pierced* might suggest that he was among those attacking the gate rather than those trying to scale the walls.

Although Thutmose must have repeatedly attempted to storm the city, in the end Kadesh's defenses held and the city did not fall.[60] The *Annals* are ominously silent regarding the outcome of Thutmose's attack against Kadesh, and even the boastful Amenemhab does not claim that they captured the city. If they had, there would have been no need for Thutmose to attack it again in regnal year 42. That attack, too, failed. The repeated Egyptian attacks undoubtedly produced high casualties, and after several failed attempts Thutmose may have thought better of it and simply withdrew. It is also possible that events elsewhere needed his attention.

Two tomb inscriptions, one from Amenemhab and the other from one Minmose the Engineer, suggest that some sort of trouble had broken out in the land of Takhsy and may have forced Thutmose to break off the attack on Kadesh to quell it. Just southeast of Kadesh, Takhsy lay between northern Canaan and Damascus, not more than two days' march away. In the area of the northern Beqqa Valley, Takhsy was well within the Egyptians' sphere of influence in Canaan. It was a land of Asiatic bedouins and Sashu, who, along with the Apiru, sometimes resorted to banditry. The texts do not reveal the nature of the problem, but it may be suspected that some of the towns in the area had fallen prey to bedouin banditry. With the assault on Kadesh meeting stiff resistance, Thutmose may have taken the news of the problem in Takhsy as an opportunity to break off the attack without losing royal prestige. It may also account for why the *Annals* are silent regarding the Kadesh operation.

The fighting in Takhsy must have been significant. Amenemhab tells us, "I fought hand-to-hand therein before the king. I brought off Asiatics, three men as living prisoners."[61] Minmose's tomb inscription conveys some additional details: "I saw how the arm of His Majesty waxed strong when he took to fighting, plundering thirty towns within the region of Takhsy whence their chiefs, chattels, and cattle were brought off."[62] Minmose's reference to towns is to be understood as bedouin villages or camps and, perhaps, small agricultural settlements. The number of settlements involved, however, suggests that Thutmose's operations in Takhsy were extensive. Perhaps they were part of a search-and-destroy campaign to punish the perpetrators and raze their logistical base.

Assuming operations in Takhsy required two weeks to complete, it was then late August, and Thutmose turned for home by overland march. From his position in the northern Beqqa Valley, the Egyptian army could have easily reached the main base at Megiddo in a few days. From there Thutmose reversed the route he had taken to Megiddo, marching up the Aruna road and across the Carmel Range to Yehem. From there it was an easy march to Gaza, then to the frontier forts at Sile, and on to Perunefer, where Thutmose boarded a boat and sailed south to Thebes, arriving in time for the October festival. The journey would have taken a little longer than a month.

It had been almost two months since Thutmose had arrived on the coast of Lebanon by sea until he reached the Euphrates. His return march took him through country that was politically hostile and past city-states that were sworn allies of the Mitannian king. One would have thought that Mitannian agents and diplomats assigned to these allies would have sent their couriers to inform their superiors that Thutmose was on the move. Why, then, was the king of the Mitanni caught by surprise? Why did the Egyptians not encounter any opposition to their river crossing? Why was there no Mitannian army to meet Thutmose in battle after the Egyptians had crossed?

The answer lies in Thutmose's brilliant use of strategic deception. Except for the occupation of the Lebanon ports, Thutmose's previous campaigns in Syria had only involved raids designed to march into an area, damage the countryside, take away what booty the Egyptian army could carry, and force the local chiefs to acknowledge him as their sovereign. These *chevauchée* raids were not intended to destroy the Syrian city-states or occupy their territory.[63] No Egyptian garrisons had been left behind in the Orontes Valley following any of the Egyptian raids. Until the time that

Thutmose skirmished outside Aleppo, which had heretofore been immune from Egyptian raids, the Mitanni might have reasonably concluded that Thutmose's most recent incursion was just another raid.

Once Thutmose bypassed Aleppo and began moving east, however, it was simply too late for the Mitanni to assemble their army in time to oppose the Egyptian crossing of the Euphrates. It is also possible that the Mitanni failed to assemble the army because they believed that the Euphrates itself presented too formidable an obstacle for the Egyptians. If so, the Egyptians might then ravage the countryside around Carchemish and withdraw. The Mitanni surely understood that the Egyptians could not long remain at the end of their extensive line of communications without incurring serious risks to their rear areas. Even if Thutmose crossed the Euphrates, the Mitanni may have reasoned, he lacked the combat power and logistics to march inland and attack their capital. This sound strategic thinking turned out to be correct.

Although Thutmose failed to take Kadesh, when reviewed as an exercise in military technique, the Euphrates campaign was a success. It represented a brilliant example of strategic deception by psychologically conditioning the Mitanni into thinking they knew the Egyptians' intentions. Thutmose's previous military expeditions had convinced the Mitanni that he harbored no strategic interests beyond southern Syria. Their assumptions permitted him to move his army to within ten days' march of the Euphrates without arousing Mitannian suspicions. By the time he arrived, however, it was too late for the Mitanni to react. Thutmose's use of the sea, the construction of river rafts, and their transport overland with four-wheeled wagons, a military technology heretofore unknown to the Egyptians, all combined perfectly to inflict strategic surprise upon the enemy and represents an excellent operational example of the projection of force in which all elements of the campaign plan were executed perfectly. The military expertise required to move an Egyptian force of 20,000 men and 6,500 animals first by sea for more than 300 miles and then overland for another 275 miles to reach the objective, without being detected, resulted in what surely stands as one of the most outstanding military feats of the Bronze Age.

And yet, when considered from a strategic perspective, the Euphrates campaign was a failure. The campaign did not achieve the strategic

7.3. CHRONOLOGY OF THUTMOSE'S EUPHRATES CAMPAIGN

Sea journey from Perunefer to Byblos	7–8	days
Cutting timber/making prefabricated rafts	15–20	days
March from Byblos to Eleutheros Valley	4	days
March through the Eleutheros Valley	5	days
March from Eleutheros Valley to Qatna	4	days
March from Qatna to Tunip	3	days
March from Tunip to Aleppo	8	days
Skirmishing and foraging at Aleppo	3	days
March from Aleppo to Carchemish	9	days
River crossing	3	days
Ravaging the Euphrates towns/carving stela	10	days
March to Niya/plundering Nukhashshe	15–20	days
Replenishing the army at Niya	7	days
March from Niya to Kadesh	8	days
Attack on Kadesh	4–6	days
Operations in Takhsy	14	days
Return march to Egypt	37	days
Total Time:	**166**	**days**

goal of bringing the army of the Mitanni to battle and destroying it. For all the effort, the Egyptians failed to alter the strategic power of the Mitanni or the strategic balance between the two great powers. The ability of the Mitanni to use their Syrian cat's-paws—Aleppo, Alalakh, Tunip, Qatna, and Kadesh—to foster trouble and instigate revolts in southern Syria was undiminished. It would not be long before Egypt would have to deal with these rebellions.

Although Qatna and Tunip had been neutralized by diplomacy, in the absence of Egyptian garrisons none but the most optimistic observers reasonably expected the peace agreements to hold for very long once Egyptian troops had withdrawn. Aleppo and Alalakh remained strong and loyal allies of the Mitanni, and Thutmose's ravaging of their agricultural areas only strengthened this alliance. The reality was that Egyptian security goals in Syria and the concomitant decline in Mitannian influence there could not be achieved as long as the powerful Syrian city-states could not be captured and garrisoned with Egyptian troops. Thutmose could launch one chevauchée after another, ravaging the cities' agricultural areas as he went, but in the end Egypt lacked the military technology to successfully overcome the stone walls and other defenses of the Syrian cities. Without a siege capability, the Egyptians could make the farmers and vassals of the Syrian rulers suffer from time to time, but the Syrian rulers themselves and their military garrisons remained safe behind the city walls, willing and able to defy the Egyptians' control once their armies left.

In short, Egypt lacked the national power to bring about a strategic decision in southern Syria. At the end of the Euphrates campaign, the sphere of Egyptian influence was pretty much as it had been before the campaign began, that is, mostly confined to Canaan and coastal Lebanon. The Euphrates campaign remains, however, a classic example of the failure, repeated throughout history, to recognize that military force is effective only when it aims at achievable strategic goals. Otherwise, it becomes merely an exercise in technique from which little of strategic value is likely to result. Thutmose's experience in the Euphrates campaign is but the first example in history in which we see the truth of Carl von Clausewitz's later famous dictum that "war is the continuation of policy by other means."

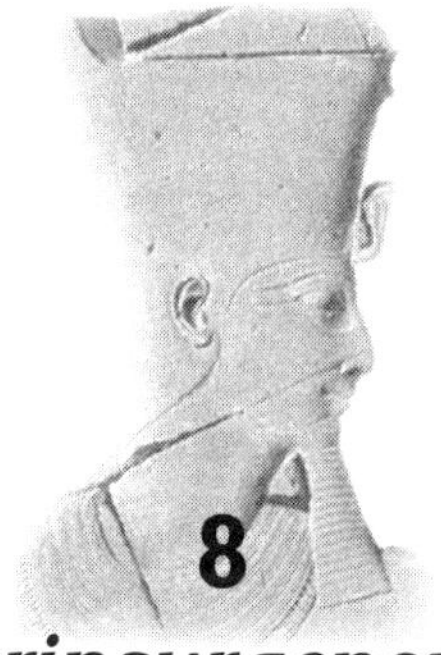

8
The Counterinsurgency Campaign

Thutmose had spent more than a decade carving out an Egyptian sphere of imperial influence in Asia by force of arms. Now he faced the problem of maintaining it. He clearly intended to annex the area of southern Syria at least as far north as Niya and to transform it into an area of Egyptian control, tying it tightly to Egypt perhaps in a manner similar to Nubia. Integrating Syria into the Egyptian realm presented far more difficulties, however, than did Nubia. The military capabilities of the Syrian city-states and principalities were far more formidable than those in Nubia. The key city-states were ruled by professional maryannu warrior castes that had imposed themselves upon the locals more than a century earlier during the Mitannian-Hurrian sweep through Canaan and Egypt. After the warrior pharaohs drove them out of Egypt, some maryannu warrior castes settled in northern Canaan and southern Syria.[1] These warrior castes were capable fighters and unwilling to submit to Egyptian rule.

Lacking a powerful ally willing to support the Nubians' resistance to Egyptian rule facilitated the Egyptians' exertion of control over Nubia. The Syrian city-states and their vassals, however, had the strong support of the Mitanni, a great power that was also geographically contiguous with the Syrian arena of conflict and could be relied on to back a Syrian insurgency. The Mitanni regarded its vassals in Syria as important geopolitical assets to its own national security strategy. These vassal states were located far forward of the Mitannian homeland and made up a strategic buffer zone within which the Mitanni could intercept and engage any attempts from the west by Egypt, and later by the Hittites, to attack the homeland itself. The Syrians knew they could rely on the Mitanni to resist the Egyptians' efforts to establish a sphere of influence in Syria at every opportunity, including encouraging revolts and sending troops to support its Syrian vassals.

Thutmose's efforts to control Syria were further hampered by other factors. The Egyptian army does not appear to have made any improvements in its siege capability that would permit it to quickly reduce the defenses of the major Syrian cities. This shortcoming was not unique among the armies of the day, and not until the Assyrians introduced the battering ram some six centuries later would armies be able to easily defeat the stone-faced casement walls characteristic of Syrian cities.[2] Egypt's ineffectual siege capability meant that the major Syrian city-states were practically invulnerable to Egyptian attacks. The Egyptians could ravage the countryside at will, but they could not crack the cities themselves.

Moreover, no matter how many times Thutmose put down a Syrian revolt or defeated an allied force of the Mitanni in the field, the arena of conflict remained limited to southern Syria. Egypt was unable to project sufficient forces over long distances to invade and defeat the Mitanni in their own homeland. No matter how many expeditions Thutmose undertook, the insurgents knew that at the end of the campaign season the Egyptians would leave and the insurgents would remain to fight another day. Thutmose could fight and defeat the insurgents again and again, but he lacked the means to bring about a strategic decision by defeating the fortified cities or the Mitanni in a decisive manner.

Thutmose's Euphrates campaign did produce some significant diplomatic results, however. The other major states in the region that had strategic security concerns with the Mitanni were quick to normalize or open diplomatic relations with Egypt after its expedition to the Euphrates. Babylon, Assyria, and the Hittites saw the Euphrates campaign as a significant projection of force by a new power in the regional political game, a power that could be used, perhaps, to counter the Mitannian threat. In the short run at least, these states were of no military consequence to Egyptian efforts, although their political support helped legitimize Egyptian control of its possessions in Syria. In the long run, however, the Hittites' support of Egyptian ambitions proved decisive in weakening the Mitanni.

The Strategy

Unable to deliver a strategic blow to the Mitanni, Thutmose embarked on a Syrian policy that today we would call a counterinsurgency strategy. The first goal of Egypt's operational design was to isolate the Syrian city-states from their Mitannian allies, a policy intended to deprive them of the Mitannian political and military support they had been receiving for years. At the same time, Egypt conducted military expeditions in the Mitanni border zone that were intended to keep the Mitanni off balance and force them to guard against the possibility of another military strike at the Euphrates border and perhaps beyond into the homeland itself. The second element of Thutmose's Syrian policy was to conduct frequent military incursions into Syria to demonstrate the Egyptians' willingness to retain their position in the country and to intimidate the Syrian principalities into a grudging acceptance of Egyptian control. This plan involved formal meetings with assembled Syrian rulers, who were obliged to present their tribute to Pharaoh. Whenever a city or town became so reckless as to rise in open revolt, Thutmose moved quickly to crush it. Thutmose intended to convince the rulers of the Syrian principalities that they faced the dilemma of a single alternative; that is, there was no alternative to Egyptian rule.

In 1470 BCE, the year after the Euphrates campaign, Thutmose put his new policy into effect and led an expeditionary force into Syria. The texts tell us that "all the harbors of His Majesty were stocked with every good thing," suggesting that the Egyptians came by sea and still controlled the coastal ports. The expedition's size is not recorded, but it was certainly much smaller than the army of the Euphrates campaign. Perhaps it included a single infantry division and a few companies of chariots, or a force of some five thousand to six thousand men. The Egyptians marched through the Eleutheros Valley; past Kadesh, which they had attacked the year before; and down the Orontes River to Qatna, where they crossed the river and entered the region known as Nukhashshe.

Nukhashshe was a triangle-shaped district formed by a line running north from Qatna and northeast of Aleppo (92 miles), then directly east to Emar (which the Egyptians called Donkey-town) on the western edge of the Great Bend of the Euphrates (46 miles), and back southwest to Qatna (100 miles).[3] The area is mostly a steppe and is inhabited by nomadic and pastoral people who are organized into clans and tribes with no other higher form of political organization. The Egyptians called the area a district instead of a foreign land, and although the texts refer to the sheikhs as kings, they were in fact little more than clan or tribal leaders. Nukhashshe's value to the Egyptians was purely geographic.

The triangle-shaped steppe served as a barrier to the Mitannian military's travel and their diplomatic and commercial intercourse with the states of southern Syria, especially those along the Orontes River. Periodically making their military presence felt in the district, the Egyptians intended to keep the Mitanni off balance and force them to deal with the possibility of an Egyptian attack on their borderlands. The distance to the Euphrates through Nukhashshe was much shorter than the western route around Aleppo that Thutmose had taken during the previous Euphrates campaign. Part of the Egyptian plan was to assemble a friendly coalition of tribal sheikhs to serve as Egyptian allies and intelligence sources in the region. In Nukhashshe, Thutmose sacked three towns and carried off a small amount of plunder, mostly sheep, cattle, and donkeys.[4]

Thutmose was back the next year, this time in force. Having met no opposition to his previous encroachment, it is likely that Thutmose's army was larger this time to render his threat of an invasion of the Mitanni more credible. The Mitanni had once made the mistake of ignoring an Egyptian army as it marched into northern Syria only to see it continue its march to the Euphrates and attack the homeland. The size and direction of Thutmose's march, to the north and east of Aleppo, along with the Mitanni intelligence efforts, convinced them that Thutmose intended to undertake yet another march on their country. They moved quickly to prevent it.

The two armies met at the town of Ar'anu. The location of this town is unknown, but it may have been some twenty miles east of Aleppo and only thirty or so miles from the Euphrates.[5] The texts record, "Now His Majesty arrived at the town of Ar'anu and that vile doomed one of Naharin had collected horses with their people and . . . their armies . . . of the ends of the earth. . . . They were more numerous than the sands of the seashore . . . intent on fighting His Majesty."[6] The texts imply that the Mitanni were already in position and that some allied units, perhaps from Aleppo, which was the closest city to the battlefield, had taken the field with them. The combined force was substantial and comprised infantry and chariots. If the Mitanni had been watching the Egyptians' advance to the north, as seems likely, they would have known the size and composition of the Egyptian army and deployed an army of their own of sufficient size to meet it.

The texts describe the battle at Ar'anu as follows:

> Then His Majesty closed with them; and then the army of His Majesty performed the charging maneuver with the cry, "Let's go get 'em!" Then His Majesty overpowered these foreigners through the power of his father Amun and made a great slaughter among those doomed ones of Naharin. They proceeded to flee, stumbling one upon the other, in front of His Majesty.[7]

This particular text is one of the few Egyptian records that describes a tactical maneuver.

The list of equipment taken after the battle clearly suggests that Thutmose got the better of the fight. The captured equipment includes bronze helmets, suits of mail, composite bows, 180 horses, and 60 chariots. Ten prisoners were also taken.[8] The numbers are relatively small, however, and there is no mention of the number of enemy dead. This omission suggests that the battle went off quickly and that perhaps the text is accurate when it suggests that some sort of charge, either infantry or chariotry, may have shattered elements of the enemy formation and then touched off a general rout. Under these conditions, it would not be unusual for the numbers of dead and captured to be small. The horses and chariots may have been confiscated in the rear areas, having been left behind as the enemy fled.

Thutmose did not press farther toward the Euphrates. In all likelihood his intention was never to mount an assault on the Mitannian homeland; instead, he may have wanted to deploy a significantly large army as a reconnaissance in force to determine if the Mitanni would react. If they did not, he may have reasonably concluded that he had a free hand in Nukhashshe, that his policy of isolating the Mitanni was succeeding, and that geographic control of the Nukhashshe district had driven a wedge between the Mitanni and its Syrian clients. The reaction of the Mitanni made it clear, however, that they still had a strong presence in the district.

Moreover, they continued to play an important role in encouraging and supporting Syrian insurgencies for years to come.

The records for the years 1471 and 1470 BCE are mostly lost, but surviving fragments imply that Thutmose was once again in the field in Nukhashshe, trying to encourage the friendly tribes and clans to forge a coalition and support Egyptian interests there. At one point Thutmose went so far as to attempt to create some sort of polity in the region by installing a clan chief named Takuwa as king of the district. In a reversal of the usual order of obligations between lord and vassal, Thutmose promised to come to the vassal king's aid if he was attacked.[9] If Thutmose was trying to establish some sort of political entity that could act as an Egyptian cat's-paw in the area—perhaps to serve as a base, a source of manpower, and a source of intelligence—the fragmented social structure of the nomadic peoples in Nukhashshe almost guaranteed failure. As it was, nothing of significance seems to have come from the Egyptian's effort.

Presumably during this time the other principalities of southern Syria remained calm, and there is no record of revolts or other difficulties with them. The Lebanon ports also remained secure and well supplied. Thutmose's expeditions in Nukhashshe required him to cross the Orontes River at Qatna, indicating that Qatna, which had come over to the Egyptians before the Euphrates campaign, remained friendly. In 1469 BCE Thutmose mounted another raid during which "His Majesty destroyed the towns . . . which were in the district of Nukhashshe."[10] Once again Thutmose was showing the flag and keeping the Mitanni focused on his movements in Nukhashshe. The most important event of the year's expedition, however, came when the chief of Alalakh sent gifts to Pharaoh.[11] Alalakh was located near the Syrian coast north and west of Aleppo and had been a loyal ally of the Mitanni. Of all the Mitannian allies in Syria, Alalakh was among the farthest from the border with the Mitanni. Its location may have made it vulnerable to Egyptian pressure, especially in light of Thutmose's willingness to mount annual military expeditions into Syria. The rulers of Alalakh may have been hedging their bets in the event that the Egyptian policy succeeded.

One indication that Alalakh's ties with the Mitanni had weakened was that the principality of Niya, formerly a vassal of Alalakh, was detached and transformed into an independent principality, probably at

Egyptian insistence. Yet another indication of the Egyptians' success in this arena was the stationing of an Egyptian garrison for the first time in the important coastal city of Ugarit.[12] Until then Ugarit had remained neutral, relying on its trade and commercial value to avoid being drawn into the great power conflict between Egypt and the Mitanni. Now it had been clearly drawn into the Egyptian orbit. The Egyptian policy of isolating the Syrian principalities from their Mitannian supporters and encouraging them through political means to accommodate themselves to Egyptian dominance of the region, a seduction certainly backed by the threat of force, seemed to be working.

In Thutmose's thirty-ninth regnal year, 1465 BCE, "His Majesty was in the land of Retjenu on the fourteenth victorious expedition, after this going to defeat the fallen ones of Shasu."[13] This text refers to a raid against the Shasu bedouin that probably occurred not in Syria but in northern Canaan. Although the text is missing, it is generally agreed that in the next year, regnal year 40, Thutmose mounted yet another expedition in northern Canaan.[14] In regnal year 41 he was again in the field, but we are not certain whether he ventured to Canaan or Syria. All that the texts tell us is that "His Majesty was in the land of . . . on his fifteenth victorious campaign. Then His Majesty sacked the town of . . ."[15] Once more Pharaoh collected tribute from the chiefs of Retjenu, and once more it is noted that his coastal harbor depots were well supplied.

Mounting eight consecutive military expeditions in as many years is testimony to Thutmose's relentless desire to pacify Syria and turn it into an Egyptian province. More evidence of his strong interest is reflected in the fact that Thutmose led each of these expeditions personally, receiving the tribute of the Syrian rulers each year to remind them that their fate was closely tied to their obedience to Egypt. His willingness to show the flag in person as well as to use force against recalcitrants, whether in Nukhashshe or Canaan, was designed to convince the local rulers of their vulnerability to Egyptian power. Thutmose's counterinsurgency policy was intended to instill a sense of political and military inevitability in Syria's rulers that Egypt was not going to leave and that it was in their interests to accommodate themselves to this reality. By 1462 BCE, Thutmose's forty-second regnal year, his many years of Egyptian political and military effort seemed to have paid off.

Revolt and Suppression

In that same year, however, a number of cities and towns in southern Syria suddenly exploded into open revolt. The rebellion was widespread and included the major city-states of Tunip and Kadesh as well as some of their vassals. That the Mitanni were involved seems clear in that the Egyptians were forced to fight Mitannian troops occupying towns around Kadesh that had been sent to support the rebellion. Other garrisons of the Mitanni may have been sent in support of other towns as well, but we have no evidence. That so many towns and two major city-states were involved in the fighting also suggests that the rebellion was a coordinated effort and not some spontaneous outbreak. There does not seem to have been a single precipitating event for the revolt. It may have been that the three previous Egyptian expeditions had been small-scale operations and had been conducted in northern Canaan and not in Syria itself. This set of circumstances may have led the Mitanni and their allies to conclude both that the Egyptians' power and will were weakening and that the time to challenge Egyptian control had come.

The rebellion seems to have caught the Egyptians by surprise, forcing Thutmose to react quickly and with a force capable of suppressing the large-scale revolt. The 350-mile overland march from Egypt to Lebanon would have taken more than a month to accomplish. Since Egypt still controlled the harbors on the Lebanon coast, it is not surprising that Thutmose again decided to travel by sea as he had done so many times before.[16] The texts tell us as much: "Regnal year 42. Now His Majesty ferried over to the lands of Fenkhu." The size of the Egyptian army is not recorded, however. Given the extent of the revolt and the involvement of the major city-states of Tunip and Kadesh as well as of the Mitanni, it would have to have been quite large to suppress the outbreak. A force of ten thousand men and at least one brigade of chariots would have been required. It would have taken at least two months to assemble and transport the army to the Lebanon ports, so Thutmose probably landed sometime in mid-May.

Thutmose most likely landed at Simyra, an Egyptian-controlled port city close to the Eleutheros Valley, from which he could easily attack the towns on the Arka Plain that had gone over to the rebels. The texts tell us, "Now His Majesty was upon the coastal road with the intent of destroying the town of Irkatu together with the towns which were in its district."[17]

Breasted notes that Irkatu is the same town as Irkata of the Amarna texts and was located twelve miles inland southeast from Sumur, across the Great River in the Eleutheros Valley on the Arka Plain.[18] It was not far from Simyra, and the texts' reference to the "coastal road" most likely refers to Thutmose's march up the coast from Simyra to the mouth of the valley before turning inland to attack the towns.

Thutmose attacked Irkata and destroyed it, also laying waste to the agricultural settlements "in this district" before moving on to attack another town on the Arka Plain. The name of this second town is lost; only part of its name, "—kana," has survived. But the text is clear in noting that Thutmose "destroyed this town together with its district."[19] The term *destroyed* suggests that Thutmose punished the rebel towns by fire and sword, ravaging their farms, orchards, and crops.

Having regained control of the Arka Plain, Thutmose then moved against Tunip, one of the two major city-states that had broken into open revolt. Tunip had been brought under Egyptian influence during the Euphrates campaign. Thutmose had purchased its loyalty by returning the ruler's son, whom Thutmose had captured at Ullaza earlier. Its loyalty had never been secure, and it is not difficult to imagine the king of Tunip had waited for the opportunity to slip the humiliating Egyptian leash.

Thutmose's decision to attack Tunip is interesting. Kadesh was only four days' march down the Eleutheros Valley. Why not strike at Kadesh first? Thutmose had at least two reasons. First, the fortifications of Kadesh were more substantial than those at Tunip. Thutmose had attempted but failed to breach Kadesh's walls a few years earlier upon his return march from the Euphrates. Moreover, he could hardly afford to get caught up in a siege of Kadesh while the rest of Syria simmered with rebellion and resentment. If his campaign of suppression was to succeed, it had to be done quickly, and Tunip was the easier nut to crack. Second, most certainly the Egyptian intelligence service had detected the presence of Mitannian troop garrisons in and around the defenses of Kadesh. Indeed, it might have been the establishment of these garrisons in the first place that signaled the Syrian revolt. These professional warriors could be expected to put up a stout fight, presenting the risk of bogging down the Egyptian army and inflicting high casualties upon it. For these reasons, if Thutmose planned to attack Kadesh, he would have to do so at the end of the campaign, not at the beginning, and only after the other rebel towns had been brought to heel.

To attack Tunip and avoid a confrontation with Kadesh and the Mitannian garrisons near the city, Thutmose could not advance on Tunip by the usual route of marching through the Eleutheros Valley, turning north on the Kadesh Plain, and following the Orontes River. Instead, he had to take the alternative route to Tunip: march north across the Arka Plain, turn inland to follow the valleys across the mountains, and debouch on the Orontes flood plain through the gap where the Crusaders would later build the fortress of Krak des Chevaliers southwest of modern Homs. It was thirty miles from the Arka Plain to the gap. From there, a march of thirty-seven miles would bring the Egyptian army outside the walls of Tunip without having to deal with Kadesh.

The texts say that Thutmose "arrived at Tunip; destroying the town, uprooting its grain and chopping down its orchards." The fact that the grain was still in the ground suggests that the attack came sometime in mid-June when the harvest was not yet in. On the one hand, if we take the text literally, we may conclude that the Egyptians had captured Tunip for the first time. There is some supposition that Thutmose himself even occupied the city and that he used it as his headquarters while his troops were ravaging the countryside.[20] On the other hand, there is nothing to suggest the Egyptians had made any improvements in their siege capabilities, which in turn would lead us to believe that Tunip's defenses were overcome and the city itself destroyed. The assertion that Egypt destroyed Tunip is unaccompanied by a booty list of casualties, prisoners, and the usual captured war paraphernalia of horses, armor, weapons, and chariots, suggesting that the claim may be an exaggeration. There is no doubt, however, that the Egyptians ravaged the countryside, destroying farms, orchards, and livestock as well as the settlements and towns in the larger district. One way or another, Tunip was made to pay heavily for its treachery.

Thutmose next marched south and upstream along the Orontes River, destroying any town, settlement, or farm that had dared to join the revolt. The texts' tone suggests his attack upon these places demonstrated a level of ferociousness that is unusual in Egyptian military accounts. The scribe who composed the accounts used the verb *sksk* to describe the manner in which the towns were attacked, and the term implies an unusual degree of ferocity and slaughter.[21] Some towns seem to have been turned over to the army to do with them as it wished. In these instances, the troops were allowed to keep whatever they could loot and carry. Thutmose was outraged by the Syrian rebellion. He was determined to subdue it with a deliberate vengeance both to punish those who had participated in it and to send a strong message to others that they would suffer a similar fate should they oppose Egypt's will. By rendering terrible destruction as he marched, Thutmose conducted a psychological warfare campaign to weaken the will of the towns that still lay before him.

Leaving a trail of blood and fire in his wake, Thutmose arrived outside Kadesh. The garrisons of the Mitanni were deployed in three towns guarding the approaches to the city. Thutmose immediately attacked them. The texts say, "Coming in safety; arrival at the district of Kadesh; plundering three towns therein."[22] The Egyptians stormed the towns and captured their Mitannian garrisons, or "troops of vile Naharin who (functioned) as garrison troops."[23] Twenty-nine enemy soldiers were killed and 691 taken prisoner. They also captured forty-eight horses and sixteen chariots. It is noteworthy that the texts do not claim that Kadesh itself was captured, a claim that surely would have been included in the official *Annals* and recorded on the walls of Karnak had such an important prize been taken. Amenemhab's claim in his tomb inscriptions that Thutmose captured Kadesh refers to the previous campaign in regnal year 30, if it is true at all. Again, Redford is probably correct when he asserts that there is no convincing evidence that Thutmose ever captured Kadesh at any time during his Syrian campaigns.[24]

It was probably around the second week of July when the Egyptian army reached the walls of Kadesh. Thutmose had plenty of time left in the campaign season to lay siege to the city. Given the importance Kadesh held in the Egyptians' eyes as the primary fomenter of their troubles in Syria, it is curious that the official records make no mention of an Egyptian attempt to capture the city by storm or siege. Certainly the harvest was already in, making it unlikely that the city could be starved into submission, and taking the city by storm, with its defenses and garrisons intact and at full strength, would be a difficult task. Lacking siege capabilities, Thutmose had attempted to take the city once before and failed.

There are no records to tell us why Thutmose did not attack Kadesh, how long he remained in Syria, and what he did for the remainder of the campaign season. The record simply ends with the usual notation that "the harbors were stocked with everything in accordance with their tax quota and in accordance with their yearly custom, and the labor of Lebanon in accordance with their yearly custom."[25] Thutmose seems to have marched away from Kadesh and back through the Eleutheros Valley to reach the Lebanon coast, where he made his annual inspection of the supply depots as he had done at the end of every previous expedition. This work accomplished, he boarded a ship and sailed for home.

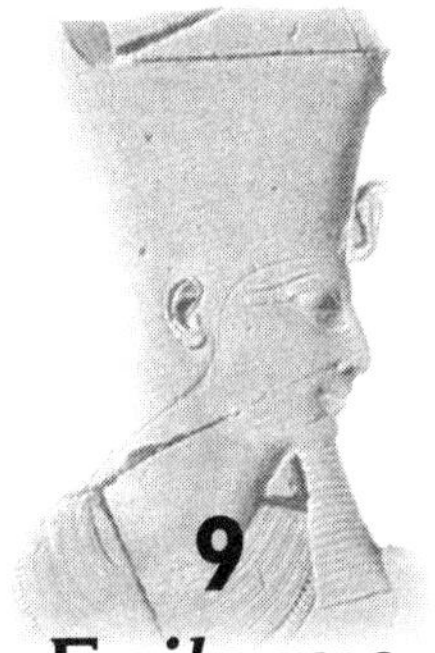

9
Epilogue

On each of his seventeen campaigns Thutmose was accompanied by an official scribe named Thaneni who recorded the accounts of the king's battles and victories in Canaan and Syria. "I followed King Menkhepperre [Thutmose III] and witnessed the victories which he won in every country. He brought the princes of Syria as living prisoners to Egypt, he captured all their cities, and cut down their groves. . . . I recorded the victories, putting them in writing according to the facts."[1] At the end of his Syrian campaigns in his forty-second regnal year, Thaneni wrote, "Behold His Majesty commanded to record the victories which he won from the year twenty-three until the year forty-two, when this inscription was recorded upon this sanctuary, that he might be given life forever."[2] The battle diaries of Thutmose's campaigns were inscribed on the walls of the great temple of Amun at Karnak, which also contained the leather scroll upon which Thaneni had written the accounts of the king's military adventures.

Thutmose lived for another twelve years, but there are no further accounts of his military activities recorded in the *Annals*. Why did the king's battle diaries stop at year 42? The answer may be that following almost twenty years of continuous military activity, Thutmose had succeeded in establishing an effective Egyptian security zone in Canaan and Syria to provide sufficient strategic depth and warning time for Egypt to defend its eastern border from any future attack. The ultimate goal of Thutmose's national defense policy was to protect Egypt from another Hyksos invasion. As long as Egypt controlled the Lebanon coast, southern

Syria, and Canaan, any attempt by the Mitanni or a coalition of Syrian maryannu princes to mount an invasion could be intercepted in ample time and at sufficient distance to shift the odds of success significantly in Egypt's favor. After the successful counterinsurgency campaign in Syria of year 42, Egyptian policy shifted from the offensive, designed to establish control over the important choke points in the forward areas of its defense zone, to the defensive, designed to maintain this control and meet any attack as far forward of the Egyptian border as possible.

Final Years

Thutmose himself no longer led military expeditions into Canaan and Syria after regnal year 42 because such expeditions were no longer necessary to maintain control in these forward areas. It is, however, unrealistic to think that once Egypt had established its position in southern Syria that it withdrew and left the area hostage to Mitannian and insurgent intentions. Rather than Thutmose himself, senior generals led Egyptian military activities after year 42. The Egyptians continued to follow the same policies in Syria that they had pursued for two decades with success in Canaan.

As they had done in Canaan, Egyptian military expeditions continued to destroy any fortifications that might be used against them in the future or that hindered movement over important terrain. They had instituted this policy at Ullaza a few years earlier and, if we can believe the texts, had done significant damage to some temporary walls constructed outside Kadesh. Certainly the towns attacked during the insurgency campaign had their fortifications reduced, and perhaps even some of Tunip's fortifications were rendered useless. As long as Egyptian sappers and miners confined their activities to areas under Egyptian control, the policy of destroying fortifications would have proceeded without much difficulty.

Thutmose's practice of securing the loyalty of Syrian chiefs by taking their sons and brothers hostage also continued, as did the practice of replacing recalcitrant rulers with Egyptian favorites who, in the normal course of things, would then witness their own children taken hostage. In Canaan, Egyptian officers oversaw the collection and transport of the harvests of the area's grain-producing lands to Egypt. In Syria, in-kind taxes, including grain, were levied and collected annually. The collection of these annual imposts would have of necessity required the presence of Egyptian authorities to ensure the specified items' delivery. It is unlikely that these authorities, scribes, and accountants would have arrived unaccompanied by military units to ensure compliance.

For almost twenty years Thutmose had kept the Canaanite and Syrian chiefs in line with annual military campaigns, with the last campaign accompanied by widespread destruction and terror. Then the annual arrival of Egyptian tax collectors, accompanied by contingents of troops, was sufficient to demonstrate the Egyptians' willingness to resort to force once more should events require it. Thus, although Thutmose no longer accompanied the army to Canaan and Syria each year, his policies continued very much in force. The result was twelve years of peace in the Egyptian security zone as even the Mitanni, now more concerned with the developing Hittite threat on its western border, withdrew from direct confrontation with Egypt in Syria.

After regnal year 42, Thutmose was occupied with numerous major construction projects undertaken at Karnak, Deir el-Bihari, Medinet Habu, Elkab, Heliopolis, and in Nubia.[3] It was also during this time that he began his program of erasing Hatshepsut's memory from all texts and public monuments in Egypt. Both programs were extensive and time consuming, and their success speaks to Thutmose's competence as an administrator. It was not until regnal year 47 that we find Thutmose once again engaged in military activities.

In that year Thutmose led a military force of unknown size into Nubia. At a place called Gebel Barkal (modern Napata) he erected a massive stela. Gebel Barkal is located some 240 miles north of Khartoum on a large bend in the Nile and was the southern boundary of Egyptian control in the south.[4] The stela describes in heroic terms many of the victories that Thutmose won over the Syrians and the Mitanni, often stressing the destruction he laid upon the lands of his enemies. The text's tone is that of a powerful oration delivered by a mighty warrior as a warning to those who might dare defy Pharaoh's will. It is probable that Egypt had seen some recent difficulties in Nubia, perhaps even revolts or refusals of the annual tribute by some recalcitrant chiefs, and that Thutmose had come to Nubia to show the flag and issue a dire warning of things to follow if circumstances did not improve.

That the stela was intended as a warning can be seen from two elements within its text. First, the text is clearly addressed to the chiefs of Nubia when it begins, "Listen, people of the southern land, which is by the Gebel Barkal. . . . Oh, you shall learn of this miracle of Amen-Re." Second, the text goes on to tell of a dream that Thutmose had in which "a star appeared to the south [Nubia]. Never had the like happened. It shone exactly towards them." The star's light is a metaphor for Pharaoh's power. The text then describes what happened to the people who had been exposed to the light: "None withstood there. I killed them like those who had never been, they lay in their blood, enemies in heaps. . . . Their horse teams were no more, they had bolted in the desert." Lest anyone miss the intent of the violence, the text goes on to say, "[All this I did] in order to make that all inhabitants of foreign lands see the might of My Majesty. . . . He [Amun] instilled fear of me among all the inhabitants of foreign lands. They fled before me. Everything on which the sun shines is bound under my soles."[5]

Thutmose had not visited Nubia for more than twenty years when he made this visit to Gebel Barkal. The inscriptions at Karnak record regular tribute payments from Wawat (Lower Nubia) and Kush (Upper Nubia) during that period, but there is nothing in the records that tells us what may have prompted Thutmose to return to Nubia after such a long absence. Perhaps the prolonged absence itself was the reason for the royal visit. Thutmose may have wanted a tour of inspection to reinvigorate the local magistrates or to ensure that the Nile canals around the cataracts were in working order and that the construction projects he had ordered were proceeding accordingly. Still, the construction of the stela and the tone of the text lead one to suspect that there may have been difficulties of some sort in Nubia that required Pharaoh's attention.

Three years later, in regnal year 50, Thutmose was back in Nubia, this time at the head of an army. He left Thebes in September, the time of year when Egyptian armies usually set out for Nubia because it was the season of the flood and the cataracts were most easily navigable. He remained in Nubia for eight months before returning to Egypt in April. On the way back, he found the canal around the First Cataract blocked by stones and ordered it dredged. "His Majesty ordered the dredging of the channel, after he had found it blocked up with stones, so that no ship could sail upon it. He then sailed downstream upon it gladness of heart, having destroyed his enemies."[6] This last phrase clearly implies that Thutmose had been engaged in some sort of military campaign during his stay in Nubia.[7] The length of time in the field—eight months—and the fact that the king had personally led the army suggest a serious military undertaking. Unfortunately, we have no information as to what it involved.

That the situation in Nubia was unsettled during Thutmose's final years seems clear from other evidence. Near the end of his reign, perhaps in the final two years of his life, Thutmose appointed his son Amenhotep II co-regent. Amenhotep was born in regnal year 35 and was probably eighteen years old when he became co-regent.[8] Sometime shortly thereafter, perhaps in Thutmose's final year of life, a revolt broke out in northern Canaan, and Amenhotep led an army to suppress it. He pacified Canaan with great brutality. Then, "after His Majesty came back from Upper Retenu . . . having slain with his own mace the seven chiefs who were in the district of Takhsy . . . [he] had the other doomed one taken south to Nubia and hung on the wall of Napata."[9] He exacted this punishment no doubt as a warning of what horrors might follow should events in Nubia become intolerable. A few years after his father's death, Amenhotep led an army into Nubia 650 miles upstream from Elephantine, where he put down a rebellion and established Egyptian control as far south as the Fourth Cataract.[10]

Thutmose III, Egypt's greatest warrior pharaoh, died on the thirtieth day of the seventh month of the year—March 17, 1450 BCE—or one month and four days short of concluding his fifty-fourth regnal year.[11] His death seems to have precipitated a revolt among some of the Syrian principalities, and Amenhotep again moved quickly and brutally to put it down. Over the next decade, Amenhotep led other punitive expeditions into Syria to control the violence. On one of these campaigns, probably in regnal year 9, Amenhotep tells us that he uprooted and deported 15,070 people from the district of Nukhashshe alone.[12] Whether the Mitanni supported these revolts as a way of testing the new Egyptian king is not clear. It is likely, however, that Amenhotep's speed and fierceness in suppressing the revolts along with the growing concern regarding the Hittites' intentions led the Mitanni to send a delegation to Egypt and offer a peace agreement. The king of the Mitanni, probably Saussatar, sent a delegation to Egypt "with proposals of brotherhood," that is, an alliance and a renunciation of hostilities. A treaty was eventually concluded between the two states a short time later.

Legacy

Thutmose III left behind a legacy of greatness. He had taken an isolated, defeated, and fearful nation and made it a true imperial power that continued to play a central role in the politics and wars of the Levant for more than five centuries. His national defense strategy guided the foreign policy of Egypt's rulers for five hundred years after his death. In this time, no foreign army trod the black earth of the Egyptian homeland. Thutmose had also constructed a professional and technologically well-equipped military force from what had been only a militia army, forged and tempered it in the crucible of war for more than two decades, and then bequeathed it to his successors to be used as the primary instrument of Egypt's defense. He had restored Egyptian national power and prestige, and he himself became the personification of the nation and its power. From his time forward, every pharaoh regarded himself as a warrior king whose primary responsibility, to protect the nation, was bestowed upon him in trust by his divine father, Amun.

It is no exaggeration to say that Thutmose established the Egyptian Empire. From the Libyan border in the west, south to the Second Cataract, and in Syria as far north as the Great River of the Eleutheros Valley and east to the Beqqa Valley, no foreign power challenged Egyptian control of its realm for four centuries. It was Thutmose who first established the rudiments of a genuine imperial administration in the conquered territories, often appointing old comrades to oversee the operations of government in the very lands they had helped subdue. Thus, he opened Egypt to the world, with the result that new cultural forces from all over the region began to flow into Egypt, expanding the horizons of its craftsmen, artists, and architects. Thutmose III was the greatest warrior king that Egypt had ever known or ever was to know in its long and varied history on this earth.

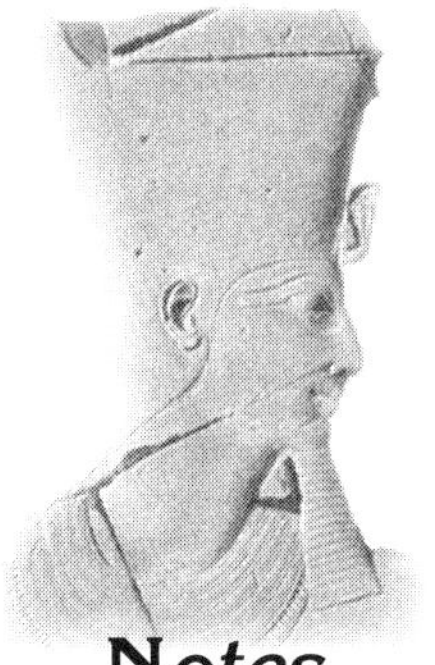

Notes

1. WARRIOR PHARAOH

1. Dennis Forbes, "Menkheperre Djehutymes: Thutmose III, a Pharaoh's Pharaoh," *KMT* 9, no. 4 (Winter 1998–99): 63.
2. Ibid., 62.
3. R. B. Partridge, *Faces of Pharaohs: Royal Mummies and Coffins from Ancient Thebes* (London: Rubicon Press, 1994), 77–80.
4. Ibid.
5. David O'Connor, "Thutmose III: An Enigmatic Pharaoh," in *Thutmose III: A New Biography*, ed. Eric Cline and David O'Connor (Ann Arbor: University of Michigan Press, 2008), 5–6.
6. Ibid.
7. Donald B. Redford, "The Northern Wars of Thutmose III," in Cline and O'Connor, *Thutmose III: A New Biography*, 325.
8. Arielle P. Kozloff, "The Artistic Production of the Reign of Thutmose III," in Cline and O'Connor, *Thutmose III: A New Biography*, 292.
9. Dimitri Laboury, "Royal Portrait and Ideology: Evolution and Signification of the Statuary of Thutmose III," in Cline and O'Connor, *Thutmose III: A New Biography*, 261.
10. Kozloff, "The Artistic Production of the Reign of Thutmose III," 294.
11. Dennis Forbes, "Menkheperure Djehutymes: The Fourth and Final Thutmose," *KMT* 9, no. 2 (Summer 2002): 74.
12. Donald B. Redford, *History and Chronology of the Eighteenth Dynasty of Egypt: Seven Studies* (Toronto: University of Toronto Press, 1967), 85.
13. Kozloff, "The Artistic Production of the Reign of Thutmose III," 317.
14. Forbes, "Menkheperre Djehutymes," 183.
15. Ibid., 54.
16. Piotr Laskowski, "Monumental Architecture and the Royal Building Program of Thutmose III," in Cline and O'Connor, *Thutmose III: A New Biography*, 229. See also in the same volume, Catharine H. Roehrig, "The Building Activities of Thutmose III in the Valley of the Kings," 238–59.

17. R. J. Forbes, *Studies in Ancient Technology* (Leiden, the Netherlands: Brill, 1964), 214.
18. Betsy M. Bryan, "Administration in the Reign of Thutmose III," in Cline and O'Connor, *Thutmose III: A New Biography*, 69.
19. Ibid., 113.
20. See S. R. Morcos and W. R. Morcos, "Diets in Ancient Egypt," *Progress in Food and Nutrition Science* 2 (1977): 457–71; they give six million to eight million people as Egypt's population in antiquity. Both of these researchers are staffers at the National Research Center in the Food Science and Nutrition Department in Cairo. O'Connor, citing K. W. Butzer, *Early Hydraulic Civilization in Egypt: A Study in Cultural Ecology* (Chicago: University of Chicago Press, 1976), 83, says the population was between four million and five million people.
21. I have accepted the dates of 1505–1451 BCE as those of Thutmose III's life, relying upon Redford even though the issue is far from settled among Egyptologists. Cline and O'Conner's book features the most recent research regarding Thutmose III and place his dates at 1479–1425. Other regnal dates suggested by other analyses are 1490–1436, 1483–1429, 1479–1425, and 1504–1450 BCE.
22. See the classic work by Adolf Erman, *Life in Ancient Egypt*, trans. H. M. Tirard (New York: Dover Books Reprint, 1971), especially chapter 14, "Learning," 328–68, for an examination of ancient Egypt's educational system. Also of interest in this regard is Barbara Mertz, *Red Land, Black Land: Daily Life in Ancient Egypt* (New York: Peter Bedrick Books, 1990), chapter 7.
23. Some idea as to how extensive the temples' libraries were can be gained from the example of Manetho, the high priest of Ptah at Memphis. When Ptolemy assumed control of Egypt in the wake of Alexander's conquests, he asked Manetho to produce a history of Egypt. In a few short months he was able to produce a comprehensive account of Egyptian history, reaching back to the third millennium BCE, by drawing on the historical records in the temple library.
24. See Richard A. Gabriel, *The Military History of Ancient Israel* (Westport, CT: Praeger, 2003), 129–31, for circumcision as a military ritual. See also James B. Pritchard, ed., *Ancient Near Eastern Texts Relating to the Old Testament* (Princeton, NJ: Princeton University Press, 1955), 326, for an Egyptian letter dating to 2300 BCE that suggests that the ritual was carried out on groups of recruits entering military service.
25. William Petty, "Hatshepsut and Thutmose III Reconsidered," *KMT* 8, no. 1 (Spring 1997): 47.
26. O'Connor, "Thutmose III: An Enigmatic Pharaoh," 20–21; and Dennis Forbes, "Akheperenre Djehutymes: The All-But-Forgotten Second Thutmose," *KMT* 11, no. 2 (Summer 2000): 75.
27. Peter F. Dorman, "The Early Reign of Thutmose III: An Unorthodox Mantle of Coregency," in Cline and O'Connor, *Thutmose III: A New Biography*, 39–68.
28. O'Connor, "Thutmose III: An Enigmatic Pharaoh," 5.
29. Petty, "Hatshepsut and Thutmose III Reconsidered," 46–48.
30. Ibid., 47.
31. Redford, *History and Chronology of the Eighteenth Dynasty of Egypt*, 81.

32. Ibid., 60.
33. Petty, "Hatshepsut and Thutmose III Reconsidered," 48.
34. Ibid.
35. Redford, *History and Chronology of the Eighteenth Dynasty of Egypt*, 60.
36. Petty, "Hatshepsut and Thutmose III Reconsidered," 48.
37. Dorman, "The Early Reign of Thutmose III," 58.
38. The contributions of Egyptian religious thought to the main Western religions of Judaism and Christianity are discussed at length in Richard A. Gabriel, *Gods of Our Fathers: The Memory of Egypt in Judaism and Christianity* (Westport, CT: Greenwood Press, 2002).
39. Redford, "The Northern Wars of Thutmose III," 325.
40. Ibid.
41. For the tactical roles of infantry and cavalry in the armies of Philip and Alexander, see Richard A. Gabriel, *Empires at War: A Chronological Encyclopedia*, vol. 1, *From Sumer to the Persian Empire* (Westport, CT: Greenwood Press, 2005), 325–29.
42. For more on the Egyptian navy in the New Kingdom, see chapter 3 of this book.
43. An analysis of the successor armies after Alexander can be found in Gabriel, *Empires at War*, vol. 2, *From Carthage to the Normans*, chapter 13.
44. Anthony J. Spalinger, *War in Ancient Egypt* (Malden, MA: Blackwell, 2005), 62.
45. The Egyptianizing of the Ptolemaic Greeks is discussed at length in Richard A. Gabriel, *Jesus the Egyptian: The Origins of Christianity and the Psychology of Christ* (New York: Universe, 2005), chapter 3.
46. Redford, "The Northern Wars of Thutmose III," 325.
47. Forbes, "Menkheperre Djehutymes," 62.
48. O'Connor, "Thutmose III: An Enigmatic Pharaoh," 33–34. See also Kozloff, "The Artistic Production of the Reign of Thutmose III," 292–324.
49. Donald B. Redford, "The Coregency of Thutmose III and Amenophis II," *Journal of Egyptian Archaeology* 51 (1965): 107–22.

2. STRATEGIC SETTING

1. Robert J. Wenke, *Patterns in Prehistory: Mankind's First Three Million Years* (New York: Oxford University Press, 1980), 468.
2. Yigael Yadin, *The Art of Warfare in Biblical Lands in Light of Archaeological Study*, trans. M. Pearlman (New York: McGraw-Hill, 1963), 2:313–28.
3. Ibid., 1:150–51.
4. For an examination of Egyptian religion from 4000 BCE through the period of the Greek conquests, see Gabriel, *Gods of Our Fathers*, 202.
5. See page xx in Eliezer D. Oren, ed., *The Hyksos: New Historical and Archaeological Perspectives* (Philadelphia: University of Pennsylvania Museum Press, 1997), for an understanding of the term *Hyksos*.
6. Ibid., 48, for the date of the Hyksos invasion.
7. Some Egyptologists argue that the Hyksos occupation of the Nile Delta was accomplished not by armed invasion but by peaceful infiltration. For this view see ibid., xxii. I agree with Redford that the evidence is overwhelming in support of a violent invasion. For this view see Donald B. Redford, *Egypt,*

Canaan, and Israel in Ancient Times (Princeton, NJ: Princeton University Press, 1992), 101–10.

8. See page 48 of David O'Connor, "The Hyksos Period in Egypt," in Oren, *The Hyksos,* for the length of the Hyksos occupation at 108 years.
9. See ibid., 62, on the psychological impact of the Hyksos occupation.
10. Alan H. Gardiner, "The Defeat of the Hyksos by Kamose: The Carnarvon Tablet, No. 1," *Journal of Egyptian Archaeology* 3 (1916): 102.
11. A good account of the campaigns of Kamose and Ahmose I in driving out the Hyksos appears in Omar Zuhdi, "A Tale of Two Ahmoses or How to Begin an Empire," *KMT* 11, no. 4 (Winter 2000–2001): 50–61.
12. Michael Grant, *The History of Ancient Israel* (New York: Charles Scribner's Sons, 1984), 13.
13. Nigel Stillman and Nigel Tallis, *Armies of the Ancient Near East, 3000 BC–539 BC* (Sussex, UK: Flexiprint Ltd., 1984), 33.
14. Yadin, *The Art of Warfare in Biblical Lands,* 1:79.
15. Grant, *The History of Ancient Israel,* 16.
16. Ibid.
17. Ibid., 17.
18. Georges Roux, *Ancient Iraq* (New York: Penguin, 1986), 235.
19. *Cambridge Ancient History* (Cambridge, UK: Cambridge University Press, 1973), 2, part 2:3.
20. See Richard A. Gabriel and Donald W. Boose, Jr., "Megiddo," in *Great Battles of Antiquity: A Strategic and Tactical Guide to Great Battles That Shaped the Development of War* (Westport, CT: Greenwood Press, 1994), chapter 2, for an explanation of Mitannian influence in Syria during the time of Thutmose III.
21. See Betsy M. Bryan, "The Egyptian Perspective on the Mitanni," in *Armana Diplomacy: The Beginnings of International Relations,* ed. Raymond Cohen and Raymond Westbrook (Baltimore, MD: Johns Hopkins University Press, 2002), 71–84, for an overview of Egyptian-Mitannian relations from Thutmose I to Thutmose III.
22. H. W. F. Saggs, *The Might That Was Assyria* (London: Sidgwick and Jackson, 1984), 38.
23. Roux, *Ancient Iraq,* 217.
24. Ibid.
25. *Cambridge Ancient History,* 2, part 2:1.
26. Ibid., 873; Saggs, *The Might That Was Assyria,* 39; and Roux, *Ancient Iraq,* 218.
27. *Cambridge Ancient History,* 2, part 2:875.
28. Ibid., 874.
29. Roux, *Ancient Iraq,* 230.
30. O. R. Gurney, *The Hittites* (London: Penguin, 1990), 86.
31. Saggs, *The Might That Was Assyria,* 196.
32. Anthony J. Spalinger, "Covetous Eyes South: The Background to Egypt's Domination of Nubia by the Reign of Thutmose III," in Cline and O'Connor, *Thutmose III: A New Biography,* 357.
33. David O'Connor, "Thutmose III: An Enigmatic Pharaoh," 10. See also S. T. Smith, *Askut in Nubia: The Economics and Ideology of Egyptian Imperialism in the Second Millennium BC* (London: Keegan Paul, 1995).

34. Spalinger, "Covetous Eyes South," 361.
35. Redford, *Egypt, Canaan, and Israel in Ancient Times,* 111.
36. Ibid., 112.
37. Spalinger, "Covetous Eyes South," 345.
38. Ibid., 348.
39. Ibid., 349.
40. Ibid., 352.
41. Redford, *History and Chronology of the Eighteenth Dynasty of Egypt,* 62.
42. Ibid., 57–64.
43. Spalinger, "Covetous Eyes South," 366.

3. THE ANTAGONISTS

1. Egyptologists still disagree regarding the proper chronology of events in ancient Egypt. When all is said and done, one is forced to choose a chronology and stick to it. Thus, all relevant dates in this chapter are taken from Donald B. Redford, *The Wars in Syria and Palestine of Thutmose III* (Boston: Brill, 2003).
2. Much of the historical material in this chapter is drawn from my earlier research. Rather than clutter up the manuscript with innumerable footnotes, I have cited those works here so that the reader can refer to the relevant chapters. The later footnotes in the chapter refer to the most recent research. See Gabriel and Donald J. Boose, Jr., *The Great Battles of Antiquity*. Also see Gabriel, *The Great Armies of Antiquity* (Westport, CT: Praeger Publishers, 2002); *Great Captains of Antiquity* (Westport, CT: Greenwood Press, 2001); *The Military History of Ancient Israel*; and all three volumes of *Empires at War*.
3. This point should not be understood to mean that one man of every ten men of military age was conscripted into the army. Rather, one man of every ten at every farm, temple, or workshop was subject to conscription, resulting in a rather much smaller number. A parallel system was used in ancient Israel, where a fixed number of men were conscripted from every *eleph,* or a subdivision of the clans within the tribes.
4. Leonard Cottrell, *The Warrior Pharaohs* (New York: Dutton, 1969), 51.
5. Ibid., 18–19.
6. An excellent work on military titles in the army of ancient Egypt is Alan R. Schulman, *Military Rank, Title, and Organization in the Egyptian New Kingdom* (Berlin: Bruno Hessling Verlag, 1964), 30–86.
7. Ibid.
8. Ibid.
9. Cottrell, *The Warrior Pharaohs,* 51.
10. R. O. Faulkner, "Egyptian Military Organization," *Journal of Egyptian Archaeology* 39 (1953): 32–47.
11. Ibid.
12. Ibid.
13. Cottrell, *The Warrior Pharaohs,* 55–56.
14. *Cambridge Ancient History,* 2, part 1:57.
15. B. I. Sandor, "Tutankhamun's Chariots: Secret Treasures of Engineering Mechanics," in *Fatigue and Fracture of Engineering Materials and Structures* 27, no. 7 (2004): 637–46.

16. Ian Shaw, "Egyptians, Hyksos, and Military Technology: Causes, Effects, or Catalysts?" in *The Social Context of Technological Change: Egypt and the Near East, 1650–1550*, ed. Andrew J. Shortland (Oxford, UK: Oxbow Books, 2001), 59–71.
17. Ibid., 63–66.
18. Ibid., 65. See also S. Dalley, "Foreign Chariotry and Cavalry in the Armies of Tiglath-Pileser III and Sargon II," *Iraq* 47 (1985): 31–48.
19. Spalinger, *War in Ancient Egypt*, 8–9.
20. Shaw, "Egyptians, Hyksos, and Military Technology," 62.
21. Hatshepsut claimed that "my troops which were formerly unequipped are now well paid since I appeared as king," suggesting that she was still upgrading the army at this time. Redford, *History and Chronology of the Eighteenth Dynasty of Egypt*, 81.
22. Spalinger, *War in Ancient Egypt*, 4–5.
23. Ibid., 3.
24. Faulkner, "Egyptian Military Organization," 42.
25. "Ancient Egyptian Joint Operations in the Lebanon under Thutmose III (1451–1438 BCE)," *Semaphore: Newsletter of the Sea Power Centre of Australia* 16 (August 2006): 1. A march from Egypt to the Euphrates would have taken more than two months to complete.
26. Manfred Bietak, "The Thutmoside Stronghold of Perunefer," *Egyptian Archaeology* 26 (Spring 2005): 13–14.
27. Torgny Save-Soderbergh, *The Navy of the Eighteenth Egyptian Dynasty* (Uppsala, Sweden: Uppsala University Press, 1946), 39.
28. For more on Egyptian ships and shipbuilding see ibid.; R. O. Faulkner, "Egyptian Seagoing Ships," *Journal of Egyptian Archaeology* 16 (1940): 3–17; Erman, *Life in Ancient Egypt*, chapter 19; and John Baines and Jaromir Malek, *Atlas of Ancient Egypt* (Oxford, UK: Andromeda Books, 1980), 67–69.
29. Save-Soderbergh, *The Navy of the Eighteenth Egyptian Dynasty*, 34.
30. Ibid., 42.
31. Raymond W. Baker, *Encyclopedia Britannica*, 15th ed., s.v. "History of Egyptian Civilization."
32. Schulman, *Military Rank, Title, and Organization in the Egyptian New Kingdom*, 54.
33. Ibid.
34. Sandor, "Tutankhamun's Chariots," 639.
35. Gillian Vogelsang-Eastwood, "Textiles," in *Ancient Egyptian Materials and Technology*, ed. P. T. Nicholson and Ian Shaw (Cambridge, UK: Cambridge University Press, 2000), 292.
36. See the experiments with chariots and archers conducted by Richard A. Gabriel and Karen S. Metz, *From Sumer to Rome: The Military Capabilities of Ancient Armies* (Westport, CT: Greenwood Press, 1991), 78–79.
37. Gabriel, *Great Captains of Antiquity*, 28.
38. For an analysis of the Egyptian modifications of the chariot, see Sandor, "Tutankhamun's Chariots," 637–46.
39. Rosemarie Drenkhahn, *Die Handwerker und ihre Tatigkeiten im alten Agypten* (Wiesbaden, Germany: Harrassowitz, 1976), 130.
40. Shaw, "Egyptians, Hyksos, and Military Technology," 64.

41. Yadin, *The Art of Warfare in Biblical Lands,* 1:87–89.
42. Sandor, "Tutankhamun's Chariots," 642.
43. Ibid.
44. Ibid., 638.
45. Ibid.
46. Ibid.
47. Ibid., 639.
48. Gabriel and Metz, *From Sumer to Rome,* 77.
49. For an excellent analysis of chariot tactics see Steven Weingartner, "In the Near Eastern Bronze Age, Chariot Tactics Were More Sophisticated Than Previously Supposed," *Military Heritage* (August 2002): 18–22, 79. One of the best analyses of the chariot horse in battle is found in Deborah Cantrell, "Horsemen of Israel: Horses and Chariotry in Monarchic Israel" (Ph.D. diss., Vanderbilt University, 2008).
50. Richard A. Gabriel, "Egypt: Empire of the Sun," in *Empires at War,* 1:73.
51. Gabriel, *Great Captains of Antiquity,* 27.
52. Shaw, "Egyptians, Hyksos, and Military Technology," 66.
53. Gabriel, *Great Captains of Antiquity,* 27.
54. See Jonathan P. Roth, *The Logistics of the Roman Army at War: 264 BC–AD 235* (Leiden, the Netherlands: Brill, 1999), 62; and Spalinger, *War in Ancient Egypt,* 35, for a different estimate.
55. Weingartner, "In the Near Eastern Bronze Age, Chariot Tactics," 19–22. See also Nic Fields's *Bronze Age War Chariots* (Oxford, UK: Osprey Publishing, 2006) for more on chariot tactics.
56. For more on the horse in Egypt see Mertz, *Red Land, Black Land,* 144; Spalinger, *War in Ancient Egypt,* 11; and Catherine Rommelaere, *Les Chevaux du Nouvel Empire Egyptien: Origines, Races, Harnachement* (Brussels: Connaissance de l'Egypte Pharaonique, 1991).
57. Stillman and Tallis, *Armies of the Ancient Near East,* 24.
58. Ibid.
59. Steven Weingartner, "Chariots Changed Forever the Way Warfare Was Fought, Strategy Conceived, and Empires Built," *Military Heritage* (August 1999): 26.
60. Stillman and Tallis, *Armies of the Ancient Near East,* 25.
61. Ibid., 139.
62. Ibid., 141.
63. Ibid., 139.
64. Ibid.
65. Ibid., 141.
66. Ibid., 25.
67. Ibid., 35.
68. Yadin, *The Art of Warfare in Biblical Lands,* 1:88.
69. Ibid.
70. Stillman and Tallis, *Armies of the Ancient Near East,* 96.
71. Michael Grant, *The History of Ancient Israel* (New York: Charles Scriber, 1984), 19.
72. Stillman and Tallis, *Armies of the Ancient Near East,* 35.
73. Yadin, *The Art of Warfare in Biblical Lands,* 1:79–84.
74. Ibid., 2:108.

75. Gabriel, *The Military History of Ancient Israel*, 234–37.
76. Stillman and Tallis, *Armies of the Ancient Near East*, 35.
77. Grant, *The History of Ancient Israel*, 81.
78. Ibid., 21.
79. A good selection of models, paintings, and reliefs of Nubian soldiers can be found in Dietrich Wildung, *Sudan: Ancient Kingdoms of the Nile* (Paris: Flammarion, 1997).
80. Shaw, "Egyptians, Hyksos, and Military Technology," 65; and Dalley, "Foreign Chariotry and Cavalry," 70.
81. Spalinger, *War in Ancient Egypt*, 62.

4. THE BATTLE OF MEGIDDO

1. There is disagreement among Egyptologists as to when the battle of Megiddo occurred. The traditional date of 1479 BCE is taken from Harold Nelson's work, the first systematic treatment of the battle published in 1913. See Harold Hayden Nelson, *The Battle of Megiddo* (Chicago: University of Chicago Library, 1913), 38. Since then, other Egyptologists, Donald Redford most prominent among them, have adjusted the date to 1481 BCE. If, as Redford maintains, Hatshepsut died in the winter of 1482, then the battle of Megiddo took place the following spring of 1481.
2. Redford, *Egypt, Canaan, and Israel in Ancient Times*, 155.
3. Ibid.
4. Redford, "The Northern Wars of Thutmose III," 330.
5. Wolfgang Helck, *Geschichte des Alten Agypten* (HdO, I, 3: 1968), 154. For the contrary view, see Hans Goedicke, *The Battle of Megiddo* (Baltimore: Halgo Inc., 2000), 137.
6. Redford, *The Wars in Syria and Palestine of Thutmose III*, 14.
7. Redford, "The Northern Wars of Thutmose III," 330.
8. During Hatshepsut's reign it had become the practice for Egypt to station only small numbers of troops and commercial and diplomatic representatives in foreign kingdoms with which Egypt had relations. These Egyptian envoys mostly dealt with trade.
9. Betty Winkelman, "Buhen: Blueprints of an Egyptian Fortress," *KMT* 6, no. 2 (Summer 1995): 72–83. See also Troy Fox, "Siege Warfare in Ancient Egypt," *Tour Egypt!* (http://www.touregypt.net/featurestories/siegewarfare.htm); and Fox's "Military Architecture of Ancient Egypt" (http://www.touregypt.net/featurestories/fortresses.htm).
10. I have relied on the following translations and commentaries of the *Annals* and the Gebel Barkal stela, which contain the original Egyptian record of the Megiddo campaign. These translations include Redford's, in *The Wars in Syria and Palestine of Thutmose III*, and Goedicke's, in *The Battle of Megiddo*. In addition I have consulted and utilized the classic translations by James Henry Breasted, *Ancient Records of Egypt*, vol. 2, *The Eighteenth Dynasty* (Urbana: University of Illinois Press, 2001); and K. Sethe, *Urkunden der 18. Dynastie: Urkunden des Agyptischen Altertums*, 2nd ed. (Berlin: Akademie-Verlag, 1927–30).

11. Redford estimates the size of the army at ten thousand troops. Spalinger, in *War in Ancient Egypt,* 86, says that estimate is too high and suggests a figure of around five thousand men. Goedicke argues that both sides could not together have deployed more than a thousand men.
12. Capt. Glen R. Townsend, "The First Battle of History" (thesis, Command and General Staff School, Fort Leavenworth, KS, 1935), 28. For similar figures as they relate to the British army of the same period, see Peter Barker, "Crossing the Hellespont: A Study in Ancient Logistics," paper delivered at the VI Classics Colloquium, Classical Association of South Africa (CASA) Conference, February 2005, 8. See also General F. Maurice, "The Size of the Army of Xerxes in the Invasion of Greece, 480 BC," *Journal of Hellenic Studies* 50, part 2 (1930): 229.
13. Stillman and Tallis, *Armies of the Ancient Near East,* 100.
14. James K. Hoffmeier, "Tents in Egypt and the Ancient Near East," *Toronto Society for the Study of Egyptian Antiquities (SSEA) Journal* 7, no. 3 (1977): 13–28, for Egyptian tents. See also Mordechai Gichon, "Military Camps on Egyptian and Syrian Reliefs," *Assaph: Studies in Honor of Asher Ovadiah* (Tel Aviv: Department of Art History, Tel Aviv University, 2005), 569–93.
15. The Romans brought wheat to Egypt.
16. Barker, "Crossing the Hellespont," 2.
17. References in Egyptian literature note that the military camp had a particularly pungent smell from the horse dung used in its cooking fires. I built fires using horse dung and cow dung, the cooking fuel of Egyptian civilians, and sure enough, horse dung has an irritating, pungent smell while cow dung has a pleasant, sweet smell.
18. Radishes were used medicinally in Egypt from ancient times. Public works crews were fed radishes to ward off illness and infection. In 1948 biochemists isolated a substance called raphanin from an extract of radish seeds. Raphanin is an effective antibiotic against a number of bacteria, including *cocci* and *coli.* See Richard A. Gabriel and Karen S. Metz, *A History of Military Medicine*, vol. 1, *From Ancient Times to the Middle Ages* (Westport, CT: Greenwood Press, 1992), 82.
19. For more on the rations of ancient armies, see Richard A. Gabriel, "Rations," in *Soldiers' Lives through History: Antiquity* (Westport, CT: Greenwood Press, 2007), chapter 5.
20. A four-gallon bucket lowered into a well and raised every fifteen seconds for twenty-four hours would remove only 23,040 gallons of water a day, assuming the well did not play out, or about just enough water to supply Thutmose's army for a single day. On average, mules and horses require about eight times as much water as soldiers do.
21. Gabriel and Metz, *From Sumer to Rome,* 108.
22. M. Kerstein, M. Mager, R. Hubbard, and J. Connelly "Heat-Related Problems in the Desert: The Environment Can Be the Enemy," *Military Medicine* 149 (December 1984): 650–56.
23. R. O. Faulkner, "The Battle of Megiddo," *Journal of Egyptian Archaeology* 28 (1942): 2.
24. Ibid., 6.

25. "It is an inescapable fact of equine life that ridden or loaded horses and pack animals cannot travel more than seven consecutive days without a rest day, otherwise their backs are damaged." Barker, "Crossing the Hellespont," 6.
26. See Redford, *Egypt, Canaan and Israel in Ancient Times,* 155; and Helck, *Geschichte des Alten Agypten,* 154.
27. Israel Finkelstein, David Ussishkin, and Baruch Halpern, eds., *Megiddo III: The 1992–1996 Seasons*, vol. 2, *The Finds* (Tel Aviv: Emery and Claire Yass Publications in Archaeology, Institute of Archaeology, Tel Aviv University, 2000), 540.
28. The population estimate of Megiddo is based on Yadin's calculations of 240 people per urban acre in Canaanite cities during this period. See Yadin, *The Art of Warfare in Biblical Lands,* 2:20.
29. Until the New Kingdom, the Egyptians were able to construct walls and buildings only on flat land. The Canaanites, by contrast, could build walls and buildings to follow the contour of the land, and the walls did so at Megiddo.
30. Eric H. Cline, *The Battles of Armageddon: Megiddo and the Jezreel Valley from the Bronze Age to the Nuclear Age* (Ann Arbor: University of Michigan Press, 2000), 22.
31. Goedicke, *The Battle of Megiddo,* 108.
32. Nelson, *The Battle of Megiddo,* 38.
33. Cline, *The Battles of Armageddon,* 10. These conditions are well attested from Roman times to the present. The biblical story of Deborah's victory over Sisera in the Kishon Valley—she tricked him into leaving the heights, and entering upon the plain, his troops and chariots became stuck in the mud—suggests that these same conditions obtained in the Late Bronze Age as well.
34. Redford, *The Wars in Syria and Palestine of Thutmose III,* 34–35.
35. Nelson, *The Battle of Megiddo,* 53.
36. Ibid., 6; and Townsend, "The First Battle in History," 18, citing James Henry Breasted.
37. Goedicke, *The Battle of Megiddo,* 128.
38. Ibid., 32 and 128.
39. Redford, *The Wars in Syria and Palestine of Thutmose III,* 15.
40. Faulkner, "Egyptian Military Organization," 32–47. See also Schulman, *Military Rank, Title, and Organization*, 292.
41. Finkelstein, Ussishkin, and Halpern, *Megiddo III,* 2:535.
42. Redford, *The Wars in Syria and Palestine of Thutmose III,* 14; Faulkner, "The Battle of Megiddo," 3.
43. Redford, *The Wars in Syria and Palestine of Thutmose III,* 14.
44. Faulkner, "The Battle of Megiddo," 3.
45. Redford, *The Wars in Syria and Palestine of Thutmose III,* 22.
46. Faulkner, "The Battle of Megiddo," 7.
47. The obvious question, then, is why didn't Thutmose take the Djefty road? The usual answer is that it was too long and that it would have exposed his army's rear to attack. This answer is unconvincing. If the Aruna road was too narrow to permit Thutmose to move his army on it in anything but single file, then it is difficult to see how an Asiatic force attacking up the road from the mountains' exit could have moved its army in strength up the same road.

48. The assumption is, of course, that Thutmose's reconnaissance teams would have observed the Asiatic task forces on the plain. But even if they did not, the Egyptians were thoroughly familiar with the organization and equipment of the Canaanite armies and would surely have known that they were chariot heavy.
49. Modern Ar'arah is probably the site of ancient Aruna.
50. Nelson, *The Battle of Megiddo,* 32. Unfortunately, Nelson offers no details.
51. Goedicke, *The Battle of Megiddo,* 34.
52. Ibid., 33.
53. This estimate is purely hypothetical but seems reasonable in light of the assumption that the Asiatics expected the Egyptians to come down the widest and easiest road through Jenin on to Ta'anach.
54. Goedicke, *The Battle of Megiddo,* 51–52.
55. Faulkner, "The Battle of Megiddo," 7.
56. Nelson, *The Battle of Megiddo,* 43.
57. Townsend, "The First Battle in History," 26.
58. Goedicke, *The Battle of Megiddo,* 50.
59. Ibid., 57.
60. Ibid., 50.
61. Ibid., 57.
62. A force of ten thousand men requires just less than two square miles of ground upon which to encamp. See Maurice, "The Size of the Army of Xerxes," 214.
63. Nelson, *The Battle of Megiddo,* 50.
64. Ibid., 26. The early American railway routes also followed the natural course of rivers and streams through mountainous terrain.
65. Besides using maps and Google Earth satellite photos, I have twice walked the ground in and around Megiddo.
66. The ground on either side of the stream is flat and bare. During the rainy season, this wide path serves as the Kina's flood plain. But by June, the brook is back in its banks, and the land on either side is firm and dry.
67. Goedicke, *The Battle of Megiddo,* 49.
68. Ibid., 57.
69. Ibid.
70. Ibid.
71. Ibid.
72. Ibid., 60.
73. Goedicke's location of the Egyptian camp as being close to the bend of the Kina brook cannot be correct. The area he identifies as the camp is only 360 feet by 1,340 feet, not nearly large enough to accommodate an army of ten thousand men, horses, chariots, and so forth. They would require at least two square miles upon which to encamp.
74. In May, the sun sets in Megiddo around 7:00 p.m.
75. The only portrayals of Egyptian military camps are those of Ramses II at the battle of Kadesh. There is no good reason to think that Thutmose's camp was any different. See Gichon, "Military Camps in Egyptian and Syrian Reliefs."
76. Egyptian shields of this period appear to have a non-Argive-like grip; that is, the handle in back of the shield runs horizontally, not vertically. The first reliefs

of Argive-like grips in Egypt seem to appear on the Shardanna guardsmen's shields during the reign of Ramses II.

77. It is interesting to note that the design of the desert tabernacle described in Exodus 26–27 and 36–38 is nearly an exact copy of Ramses's war tent at the battle of Kadesh and is portrayed in the reliefs found on the wall of the Great Hall of Abu Simbel. The famous Old Testament scholar Hugo Grossman first made this observation in 1913. See Michael M. Homan, "The Divine Warrior in His Tent: A Military Model for Yahweh's Tabernacle," *Bible Review* 16, no. 6 (December 2000): 55; and Gabriel, *The Military History of Ancient Israel*, 95–98.
78. Goedicke, *The Battle of Megiddo*, 64.
79. Faulkner ("The Battle of Megiddo," 11) and Goedicke (*The Battle of Megiddo*, 67) differ on the meaning of this phrase.
80. Goedicke, *The Battle of Megiddo*, 67.
81. Ibid.
82. Ibid., 71.
83. Townsend, "The First Battle in History," 29.
84. Weingartner, "Chariots Changed Forever the Way Warfare Was Fought," 18–26; and by the same author, "In the Near Eastern Bronze Age, Chariot Tactics," 18–22, 79. Weingartner's book *Chariots as a Whirlwind* (Westport, CT: Praeger, forthcoming 2009) promises to be the definitive work on chariot tactics.
85. I am indebted to Steve Weingartner for the idea that horse movements in a chariot battle were much like those in a polo match.
86. Goedicke, *The Battle of Megiddo*, 75.
87. Their panic did not lead them to abandon their chariots on the battlefield, which, of course, would have been suicidal. The Asiatics fled in their chariots toward the city. As the charioteers scrambled over the city's walls, they abandoned the chariots, which the Egyptians gathered up later.
88. Redford, *The Wars in Syria and Palestine of Thutmose III*, 30; and Goedicke, *The Battle of Megiddo*, 72.
89. This conclusion is based on a study of the nature and type of casualties suffered in the infantry-chariot melee in Ramses II's camp at the battle of Kadesh. It seems that the poor bloody infantry always gets the worst of it! See Gonzalo M. Sanchez, "Injuries in the Battle of Kadesh," *KMT* 14, no. 1 (Spring 2003): 58–65.
90. Goedicke, *The Battle of Megiddo*, 80.
91. Yadin, *The Art of Warfare in Biblical Lands*, 2:20.
92. See Goedicke, *The Battle of Megiddo*, 91 and 128, for the problems associated with determining the length of the siege.
93. Redford, *The Wars in Syria and Palestine of Thutmose III*, 37–39; and Spalinger, *War in Ancient Egypt*, 95. The problem of the location of these towns is dealt with in chapter 5. As Breasted notes, they have been misidentified as being located in north Jordan when in fact they are located near the Litani River in south Lebanon. As chapter 5 makes clear, Thutmose captured these towns during his incursion into Lebanon later that summer.
94. Redford, *The Wars in Syria and Palestine of Thutmose III*, 39–39.
95. Goedicke, *The Battle of Megiddo*, 92.
96. Ibid., 96.

97. Since the story of the town's establishment appears only on the Gebel Barkal stela it cannot be taken as certain. See ibid., 123. Some sort of town and cultic center had existed at or near Beth Shean probably for millennia. Thutmose may have turned the site into a fortified town for the Egyptian military's use.

5. THE CAMPAIGN IN CANAAN

1. Redford, *The Wars in Syria and Palestine of Thutmose III*, 219.
2. A. T. Olmstead, *History of Palestine and Syria to the Macedonian Conquest* (Westport, CT: Greenwood Press, 1972), 76. I have relied on this classic work for its description of the geography of Lebanon and Syria and for its analysis of the archaeological evidence for the descriptions of the ancient cities of Kadesh and Qatna.
3. Petrie's claim that these cities were first encountered by Thutmose near Megiddo and that they must therefore have been in the Jordan Valley is incorrect. See Breasted, *Ancient Records of Egypt*, 2:187; and Nicolas Grimal, *A History of Ancient Egypt*, trans. Ian Shaw (Oxford, UK: Blackwell, 1988), 213.
4. Breasted, *Ancient Records of Egypt*, 188. I have relied on Breasted's work for the translation of the original inscriptions. He was the first to publish these translations in 1906. Most of the footnotes from this source that appear herein are references to the original texts.
5. Ibid., 186.
6. Ibid., 220.
7. Redford, *The Wars in Syria and Palestine of Thutmose III*, 144.
8. Ibid., 195.
9. Olmstead, *History of Palestine and Syria to the Macedonian Conquest*, 144.
10. It is interesting to speculate where Thutmose III might have learned about his grandfather's exploits and, more specifically, his strategic thinking. He may have listened to tales about the old man from Thutmose I's former generals and even from Hatshepsut herself. She seems to have idolized her father, even going so far as to have his sarcophagus moved into her tomb. The Egyptians were well aware of their history and kept historical records. Thutmose would have had access to the temple library when he was sent there to learn to read and write and become a priest of Amun.
11. Redford, *The Wars in Syria and Palestine of Thutmose III*, 199.
13. This is Olmstead's view of the matter. Olmstead, *History of Palestine and Syria to the Macedonian Conquest*, 135.
14. Breasted, *Ancient Records of Egypt*, 198.
15. Redford, *The Wars in Syria and Palestine of Thutmose III*, 71.
16. Ibid., 170.
17. Olmstead, *History of Palestine and Syria to the Macedonian Conquest*, 143.
18. Ibid. See also Laskowski, "Monumental Architecture and the Royal Building Program of Thutmose III," 183–237.
19. The use of regnal years to chronicle events is sometimes confusing. Pharaohs counted their reigns as beginning from the year in which they actually came to the throne. Thutmose's father had died when Thutmose was an infant, so he officially assumed the throne then even though Hatshepsut ruled as regent.

Thus, when he assumed the throne in his own right, it was in his twenty-third regnal year.

20. Redford, *The Wars in Syria and Palestine of Thutmose III*, 131, 214. The "lands of Fenkhu" are generally identified with the Phoenician coast, most particularly the coast north of Carmel.
21. Ibid.
22. T. L. Thompson, *The Settlement of Palestine in the Late Bronze Age* (Wiesbaden, Germany, 1979), 59.
23. Breasted, *Ancient Records of Egypt*, 191–92.
24. Ibid., 193.
25. Ibid.
26. Olmstead, *History of Palestine and Syria to the Macedonian Conquest*, 135–36; and Breasted, *Ancient Records of Egypt*, 195.
27. See Gabriel, "The Dawn of Conscience," in *Gods of Our Fathers*, chapter 1, for Pharaoh's role in maintaining universal order. See also James Henry Breasted, *Development of Religion and Thought in Ancient Egypt: Lectures Delivered on the Morse Foundation at Union Theological Seminary* (New York: Charles Scriber's Sons, 1912), chapter 6.
28. Redford, *The Wars in Syria and Palestine of Thutmose III*, 217.
29. The name of Eleutheros Valley is taken from Strabo, *Histories*, xvi, 2, 12, and was used throughout classical times. The name appears in the Bible (Maccabees 11:7 and 12:30), but we do not know by what name it was known to the Egyptians.
30. Olmstead, *History of Palestine and Syria to the Macedonian Conquest*, 73–74.
31. Donald W. Engels, *Alexander the Great and the Logistics of the Macedonian Army* (Berkeley: University of California Press, 1978), 155.
32. Two of those rivers, the Crocodile and the Gihon, still flow through the area. The Crocodile River has provided water to Caesarea since Roman times.
33. The swamp remained a major obstacle until Roman times when it was drained and turned into farmland. After the Arab conquest, the drainage system was allowed to decay and the swamp once more covered the land until the Israelis repaired the drainage system in the 1950s.
34. Breasted, *Ancient Records of Egypt*, 197–98.
35. "Arvad [is] a bare rock in the center of a north and south line of reefs, two and a half miles from shore. A half mile long and quarter mile wide, its surface rose but a few feet above the waves. . . . On all sides but the east were reefs whose dangers only the local pilots knew. The bare rocks were leveled off with stones and concrete, and to west and south rose a great seawall above the moat." Olmstead, *History of Palestine and Syria to the Macedonian Conquest*, 137. It was very close to the modern port of Tartus.
36. Breasted, *Ancient Records of Egypt*, 196.
37. Ibid., 196–97.
38. Ibid.
39. Redford, *The Wars in Syria and Palestine of Thutmose III*, 217.
40. Spalinger, *War in Ancient Egypt*, 57.
41. Olmstead, *History of Palestine and Syria to the Macedonian Conquest*, 136.

42. Breasted, *Ancient Records of Egypt*, 196.
43. Ibid.

6. THE CAMPAIGN FOR THE LEBANON COAST

1. Save-Soderbergh, *The Navy of the Eighteenth Egyptian Dynasty*, 30.
2. Redford, *The Wars in Syria and Palestine of Thutmose III*, 218. The term *palatine cities* refers to the fact that these small towns were based on small palace economies.
3. Ibid.
4. George W. Houston, "Ports in Perspective: Some Comparative Material on Roman Merchant Ships and Ports," *American Journal of Archaeology* 92, no. 4 (1988): 559. See also Avner Raban, "Minoan and Canaanite Harbours," *Aegaeum* 7 (1991): 129–46.
5. Olmstead, *History of Palestine and Syria to the Macedonian Conquest*, 119.
6. Ibid. More recent archaeological research carried out by a Syrian-Italian team at Qatna in 2008 confirms the dimensions of the city that Olmstead had noted in his earlier work.
7. Save-Soderbergh, *The Navy of the Eighteenth Egyptian Dynasty*, 34.
8. Faulkner, "Egyptian Seagoing Ships," 3.
9. Richard A. Gabriel, *Scipio Africanus: Rome's Greatest General* (Washington, DC: Potomac Books, 2008), 152; and Houston, "Ports in Perspective," 559.
10. Faulkner, "Egyptian Seagoing Ships," 3.
11. Save-Soderbergh, *The Navy of the Eighteenth Egyptian Dynasty*, 34.
12. Spalinger, *War in Ancient Egypt*, 6.
13. Bietak, "The Thutmoside Stronghold of Perunefer," 13–17.
14. Save-Soderbergh, *The Navy of the Eighteenth Egyptian Dynasty*, 90.
15. Ibid., 37.
16. James Hornell, "Naval Activity in the Days of Solomon and Ramses III," *Antiquity* 21 (1947): 66.
17. Save-Soderbergh, *The Navy of the Eighteenth Egyptian Dynasty*, 46.
18. Faulkner, "Egyptian Seagoing Ships," 4. The dates are taken from Sir Alan H. Gardiner, *Egypt of the Pharaohs* (Oxford, UK: Oxford University Press, 1961), 434–35.
19. William F. Edgerton, "Ancient Egyptian Ships and Shipping," *American Journal of Semitic Languages and Literature* 39, no. 2 (January 1923): 116–17.
20. William F. Edgerton, "Dimensions of Ancient Egyptian Ships," *American Journal of Semitic Languages and Literature* 46, no. 3 (April 1930): 146.
21. Faulkner, "Egyptian Seagoing Ships," 7–8.
22. Edgerton, "Ancient Egyptian Ships and Shipping," 121.
23. Faulkner, "Egyptian Seagoing Ships," 4.
24. Edgerton, "Dimensions of Ancient Egyptian Ships," 146.
25. Faulkner, "Egyptian Seagoing Ships," 3–4.
26. Spalinger, *War in Ancient Egypt*, 54.
27. Faulkner, "Egyptian Seagoing Ships," 8.
28. Ibid.
29. Edgerton, "Dimensions of Ancient Egyptian Ships," 149.

30. William F. Edgerton, "Ancient Egyptian Steering Gear," *American Journal of Semitic Languages and Literature* 43, no. 4 (July 1927): 255–65.
31. Edgerton, "Ancient Egyptian Ships and Shipping," 116.
32. Faulkner, "Egyptian Seagoing Ships," 7.
33. Gabriel, *Empires at War,* 1:88.
34. Lionel Casson, "Seasons and Winds, Sailing, Rowing Speed," in *Ships and Seamanship in the Ancient World* (Princeton, NJ: Princeton University Press, 1971), 270.
35. Ibid. See also H. Koster, *Das antike Seewesen* (Berlin, 1923), 125.
36. Koster, *Das antike Seewesen,* 125; and Connie Lambrou-Phillipson, "Seafaring in the Bronze Age Mediterranean," *Aegaeum* 7 (1999): 11–19.
37. Raban, "Minoan and Canaanite Harbours," 129–46; and Houston, "Ports in Perspective," 559.
38. Redford, *The Wars in Syria and Palestine of Thutmose III,* 205. See also R. P. Duncan-Jones, "Giant Cargo Ships in Antiquity," *Classical Quarterly* 27, no. 2 (1977): 331–36.
39. An approximate model of a Roman era transport of eighty to a hundred tons burden can be found in the entrepot vessels that plied the New England coast in the 1870s. These vessels were ninety feet long, sixteen feet wide, and fourteen feet deep from keel to deck. They were shallow-draft boats drawing less than two feet of water when empty and were capable of carrying a hundred tons of firewood, lumber, or coal. My thanks to Paul Rollins of York, Maine, a naval architect and shipbuilder, for the information on New England entrepots.
40. The name of one of these transports was *The Stable,* clearly suggesting it was a horse transport. Save-Soderbergh, *The Navy of the Eighteenth Egyptian Dynasty,* 42.
41. Gabriel, *Soldiers' Lives through History,* 10. See also Roth, *The Logistics of the Roman Army at War,* 9.
42. Alcohol served the important purpose of calming the nerves of the soldiers, many of whom had never seen the sea and had surely never sailed on it.
43. I owe a debt of gratitude to Ms. Alison Galliardi of Maine, an accomplished horsewoman, for these figures. Those interested in more information about the horse in ancient Egypt should see Spalinger, *War in Ancient Egypt,* 8–11.
44. Roth, *The Logistics of the Roman Army at War,* 66–67.
45. Gabriel, *The Military History of Ancient Israel,* 120.
46. For example, the complete sarcophagus for the burial of the sacred Apis bull was quarried of black Aswan granite and weighed twenty-five tons. Egyptian sailors transported the sarcophagus from Aswan to Memphis, a distance of six hundred miles, by boat.
47. Although Egyptians were constructing ships for millennia before Roman times, there persisted an impression in modern scholarship that they were not a seafaring people. In "Ancient Egyptian Ships and Shipping," 134, Edgerton notes, "At some time between the 18th Dynasty and the period represented by the oldest surviving Greek traditions, Egyptian shipping disappeared from the sea and has never been revived; we still have to combat the myth that the ancient Egyptians were never a sea-faring people." The reasons for the demise

of Egyptian shipping are complex but include the gradual weakening of Egyptian authority in Asia during the Amarna period and the shift to ground warfare in Asia, which did not require an amphibious capability. It is now clear from recent research that the Egyptians designed and constructed ships that were later used by the Phoenicians. See Mertz, *Red Land, Black Land,* 231.

48. Breasted, *Ancient Records of Egypt,* 197.
49. Ibid., 198.
50. Ibid., 232.
51. Olmstead, *History of Palestine and Syria in the Macedonian Conquest,* 118.
52. Ibid., 119.
53. Yadin, *The Art of Warfare in Biblical Lands,* 2:20.
54. Ibid.
55. Redford, *Egypt, Canaan, and Israel in Ancient Times,* 158. Redford agrees that Thutmose probably did not capture Kadesh.
56. Indeed, it was on this plain that Ramses II fought the Hittites at the battle of Kadesh in 1275 BCE.
57. Breasted, *Ancient Records of Egypt,* 198.
58. Ibid., 232.
59. It was the Egyptian practice to cut off the hand of an enemy as proof that one had killed the adversary in battle. This practice sometimes produced problems wherein the hands of the enemy wounded as well as the hands of Egyptian dead were severed and presented to superiors for rewards.
60. Breasted, *Ancient Records of Egypt,* 232.
61. Ibid., 198.
62. This location presented no problem since the Mediterranean is essentially tideless; however, it was more difficult to push a boat off the sand once it had been beached to off-load its troops or cargo.
63. Olmstead, *History of Palestine and Syria in the Macedonian Conquest,* 137.
64. Redford, *The Wars in Syria and Palestine of Thutmose III,* 218.
65. Breasted, *Ancient Records of Egypt,* 198.
66. The Egyptians symbolized their intention to remain in Arvad by erecting an obelisk on the island; it still stands. Olmstead, *History of Palestine and Syria in the Macedonian Conquest,* 138.
67. Breasted, *Ancient Records of Egypt,* 198.
68. Ibid., 199, for "the son of that foe of Tunip"; and Redford, *Egypt, Canaan, and Israel in Ancient Times,* 158.
69. Breasted, *Ancient Records of Egypt,* 199.
70. Ibid.
71. Ibid.
72. Redford, *Egypt, Canaan, and Israel in Ancient Times,* 158.
73. Breasted, *Ancient Records of Egypt,* 200.
74. Ibid.
75. Ibid.
76. Ibid.
77. Ibid., 204. The military supplies were collected as impost—that is, a direct levy—and are to be distinguished from tribute.

78. Breasted, *Ancient Records of Egypt*, 198.
79. Ibid.
80. Redford, "The Northern Wars of Thutmose III," 333.

7. THE EUPHRATES CAMPAIGN

1. Redford, *The Wars in Syria and Palestine of Thutmose III*, 220.
2. See Forbes, *Studies in Ancient Technology*, 37, for the calculations regarding the number of smiths required for an army of twenty thousand troops. Forbes bases his calculations on information found in the writings of Livy, Dionysius, and Cicero.
3. Redford, *The Wars in Syria and Palestine of Thutmose III*, 231.
4. Ibid., 232.
5. Ibid., 123.
6. Ibid.
7. The version of the Gebel Barkal stela used herein is taken from Sethe, *Urkunden der 18. Dynastie*, Bd. 2: Historisch-biographishce Urkunden, Heft 4, S. 1227-1243, and appears online at http://www.terraflex.co.il/ad/egypt/napata_stela.htm.
8. Ibid.
9. Spalinger, *War in Ancient Egypt*, 114.
10. Gebel Barkal stela, 4, in Sethe, *Urkunden der 18. Dynastie*.
11. R. O. Faulkner, "The Euphrates Campaign of Thutmose III," *Journal of Egyptian Archaeology* 32 (1947): 40.
12. Ibid.
13. Yadin, *The Art of Warfare in Biblical Lands*, 1:90.
14. Gichon, "Military Camps on Egyptian and Assyrian Reliefs," *Assaph: Studies in Honor of Asher Ovadiah* (Tel Aviv: Department of Art History, Tel Aviv University, 2005–6), 571.
15. Gabriel, *Soldiers' Lives through History*, 102. See also *Animal Management* (London: British Army Veterinary Department, 1908), 299.
16. Bernard S. Bachrach, "Animals and Warfare in Early Medieval Europe," in *Armies and Politics in the Early Medieval West*, ed. Bernard S. Bachrach (Brookfield, VT: Variorum, 1993), 717.
17. See Breasted, *Ancient Records of Egypt*, 2:227–34, for Amenemhab's biography.
18. See Redford, *The Wars in Syria and Palestine of Thutmose III*, 222–23, for the thematic argument.
19. An army of twenty thousand troops marching four abreast forms a column seven miles long. Add to this number the 6,500 animals and the wagons, and an estimate of ten miles for the length of Thutmose's column seems reasonable. See Maurice, "The Size of the Army of Xerxes," 229.
20. Redford, *The Wars in Syria and Palestine of Thutmose III*, 126–27.
21. The exact location of Tunip is unknown.
22. It is not unreasonable to suspect that part of the arrangements Thutmose made with Tunip and Qatna may also have included an agreement for the cities to provide some supplies for the Egyptian army. The alternative they faced was that Thutmose would simply plunder the agricultural countryside around the cities. Armies, after all, have to be fed.

23. R. S. Bagnall, *Egypt in Late Antiquity* (Princeton: NJ: Princeton University Press, 1993), 39. A thousand donkeys could transport 150,000 pounds of food and other supplies. See also Gabriel, "Logistics," in *Soldiers' Lives*, 107–10, for the logistics of ancient armies.
24. British staff officers in World War I invented the term *wastage* to describe the number of soldiers who became unfit for a variety of reasons each day.
25. Breasted suggests that modern Gebel Sim, a ridge 2,700 feet high that is located north and west of Aleppo, might have been the location of the battle. Breasted, *Ancient Records of Egypt*, 231.
26. Ibid.
27. Ibid.
28. Ibid.
29. For a description of the agricultural region around the area of Carchemish and the west bank of the Euphrates in antiquity, see Irene J. Winter, "Carchemish," *Anatolian Studies* 33 (1983): 177–97; T. J. Wilkinson, E. Peltenburg, A. McCarthy, E. B. Wilkinson, and M. Brown, *Archaeology in the Land of Carchemish: Landscape Surveys in the Area of Jerablus Tahtani, 2006* (London: Council for British Research Inside the Levant, 2007), 213–47; and Tony J. Wilkinson, *On the Margin of the Euphrates: Settlement and Land Use at Tell Es-Sweyhat and in the Upper Land Area, Syria* (Chicago: University of Chicago Oriental Institute Publications, 2004), 124:79
30. Breasted, *Ancient Records of Egypt*, 203.
31. A 30-foot-long, 9.8-inch-diameter modern telephone pole made from cedar weighs about 428 pounds. Twenty-four of these poles would be sufficient to fashion a raft 20 feet wide. A wagon carrying eight poles would have a load burden of 3,424 pounds. Three wagons could carry enough logs for one raft. A fourth wagon could carry the five cross poles, pegs, dowels, and papyrus rope. Thus, four wagons could carry all the materials needed to construct one raft. My thanks to Ms. Phyllis Sipe, regional manager for Koppers Incorporated, the largest supplier of telephone polls in the United States, and to Professor Jeff Schnick, chairman of the Department of Physics at Saint Anselm College, for his calculations regarding the load-carrying capacity of the rafts.
32. Gebel Barkal stela, 3, in Sethe, *Urkunden der 18. Dynastie*.
33. The king of the Mitanni may have been Barratarna. See Redford, *The Wars in Syria and Palestine of Thutmose III*, 231.
34. Ibid., 74.
35. Faulkner, "The Euphrates Campaign of Thutmose III," 40.
36. Ibid.
37. Ibid.
38. Breasted, *Ancient Records of Egypt*, 202.
39. Redford, *The Wars in Syria and Palestine of Thutmose III*, 223.
40. Ibid., 74.
41. Gebel Barkal stela, 4, in Sethe, *Urkunden der 18. Dynastie*.
42. Breasted, *Ancient Records of Egypt*, 202.
43. It is for this reason—the conquered country became part of Pharaoh's realm—that the texts frequently portray the military expeditions of the Egyptian king as "extending the boundaries of Egypt."

44. Breasted, *Ancient Records of Egypt*, 202.
45. Redford, *The Wars in Syria and Palestine of Thutmose III*, 224.
46. Ibid., 225.
47. Breasted, *Ancient Records of Egypt*, 202.
48. Gebel Barkal stela, 5, in Sethe, *Urkunden der 18. Dynastie*.
49. Breasted, *Ancient Records of Egypt*, 233.
50. For a fictional account of Thutmose's elephant hunt at Niya see my novel, *Lion of the Sun* (New York: iUniverse, 2001).
51. Breasted, *Ancient Records of Egypt*, 233.
52. Ibid.
53. Cantrell, "The Horsemen of Israel" (Ph.D. diss., Vanderbilt University, 2008), 34. See also Ann Hyland, *Equus: The Horse in the Roman World* (New Haven, CT: Yale University Press, 1990), 81.
54. Cantrell, "The Horsemen of Israel," 33–34.
55. Ibid.
56. Ibid., 32.
57. Ibid., 42.
58. Ibid., 31.
59. Breasted, *Ancient Records of Egypt*, 233–34.
60. Redford, *The Wars in Syria and Palestine of Thutmose III*, 240.
61. Breasted, *Ancient Records of Egypt*, 233.
62. Redford, *The Wars in Syria and Palestine of Thutmose III*, 174.
63. The term *chauvechée* was first used by the French during the Hundred Years War to describe the English practice of landing an army on French soil and marching inland, plundering and looting as they went, only to return to their ships, leave, and make no attempt to occupy the territory they had ravaged.

8. THE COUNTERINSURGENCY CAMPAIGN

1. A. T. Olmstead, *History of Palestine and Syria* (Westport, CT: Greenwood Press, 1972), 118–22, notes that many of the maryanna-dominated cities of Syria had military camps and fortifications outside them, remnants of the days when the maryanna first imposed themselves upon the cities.
2. Yadin, *The Art of Warfare in Biblical Lands*, 1:70, disagrees, noting that there are illustrations showing Egyptian troops using a number of siege engines, including the battering ram, long before Thutmose III's reign. O'Connor, in "Thutmose III: A Enigmatic Pharaoh," 31, argues that the successful Egyptian assaults against the Hyksos capital at Avaris and Sharuhen argue for the presence of Egyptian siege capability. The problem is that except for Megiddo, there is no claim in the texts that any major Syrian city was taken by siege. The Egyptians did have the capability to attack defensive walls but only if they were fashioned of mud brick. The walls of the Syrian cities were stone casement walls, which were another matter entirely.
3. Some researchers have included Ebla and even Niya in the Nukhashshe area. This information seems to be erroneous.
4. "Regnal year 34. Now His Majesty was in Djahy . . . his . . . capitulating to His Majesty completely and abjectly. Tally of the towns plundered in this year: two towns. Towns which capitulated in the region of Nukhashshe." See

Redford, *The Wars in Syria and Palestine of Thutmose III*, 79.
5. Wolfgang Helck, in *Die Beziehungen Aegyptens und Vorderasiens zur Agais bis 7. Jahrhundert von Chr.* (Darmstadt, Germany, 1979), 153, places Ar'anu to the west of Aleppo.
6. Redford, *The Wars in Syria and Palestine of Thutmose III*, 83.
7. Ibid.
8. Ibid.
9. Ibid., 234.
10. Ibid., 87.
11. Ibid., 89.
12. Redford, *Egypt, Canaan, and Israel in Ancient Times*, 160–61.
13. Breasted, *Ancient Records of Egypt*, 2:211.
14. Ibid., 212. Breasted argues that the spacing on Pylon VI indicates that there was probably an additional text addressing some campaign in year 40, but all that has survived are the tribute lists from Cyprus and the imposts of Kush and Wawat.
15. Redford, *The Wars in Syria and Palestine of Thutmose III*, 93.
16. Redford disagrees, suggesting that the mention of the road indicates an overland march. I am convinced that Breasted is correct on this point. Redford, *The Wars in Syria and Palestine of Thutmose III*, 95.
17. Ibid.
18. Breasted, *Ancient Records of Egypt*, 2:214. See also H. Klengel, *Syria 3000 to 300 B.C.: A Handbook of Political History* (Berlin: Akademie Verlag, 1992), 162.
19. Redford, *The Wars in Syria and Palestine of Thutmose III*, 95.
20. Redford, *Egypt, Canaan, and Israel in Ancient Times*, 162.
21. Redford, *The Wars in Syria and Palestine of Thutmose III*, 239.
22. Breasted, *Ancient Records of Egypt*, 2:215–16.
23. Redford, *The Wars in Syria and Palestine of Thutmose III*, 95.
24. Ibid., 240.
25. Ibid., 75.

9. EPILOGUE

1. Arthur Weigall, *A History of the Pharaohs* (New York: E. P. Dutton, 1927), 2:385.
2. Breasted, *Ancient Records of Egypt*, 2:217.
3. Redford, *The Wars in Syria and Palestine of Thutmose III*, 214.
4. Goedicke, *The Battle of Megiddo*, 126.
5. Sethe, *Urkunden der 18. Dynastie*, S. 1227-1243, for the complete translation of the Napata stela.
6. Weigall, *A History of the Pharaohs*, 2:394.
7. O'Connor, "Thutmose III: An Enigmatic Pharaoh," 31; and Salinger, "Covetous Eyes South," 355, support the contention that Thutmose led an expedition into Nubia in regnal year 50.
8. Redford, "The Coregency of Thutmose III and Amenophis II," 122.
9. Ibid., 243.
10. Weigall, *A History of the Pharaohs*, 2:394.
11. The regnal year of a new pharaoh usually began when the new king assumed the throne. Thus, a king who assumed the throne at age twenty would mark

that year as his first regnal year. In the case of Thutmose III, the question of when to begin his regnal years remains unsettled. If his father died when Thutmose was still an infant, as seems the case, then his regnal years would begin then, even though his stepmother-aunt, Hatshepsut, ruled as regent. If, as some maintain, his father died when Thutmose was age six or seven, then at his first regnal year he would have been age six or seven. Thus, it is possible that Thutmose was either fifty-four or sixty years of age when he died.

12. Redford, in *Egypt, Canaan, and Israel in Ancient Times,* 163, cites Peter der Manuelian, *Studies in the Reign of Amenophis II* (Leiden, the Netherlands: Hildesheim, 1987), 56.

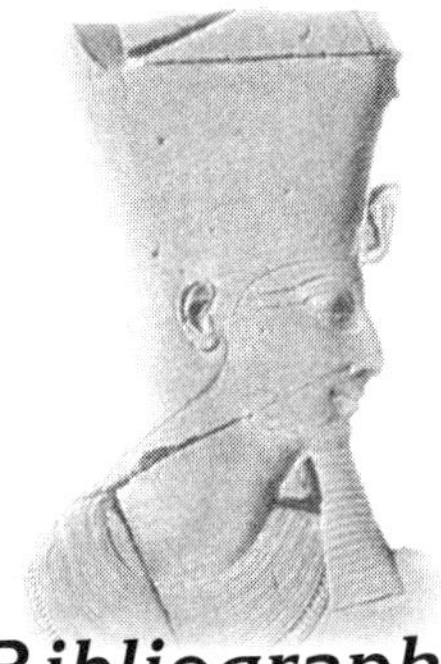

Bibliography

Aldred, Cyril. *Egyptian Art*. London: Thames and Hudson, 1980.

"Ancient Egyptian Joint Operations in Lebanon under Thutmose III (1451–1438 BCE)." *Semaphore: Newsletter of the Sea Power Centre of Australia* 16 (August 2006): 1–2 (http://www.navy.gov.au/Publication:Semaphore_-_Issue_16%2C_2006).

Animal Management. London: British Army Veterinary Department, 1908.

Bachrach, Bernard S., ed. *Armies and Politics in the Early Medieval West*. Brookfield, VT: Variorum, 1993.

Bagnall, R. S. *Egypt in Late Antiquity*. Princeton, NJ: Princeton University Press, 1993.

Baines, John, and Jaromir Malek. *Atlas of Ancient Egypt*. Oxford, UK: Andromeda Books, 1980.

Barker, Peter. "Crossing the Hellespont: A Study in Ancient Logistics." Paper delivered at VI Classics Colloquium, Classical Association of South Africa (CASA) Conference, February 2005, 1–12.

Bietak, Manfred. "The Thutmoside Stronghold of Perunefer." *Egyptian Archaeology* 26 (Spring 2005): 13–17.

Breasted, James Henry. *Ancient Records of Egypt*. Vol. 2, *The Eighteenth Dynasty*. Urbana: University of Illinois Press, 2001.

———. *Development of Religion and Thought in Ancient Egypt: Lectures Delivered on the Morse Foundation at Union Theological Seminary*. New York: Charles Scribner's Sons, 1912.

———. *A New Chapter in the Life of Thutmose III*. Leipzig: J. C. Hinrichs'sche Buchhandlung, 1900.

Bryan, Betsy M. "Administration in the Reign of Thutmose III." In Cline and O'Connor, *Thutmose III: A New Biography*, 69–122.

———. "The Egyptian Perspective on the Mitanni." In *Armana Diplomacy: The Beginnings of International Relations*, edited by Raymond Cohen and Raymond Westbrook, 71–84. Baltimore: Johns Hopkins University Press, 2002.

Butzer, K. W. *Early Hydraulic Civilization in Egypt: A Study in Cultural Ecology*. Chicago: University of Chicago Press, 1976.

Cambridge Ancient History. Vol. 2. Cambridge, UK: Cambridge University Press, 1973.

Cantrell, Deborah. "The Horsemen of Israel: Horses and Chariotry in Monarchic Israel." Ph.D. diss., Vanderbilt University, 2008.

Casson, Lionel. "Seasons and Winds, Sailing, Rowing Speed." In *Ships and Seamanship in the Ancient World*, 268–81. Princeton, NJ: Princeton University Press, 1971.

Cline, Eric. *The Battles of Armageddon: Megiddo and the Jezreel Valley from the Bronze Age to the Nuclear Age*. Ann Arbor: University of Michigan Press, 2000.

Cline, Eric, and David O'Connor, eds. *Thutmose III: A New Biography*. Ann Arbor: University of Michigan Press, 2008.

Cottrell, Leonard. *The Warrior Pharaohs*. New York: Dutton, 1969.

Dalley, S. "Foreign Chariotry and Cavalry in the Armies of Tiglath-Pileser III and Sargon II." *Iraq* 47 (1985): 31–48.

Dorman, Peter F. "The Early Reign of Thutmose III: An Unorthodox Mantle of Coregency." In Cline and O'Connor, *Thutmose III: A New Biography*, 39–68.

Drenkhahn, Rosemarie. *Die Handwerker und ihre Tatigkeiten im alten Agypten*. Wiesbaden, Germany: Harrossowitz, 1976.

Duncan-Jones, R. P. "Giant Cargo Ships in Antiquity." *Classical Quarterly* 27, no. 2 (1977): 331–36.

Edgerton, William F. "Ancient Egyptian Ships and Shipping." *American Journal of Semitic Languages and Literature* 39, no. 2 (January 1923): 109–35.

———. "Ancient Egyptian Steering Gear." *American Journal of Semitic Languages and Literature* 43, no. 4 (July 1927): 255–65.

———. "Dimensions of Ancient Egyptian Ships." *American Journal of Semitic Languages and Literature* 46, no. 3 (April 1930): 145–49.

———. "Egyptian Seagoing Ships of One Hundred Cubits." *American Journal of Semitic Languages and Literature* 47, no. 1 (October 1930): 50–51.

Engels, Donald W. *Alexander the Great and the Logistics of the Macedonian Army*. Berkeley: University of California Press, 1978.

Erman, Adolf. *Life in Ancient Egypt*. Translated by H. M. Tirard. New York: Dover Books, 1971.

Fabre, David. *Seafaring in Ancient Egypt*. New York: Periplus, 2004.

Faulkner, R. O. "The Battle of Megiddo." *Journal of Egyptian Archaeology* 28 (1942): 2–15.

———. "Egyptian Military Organization." *Journal of Egyptian Archaeology* 39 (1953): 32–47.

———. "Egyptian Seagoing Ships." *Journal of Egyptian Archaeology* 16 (1940): 3–17.

———. "The Euphrates Campaign of Thutmose III." *Journal of Egyptian Archaeology* 32 (1947): 39–42.

Fields, Nic. *Bronze Age War Chariots*. Oxford, UK: Osprey Publishing, 2006.

Finkelstein, Israel, David Ussishkin, and Baruch Halpern, eds. *Megiddo III: The 1992–1996 Seasons*. Vol. 2, *The Finds*. Tel Aviv: Emery and Claire Yass Publications in Archaeology, Institute of Archaeology, Tel Aviv University, 2000.

Forbes, Dennis. "Akheperenre Djehutymes: The All-But-Forgotten Second Thutmose." *KMT* 11, no. 2 (Summer 2000): 63–75.

———. "Menkheperre Djehutymes: Thutmose III, a Pharaoh's Pharaoh." *KMT* 9, no. 4 (Winter 1998–99): 44–65.

———. "Menkheperure Djehutymes: The Fourth and Final Thutmose." *KMT* 13, no. 2 (Summer 2002): 68–76.

Forbes, R. J. *Studies in Ancient Technology*. Leiden, the Netherlands: Brill, 1964.

Fox, Troy. "The Ancient Egyptian Navy." *Tour Egypt!* (http://www.touregypt.net/featurestories/navy.htm).

———. "Defensive Equipment of the Egyptian Army." *Tour Egypt!* (http://www.touregypt.net/featurestories/defense.htm).

———. "Military Architecture of Ancient Egypt." *Tour Egypt!* (http://www.touregypt.net/featurestories/fortresses.htm).

———. "Siege Warfare in Ancient Egypt." *Tour Egypt!* (http://www.touregypt.net/featurestories/siegewarfare.htm).

Gabriel, Richard A. *Empires at War: A Chronological Encyclopedia*. 3 vols. Westport, CT: Greenwood Press, 2005.

———. *Gods of Our Fathers: The Memory of Egypt in Judaism and Christianity*. Westport, CT: Greenwood Press, 2002.

———. *The Great Armies of Antiquity*. Westport, CT: Praeger Publishers, 2002.

———. *Great Captains of Antiquity*. Westport, CT: Greenwood Press, 2001.

———. *Jesus the Egyptian: The Origins of Christianity and the Psychology of Christ*. New York: Universe, 2005.

———. *The Military History of Ancient Israel*. Westport, CT: Praeger, 2003.

———. *Scipio Africanus: Rome's Greatest General*. Washington, DC: Potomac Books, 2008.

———. *Soliders' Lives through History: Antiquity*. Westport, CT: Greenwood Press, 2007.

Gabriel, Richard A., and Donald W. Boose, Jr. *The Great Battles of Antiquity: A Strategic and Tactical Guide to Great Battles That Shaped the Development of War*. Westport, CT: Greenwood Press, 1994.

Gabriel, Richard A., and Karen S. Metz. *From Sumer to Rome: The Military Capabilities of Ancient Armies*. Westport, CT: Greenwood Press, 1991.

Gabriel, Richard A., and Karen S. Metz. *A History of Military Medicine*. Vol. 1, *From Ancient Times to the Middle Ages*. Westport, CT: Greenwood Press, 1992.

Gardiner, Sir Alan H. "The Defeat of the Hyksos by Kamose: The Carnarvon Tablet, No. 1." *Journal of Egyptian Archaeology* 3 (1916): 95–110.

———. *Egypt of the Pharaohs*. Oxford, UK: Oxford University Press, 1961.

Gichon, Mordecai. "Military Camps in Egyptian and Assyrian Reliefs." *Assaph: Studies in Honor of Asher Ovadiah*. Tel Aviv: Department of Art History, Tel Aviv University, 2005–6, 569–93.

Goedicke, Hans. *The Battle of Megiddo*. Baltimore: Halgo Inc., 2000.

———. "Egyptian Military Actions in Asia in the Middle Kingdom." *Revue d'egyptologie* 42 (1991): 89–94.

Grant, Michael. *The History of Ancient Israel*. New York: Charles Scribner's Sons, 1984.

Grimal, Nicholas. *A History of Ancient Egypt*. Translated by Ian Shaw. Oxford, UK: Blackwell, 1988.

Gurney, O. R. *The Hittites*. London: Penguin, 1990.

Hansen, Kathy. "The Chariot in Egypt's Age of Chivalry." *KMT* 5, no. 1 (1994): 50–61, 82–83.

Hasel, Michael G. *Domination and Resistance: Egyptian Military Activity in the Southern Levant, 1300–1185 BC*. Boston: Brill, 1998.

Helck, Wolfgang. *Die Beziehungen Aegyptens und Vorderaisens zur Agais bis 7. Jahrhundert von Chr*. Darmstadt, Germany, 1979.

———. *Geschichte des Alten Agypten*. HdO, I, 3. 1968.

Hoffmeier, James K. "Tents in Egypt and the Ancient Near East." *Toronto Society for the Study of Egyptian Antiquities (SSEA) Journal* 7, no. 3 (1977): 13–28.

Homan, Michael M. "The Divine Warrior in His Tent: A Military Model for Yahweh's Tabernacle." *Bible Review* 16, no. 6 (December 2000): 51–57.

Hornell, James. "Naval Activity in the Days of Solomon and Ramses III." *Antiquity* 21 (1947): 66–73.

Houston, George W. "Ports in Perspective: Some Comparative Material on Roman Merchant Ships and Ports." *American Journal of Archaeology* 92, no. 4 (1988): 553–64.

Hyland, Ann. *Equus: The Horse in the Roman World*. New Haven, CT: Yale University Press, 1990.

Kerstein, M., M. Mager, R.Hubbard, and J. Connelly. "Heat-Related Problems in the Desert: The Environment Can Be the Enemy." *Military Medicine* 149 (December 1984): 650–56.

Klengel, H. *Syria 3000 to 300 BC: A Handbook of Political History*. Berlin: Akademie Verlag, 1992.

Koster, H. *Das antike Seewesen*. Berlin, 1923.

Kozloff, Arielle P. "The Artistic Production of the Reign of Thutmose III." In Cline and O'Connor, *Thutmose III: A New Biography*, 292–324.

Laboury, Dimitri. "Royal Portrait and Ideology: Evolution and Signification of the Statuary of Thutmose III." In Cline and O'Connor, *Thutmose III: A New Biography*, 260–91.

Lambrou-Philipson, Connie. "Seafaring in the Bronze Age Mediterranean." *Aegaeum* 7 (1999): 11–19.

Laskowski, Piotr. "Monumental Architecture and the Royal Building Program of Thutmose III." In Cline and O'Connor, *Thutmose III: A New Biography*, 183–237.

Manuelian, Peter der. *Studies in the Reign of Amenophis II*. Leiden, the Netherlands: Hildesheim, 1987.

Maurice, Gen. F. "The Size of the Army of Xerxes in the Invasion of Greece, 480 BC." *Journal of Hellenic Studies* 50, part 2 (1930): 210–35.

Mertz, Barbara. *Red Land, Black Land: Daily Life in Ancient Egypt*. New York: Peter Bedrick Books, 1990.

Morcos, S. R., and W. R. Morcos. "Diets in Ancient Egypt." *Progress in Food and Nutrition Science* 2 (1977): 457–71.

Nelson, Harold Hayden. *The Battle of Megiddo*. Chicago: University of Chicago Library, 1913.

Nicholson, P. T., and Ian Shaw. *Ancient Egyptian Materials and Technology*. Cambridge, UK: Cambridge University Press, 2000.

O'Connor, David. *Ancient Nubia: Egypt's Rival in Africa*. Philadelphia: University of Pennsylvania Museum Press, 1993.

———. "The Hyksos Period in Egypt." In Oren, *The Hyksos: New Historical and Archaeological Perspectives*, 43–56.

———. "Thutmose III: An Enigmatic Pharaoh." In Cline and O'Connor, *Thutmose III: A New Biography*, 1–38.

Olmstead, A. T. *History of Palestine and Syria to the Macedonian Conquest*. Westport, CT: Greenwood Press, 1972.

Oren, Eliezer D., ed. *The Hyksos: New Historical and Archaeological Perspectives*. Philadelphia: University of Pennsylvania Museum Press, 1997.

Partridge, R. B. *Faces of the Pharaohs: Royal Mummies and Coffins from Ancient Thebes*. London: Rubicon Press, 1994.

Petty, William. "Hatshepsut and Thutmose III Reconsidered." *KMT* 8 no. 1 (Spring 1997): 45–53.

Pritchard, James B., ed. *Ancient Near Eastern Texts Relating to the Old Testament*. Princeton, NJ: Princeton University Press, 1955.

Raban, Avner. "Minoan and Canaanite Harbours." *Aegaeum* 7 (1991): 129–46.

Redford, Donald B. "The Coregency of Thutmose III and Amenophis II." *Journal of Egyptian Archaeology* 51 (1965): 107–22.

———. *Egypt, Canaan, and Israel in Ancient Times*. Princeton, NJ: Princeton University Press, 1992.

———. *History and Chronology of the Eighteenth Dynasty of Egypt: Seven Studies*. Toronto: University of Toronto Press, 1967.

———. "The Northern Wars of Thutmose III." In Cline and O'Connor, *Thutmose III: A New Biography*, 325–43.

———. "On the Chronology of the Egyptian Eighteenth Dynasty." *Journal of Near Eastern Studies* 25, no. 2 (April 1966): 113–24.

———. *The Wars in Syria and Palestine of Thutmose III*. Boston: Brill, 2003.

Roehrig, Catharine H. "The Building Activities of Thutmose III in the Valley of the Kings." In Cline and O'Connor, *Thutmose III: A New Biography*, 238–59.

Rommelaere, Catherine. *Les Chevaux du Nouvel Empire Egyptien: Origines, Races, Harnachement*. Brussels: Conaissance de l'Egypte Ancienne, 1991.

Roth, Jonathan P. *The Logistics of the Roman Army at War: 264 BC–AD 235*. Leiden, the Netherlands: Brill, 1999.

Roux, Georges. *Ancient Iraq*. New York: Penguin, 1986.

Saggs, H. W. F. *The Might That Was Assyria*. London: Sidgwick and Jackson, 1984.

Sanchez, Gonzalo M. "Injuries in the Battle of Kadesh." *KMT* 14, no. 1 (Spring 2003): 58–65.

Sandor, B. I. "The Rise and Decline of the Tutankhamun-Class Chariot." *Oxford Journal of Archaeology* 23 no. 2 (2004): 153–75.

———. "Tutankhamun's Chariots: Secret Treasures of Engineering Mechanics." *Fatigue and Fracture of Engineering Materials and Structures* 27, no. 7 (2004): 637–46.

Save-Soderbergh, Torgny. *The Navy of the Eighteenth Egyptian Dynasty*. Uppsala, Sweden: Uppsala University Press, 1946.

Schulman, Alan R. "Chariots, Chariotry, and the Hyksos." *Toronto Society for the Study of Egyptian Antiquities* 110 (1980): 105–53.

———. *Military Rank, Title, and Organization in the Egyptian New Kingdom*. Berlin: Bruno Hessling Verlag, 1964.

Sethe, K. *Urkunden der 18. Dynastie: Urkunden des Agyptischen Altertums,* 2nd ed. Berlin: Akademie-Verlag, 1927–30.

Shaw, Ian. "Egyptians, Hyksos, and Military Technology: Causes, Effects, or Catalysts?" In *The Social Context of Technological Change: Egypt and the Near East, 1650–1550 BC,* edited by Andrew J. Shortland, 59–71. Oxford, UK: Oxbow Books, 2001.

Smith, S. T. *Askut in Nubia: The Economics and Ideology of Egyptian Imperialism in the Second Millennium BC.* London: Keegan Paul, 1995.

Spalinger, Anthony J. "Covetous Eyes South: The Background to Egypt's Domination of Nubia by the Reign of Thutmose III." In Cline and O'Connor, *Thutmose III: A New Biography,* 344–69.

———. "New Reference to an Egyptian Campaign of Thutmose III in Asia." *Journal of Near Eastern Studies* 37, no. 1 (January 1978): 35–41.

———. *War in Ancient Egypt.* Malden, MA: Blackwell, 2005.

Stillman, Nigel, and Nigel Tallis. *Armies of the Ancient Near East, 3000 BC–539 BC.* Sussex, UK: Flexiprint Ltd., 1984.

Thompson, T. L. *The Settlement of Palestine in the Late Bronze Age.* Wiesbaden, Germany, 1979.

"Thutmose III: The Napata Stela." *Introduction to the History and Culture of Pharaonic Egypt* (http://www.terraflex.co.il/ad/egypt/napata_stela.htm).

Townsend, Capt. Glen R. "The First Battle in History." Thesis, Command and General Staff School, Ft. Leavenworth, KS, 1935.

Vogelsang-Eastwood, Gillian. "Textiles." In Nicholson and Shaw, *Ancient Egyptian Materials and Technology,* 289–94.

Weigall, Arthur. *A History of the Pharaohs.* New York: E. P. Dutton, 1927.

Weingartner, Steven. *Chariots as a Whirlwind.* Westport, CT: Praeger, forthcoming 2009.

———. "Chariots Changed Forever the Way Warfare Was Fought, Strategy Conceived, and Empires Built." *Military Heritage* (August 1999): 18–26.

———. "In the Near Eastern Bronze Age, Chariot Tactics Were More Sophisticated Than Supposed." *Military Heritage* (August 2002): 18–26, 79.

Wenke, Robert J. *Patterns in Prehistory: Mankind's First Three Million Years.* New York: Oxford University Press, 1980.

Wildung, Dietrich. *Sudan: Ancient Kingdoms of the Nile.* Paris: Flammarion, 1997.

Wilkinson, Tony, ed. *On the Margin of the Euphrates: Settlement and Land Use at Tell Es-Sweyhat and in the Upper Lake Assad Area, Syria.* Chicago: University of Chicago Oriental Institute Publications, 2004.

Wilkinson, T. J., E. Peltenburg, A. McCarthy, E. B. Wilkinson, and M. Brown. *Archaeology in the Land of Carchemish: Landscape Surveys in the Area of Jerablus Tahtani, 2006.* London: Council for British Research in the Levant, 2007.

Winkelman, Betty. "Buhen: Blueprints of an Egyptian Fortress." *KMT* 6, no. 2 (Summer 1995): 72–83.

Winter, Irene J. "Carchemish." *Anatolian Studies* 33 (1983): 177–97.

Yadin, Yigael. *The Art of Warfare in Biblical Lands in Light of Archaeological Study.* Translated by M. Pearlman. New York: McGraw-Hill, 1963.

Zuhdi, Omar. "A Tale of Two Ahmoses or How to Begin an Empire." *KMT* 11, no. 4 (Winter 2000–2001): 50–61.

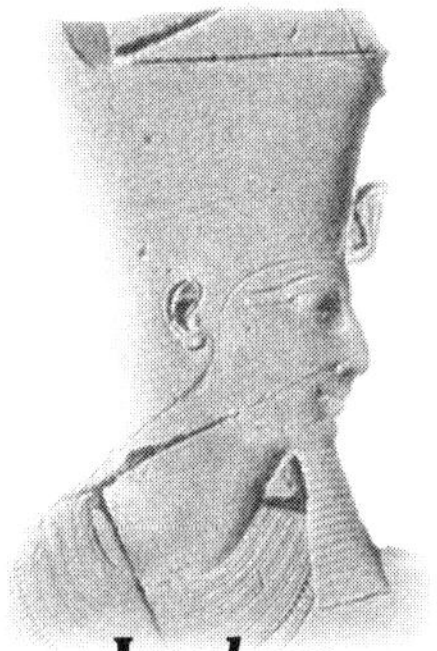

Index

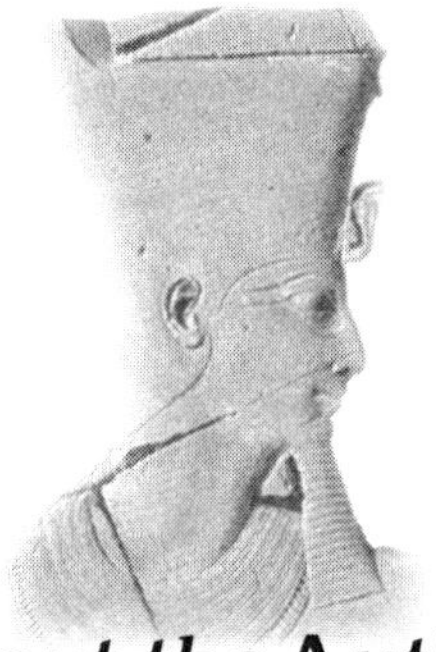

About the Author

Richard A. Gabriel is a distinguished adjunct professor in the Department of History and War Studies at the Royal Military College of Canada in Kingston, Ontario, and the Department of Security Studies at the Canadian Forces College in Toronto. He was a professor of history and politics at the U.S. Army War College and held the Visiting Chair in Ethics at the Marine Corps University. He is a retired U.S. Army officer and the author of forty-four books and eighty published articles on military history and other subjects. His books have been the subject of a number of television programs on the History Channel, most recently the eight-part series *Battles B.C.* and *The Art of War*, a study of Sun Tzu's principles applied to modern war. Dr. Gabriel's most recent books are *Subotai the Valiant: Genghis Khan's Greatest General* (2006), *Muhammad: Islam's First Great General* (2007), and *Scipio Africanus: Rome's Greatest General* (2008). He lives in New Hampshire, where he flies his antique open-cockpit airplane.